The Sociology of Health Inequalities

Sociology of Health and Illness Monograph Series

Edited by Jonathan Gabe
Department of Social Policy and Social Sciences
Royal Holloway
University of London

Current titles:

Health and the Sociology of Emotion
Edited by Veronica James and Jonathan Gabe

The Sociology of Medical Science
Edited by Mary Ann Elston

Medicine, Health and Risk
Edited by Jonathan Gabe

The Sociology of Health Inequalities
Edited by Mel Bartley, David Blane and George Davey Smith

Forthcoming titles:

Sociological Perspectives on the New Genetics
Edited by Peter Conrad and Jonathan Gabe

Rethinking the Sociology of Mental Health
Edited by Joan Busfield

The Sociology of Health Inequalities

Edited by Mel Bartley, David Blane and George Davey Smith

Blackwell Publishers/Editorial Board

Copyright © Blackwell Publishers Ltd/Editorial Board 1998

ISBN 0–631–20929–8

First published in 1998

Transferred to digital print 2005

Blackwell Publishers Ltd
108 Cowley Road, Oxford OX4 1JF, UK
and
350 Main Street,
Malden, MA 02148, USA

British Library Cataloguing in Publication Data

A CIP catalogue record for this book is available from he British Library

Library of Congress Cataloging-in-Publication Data

applied for

This book is printed on acid-free paper.

Acknowledgements

The monograph editors would like to acknowledge all those who have been involved in the production process: Susan Gregory for editorial assistance, Anthea Holmes for copy editing, Jonathan Gabe and the editorial board of SHI for their support and guidance. Tricia Crowley of the International Centre for Health and Society gave invaluable administrative assistance. As always, an exercise such as the production of this volume is dependent upon the generous work of anonymous referees, and we thank ours for their prompt and helpful reports.

Contents

Introduction: beyond the Black Report

Mel Bartley, David Blane and George Davey Smith

This is an opportune moment to be producing a book on the sociology of health inequalities. Almost 20 years after the Black Report, the classic document which was commissioned by the last Labour administration in the UK in the late 1970s and shelved by the Conservative successors in 1980 (DHSS 1980), a new Labour administration has commissioned the Independent Inquiry into Health Inequality. In the interim, many nations have followed the UK in turning away from social democratic corporatism towards a greater emphasis on free market economics. These changes took place through the ballot box, and were widely thought to signal public disenchantment with redistributive social policies (*e.g.* Johnson 1987). At the same time, some commentators have pronounced the death of social class as a force in economy, society and human biology (Clark and Lipset 1991, Phoenix and Tizard 1996). Those who continued to do research on social inequality in health were therefore under a heavy obligation of rigour in their work. It was a lonely time to be doing such work in many ways, but also a highly challenging one, in which all assumptions were questioned and sometimes tested to destruction.

Two of the assumptions to come under attack were that health inequalities existed at all (Bloor *et al.* 1987) and that there was any causal relation between social conditions and health (Illsley 1955, 1985, 1987, Macintyre and West 1991). It was argued that, as sociologists have previously shown in other cases (Douglas 1967), an apparent 'social fact' may merely be an artifact of official statistics gathering processes. And even if this were not the whole truth, what evidence was there that unhealthy individuals had not been simply left behind in the less privileged social groups during the rapid expansion of managerial, technical and professional occupations of the 1960s, 70s and 80s? The editors of this book have been fortunate in having worked together in this intellectual field over a 10-year period when new data and new methods, together with the explosion in computing power, have allowed these questions to be settled. It has been possible to carry out analyses which, to the pioneers we have followed, would have been either unthinkable or, perhaps more often, thinkable but unfeasible (Morris and Titmuss 1944).

Since 1980 a number of developments have changed our perception of health inequalities. In Britain an important example was the instigation of the Office of Nations Statistics' Longitudinal Study (the LS) (Fox and Goldblatt 1982). This was no accident, as the LS has its origins in the discovery that mortality differences between the most and least privileged groups according to the Registrar-General's social classes seemed to have widened between 1961 and 1971 (OPCS 1975, 1978). This was shocking to some (Wilkinson 1976) and to others simply unbelievable (Illsley 1986). How could this be happening in a Britain that had 'never had it so good', in which the political complaints given most air time were to do with excessive equalisation, too much public spending, and excessive generosity to the poor (Deacon 1978, Ditch 1986)? Perhaps the method used in the Decennial Supplements, which simply collected death certificates for the three years around each census and divided the numbers of deaths in each class by the numbers in that class in the population, was at fault? The purpose of the LS was to get round this. It sampled one per cent of everyone at the 1971 census and linked the death certificates (or cancer registration certificates, or birth certificates of any children they might have) to the information they gave at the previous census. In future years, this same one per cent's 1971 census data was then linked to the 1981 and 1991 censuses. The health inequalities seen using this method duly confirmed that health inequalities existed, were not due to statistical bias, and that they were continuing to get wider (Fox et al. 1985, Goldblatt 1990, Drever and Whitehead 1997).

The second major development was the maturing of the two earliest British birth cohorts, the 1946 National Study of Health and Development, and the 1958 National Child Development Study. By their very nature, these data sets were bound to show the ways in which early life influenced later health. This allowed direct testing of the degree to which social mobility of children with long term illness accounted for inequalities in illness in early and middle adulthood (Power et al. 1996, Wadsworth and Kuh 1997). Yet the story is not a simple one, and continues to unfold in a complex manner (Kuh and Ben-Shlomo 1997, Marmot and Wadsworth 1997). Early life experiences do not have the same effect on later health in all people. Those with greater social advantage may shrug off early health problems, whereas those with a combination of health and social disadvantage may find themselves in a downward spiral which is far more difficult to escape. The influence of these studies was combined with a renewed interest in early life influences on adult disease (Kuh and Davey Smith 1993), following the Southampton studies showing that low birthweight babies, quite independently of later social position, were at higher risk of a number of serious chronic diseases (Barker 1992). Debate continues over the extent to which low birthweight and its consequences may be a result of social patterns which our methods are at present too crude to discern (Bartley et al. 1994), and also over the policy implications of these findings (Bartley et al. 1997). The longitudinal studies have shown that high morbidity and mortality of those in disadvantaged social groups cannot be attributed to health related social mobility alone. In fact there is evidence that social mobility in adult life acts to constrain rather than to produce health gradients (Bartley and

Plewis 1997, Hart *et al.* 1998). The extent to which the debate has moved beyond an argument about selection and artifact has, as pointed out in the contribution to this collection by Popay *et al.*, been summarised by Macintyre's call for a re-focusing of research onto a more finely detailed understanding of the manner in which social structure influences individuals' health risks (Macintyre 1997). The lifecourse approach to health inequalities similarly encourages an attempt to embrace the complexity of social causation, rather than the production of simple but inadequate unitary explanations.

Relative or absolute?

Of course, as the old debates die away, new ones have arisen. One of the most prominent of these is reflected quite strongly among the papers in this issue. It is the question of how to reconcile the discovery of the 'fine grain' of health and mortality, that is, health inequalities stretching right up the social scale (Blane *et al.* 1997), with the findings of the research programme of Wilkinson and others who point out that it may not be income alone, but also the degree of income inequality which matters for health (Wilkinson 1989, 1990, 1994, 1997b, Kennedy *et al.* 1996, Kaplan *et al.* 1996, Kawachi & Kennedy 1997). Health inequalities are not found only between rich and poor, or between 'the deprived' and everyone else. We use the term 'fine grain' to refer to the fine level of social differentiation in health risks. Life expectancy is greater in those who own their own homes and two cars than in home-owners with only one car (Goldblatt 1990): in those with a car and a garden than in those with only a car (Davey Smith and Shipley, unpublished observation). However, the fine grain of the health gradient has emerged from research into populations or sub-populations within a single nation at a time (Davey Smith *et al.* 1990, Marmot *et al.* 1991, Davey Smith *et al.* 1996a, b). Comparing life expectancy between nations, several research teams now confirm the findings Wilkinson first reported in the 1980s that the average amount of income available to each member of a population, is less strongly related to life expectancy in whole countries than is the distribution of that income (Wilkinson 1986). At around the same average income per person, a more equal distribution of income seems to produce higher life expectancy. If it is not the case that the health of whole nations improves incrementally with increases in average income, why do we find that, at the level of individuals, the higher the material living standard, the better their health?

The international income distribution and health studies suggest that the same amount of income may benefit even those who are reasonably well off less when they live in a country with a high level of income inequality. To some authors, this suggests that the effect of income and other material goods is not directly material, but psychological (Wilkinson 1997, 1977a, b).

In this book, two of the leading proponents of the income-distribution programme, Wilkinson and Kawachi, have co-authored a chapter setting out,
with vivid qualitative and quantitative illustrations, their ideas on one possible mechanism by which this relationship may operate. In essence, the
argument is that greater inequality makes it more difficult to maintain social
bonds and self esteem. In the absence of social integration, dominance takes
on greater importance, and those experiencing sharp relative deprivation
may have few options but to maintain their 'social honour' by means of
aggression. Furthermore, the same amount of income may have very different effects on individual health and well-being if a high proportion of it is
needed to protect oneself against the consequences of other people's deprivation (Hutton 1996: 172–81).

Linking well with Wilkinson and Kawachi's chapter, Elstad provides a
comprehensive review of psychosocial theories linking health to the social
environment, showing how the older stress theories relate to newer ideas
about the emotions and social cohesion. He opens up the possibility that
societies with different income distributions are ones in which different levels
of assistance are given out to those who are experiencing life events, including perhaps the universal but difficult transitions from school to work, childhood to sexual maturity, parenthood, and old age. Will the individual be
helped and protected during these events and processes? How much can the
uncertain emotions which accompany them be openly shared, in the expecta-
tion that support of both an emotional and material kind will be available if
things go wrong? How far, does each individual need to fear they might fall
if things go wrong? Surely these are aspects of material inequality in a society
which will prove relevant for health and illness. And they will be relevant not
only for 'the poor', as we all face life events and transitions: perhaps what
inequality does is condition the experience of these critical moments over the
life course. Popay and colleagues in their contribution remind us of the now
neglected concept of the 'social wage' resulting from public spending on
common services such as health, education, housing and transport. As the
social wage is cut, individuals need increasingly greater amounts of personal
or household income in order to maintain the same standard of living. Yet
historically we find that reductions of the social wage and the amount of
income available to non-privileged households take place in parallel. Even
well-off middle class families might quail at the full costs of covering all the
necessary schooling, higher education, health care and elder care likely to be
needed by private insurance policies alone. This has been estimated to cost
around £500 per week at 1997 prices before any income even began to be
available for food and housing costs (Hutton 1996).

We should not forget that, as Elstad points out, the concept of relative
deprivation was used in studies of political attitudes and behaviour long
before it was used in health studies. Runciman's (1966) *Relative Deprivation
and Social Justice* was concerned with the reasons for social unrest and

revolutionary uprisings. When we look at the high levels of life expectancy in countries such as Germany, Japan and South Korea, we need to bear in mind the importance historically to American policy makers of their proximity to the giants of the Eastern bloc. This, and their potential for political turbulence was reflected in the granting of Marshall Aid and 'most favoured trading nation' status in the late 1940s, at the inception of the Cold War. The strength of dissident social movements may have influenced demographic trends in a number of ways. Countries where such movements persist tend to be more likely to respond by setting up more extensive welfare provision of various kinds (Esping-Anderson 1990): from clean piped water, electricity and sewage to trade union rights and income supplementation for the unemployed and those unable to work for other reasons. The existence of such financial provisions will no doubt serve to reduce the degree of income inequality, but is it the financial or the socially integrative effect of citizenship in a country where less privileged groups engage in organised collective activity that is more important?

Structure and agency

The classic sociological problem of structure and agency is well exemplified in this collection. Health inequality research needs to acknowledge that it is not just the nature of the social environment, but its dynamics which must be understood. Modern industrial economies work by getting at least some people to produce more than the value of the wages they are paid. This surplus is retained by employers (or ruling bureaucracies) and forms the basis of profit, the driving mechanism of the economic system. The fact that some citizens are poorer than others is therefore not an accident of bad planning or even individual greed. The reason for increasing numbers of 'excluded' people in late 20th century advanced industrial society is the increasing power of technology to produce ever more goods with ever fewer human workers. One result is 'social exclusion'. Like the Native Americans in the 19th century (Higgs and Scambler 1998), the traditional (especially male) working class is becoming surplus to economic requirements in the late 20th century. The native American people were confined to reservations and granted small amounts of land and welfare payments: significantly the destruction of their communities was brought about in its later phases not by overt genocide but by the health consequences of utter demoralisation. Although inequality may take new forms, the chapters in this book show the implausibility of the idea that 'class has disappeared'. They add to the evidence of large social differences in quality of residential environment, political attitudes, voting, car and home ownership as well as the very different patterns of educational and career attainment among children from different social backgrounds. People from mining areas may no longer wear cloth caps, but the waning of stereotyped cultural signals co-exists with a wide belief that class distinction is alive and well in Britain today (Marshall *et al.* 1988).

Popay and her colleagues criticise the concentration of many studies of health inequality on individuals' 'risk factors' and 'risk behaviour' to the relative neglect of the macrosocial environment. However, they also call for greater understanding at the micro level. They take up a question implicit in the essay of Wilkinson and Kawachi: why is it that people located within the social structures where we find them behave in the way they do? The continuity of social structure is itself produced by myriad individual decisions and actions. Most people who decide whether or not to take a school exam or aim for promotion at work are not consciously reproducing the class system: they are doing what seems best to them at the time. Similarly most people lighting up a cigarette or going out jogging are not aiming to reproduce the pattern of health inequality. Once health education has disseminated information about the risks of behaviours such as smoking and inadequate diet, we still need some explanation of why those in the most socially disadvantaged positions seem least able to adopt healthier lifestyles; studies show that they are equally willing to do so (Lee *et al.* 1991).

We understand very little about these patterns of decision and action, perhaps in part because of the neglect of agency criticised in the chapter by Popay *et al.* The UK Economic and Social Research Council's recent initiative in funding a programme of work on Social Variations in Health will help to overcome this lack. Several of the projects funded by the programme, including ones in which Shaw and Popay and their collaborators are involved, are concentrating on an ethnographic approach, placing the researchers in the communities identified by geographical studies as having poor health, and collecting face to face data on attitudes, actions and ideas of residents. This is probably the largest amount of resources ever devoted to ethnographic study of health inequality. Hopefully in a few years, a collection of ethnographic work on the meaning of inequality in everyday life will be put together. A particularly valuable product of this research could be an increased understanding of how position in a social hierarchy may influence health in the way postulated by Wilkinson and others.

If we are to direct attention simultaneously to structure and agency, then studies of delimited areas become necessary: neighbourhoods are where individuals do encounter social structure and live out life-courses. At this point the concept of 'social capital' becomes relevant to the debate on health inequality. What is the effect on individual deprivation of the quality of social relationships? Perhaps we can discuss the concept by beginning with William Farr's formula for predicting area differences in mortality (Eyler 1979). Farr regarded the excess mortality (over and above the 'ideal' rate) in an area as determined by hygienic conditions (crowding and the 'number of germs in the atmosphere') only where the average income was greater than or equal to the price of 'necessities'. '[O]nly where [the market price of all necessities of life in an area] is greater than [the average wage] did low income exert an important influence on mortality. Under other conditions, hygiene was more important' (Eyler 1979: 126). The poorer the inhabitants, the more important was hygiene. Today some health inequality researchers might substitute 'social capital' for 'hygiene' in this model: where income is sufficient to cover bare necessities, population health depends on social cohesion. However, successive attempts to determine the real cost of the minimum basic necessities of life have conspicuously failed (Veit-Wilson 1992). Living standards are subject to a 'historical and moral component' which depends on the cost of symbolic goods needed for full social participation as well as physical subsistence (Bartley 1991). For example, where do such goods as education and health care come in this equation? In the post war welfare state these were provided as part of the social wage: now their quality, if not availability, increasingly depends on individual income. It may well be that where public provision for schools and health services is declining, the social composition of an area may make up for declining levels of social wage, that is, instead of the density of germs in the air, we would take the density of 'social capital'.

For example, consider the different performance of children in comprehensive schools according to the social makeup of the catchment area (Morris et al. 1996). Morris and colleagues found that an index of local social conditions was significantly related both to average school attainment and to local mortality rates. This ecological analysis seemed to indicate that there was some characteristic of localities which affected both the school attainment of children and the life expectancy of their elders. It is a commonplace among middle class parents in urban areas that the social composition of the school will affect the burden on a school's teachers (Buchel and Duncan 1998). What is happening is that the better-off children's families are subsidising (in terms of social support and unpaid domestic labour) the efforts of the teachers by sending out children who are already well socialised, able to read, etc. This allows more time and effort to be devoted to the less fortunate children. But surely the same will be true of all socially provided services. Because more of the overhead costs of health maintenance of middle class workers are carried by employers, in terms of sick pay, longer holidays, paid time off to visit the doctor etc., there are shorter hospital waiting lists in middle class than working class residential areas, which will of course mean that even poorer people in wealthy areas wait less long for medical care. This is not, however, the way in which 'social capital' is usually expressed (Messer 1998, Moser 1998, Woolcock 1998). It is more usually taken to be the density of social relationships amongst local residents, with the implication that higher levels of communication and support between individuals adds to the common good (Putnam et al. 1993, 1995:

664–5 cited in Wilkinson 1996). It is the contention of 'communitarianism', at least implicitly, that in a re-moralised society fewer public resources would be needed, for example, to support parents, elderly people and those who are chronically ill, as this would be done by 'the community', as part of solidaristic commitment, without cost to the employer or the state. Even the cost of goods for individual consumption, and thereby the income/ necessities ratio, would, in this view, be lowered by high levels of social capital, thus enabling a lower wage to cover the reproduction costs of labour power.

But what is it that links social conditions, however they are characterised, to the health of the individual? A message common to the chapters by Wilkinson and Kawachi and Popay and her colleagues, and shared by the wider literature on emotions and the body, is the importance of personal identity. One thing researchers are starting to ask is: What resources does each social form make available to individuals from which they may shape an identity they can live with? These considerations are most acute in the literature on disability; but they may also turn out to be crucial for health inequality research as a whole. Future research may well set out to discover how action is shaped by the narratives people construct to make sense of their own encounters with inequality. One strategy which has been well described in the literature on illness behaviour is that known as 'normalisation': rather than bear the threat to self-esteem inherent in the admission of a problem, many will find skillful ways to deny it. Improved understanding of an important source of the persistence of health inequality may well lie in the sensitive analysis of such strategies of denying the existence of subordination.

Curtis and Jones take up the issue of how to study health inequality in localities, but give more attention to the quantitative methods which have been used in existing studies. Saying that the locality is where individuals encounter social structure and the agency of others is all very well; however, evidence for an 'area effect' independent of individual characteristics remains elusive and contradictory. Some might be wary of the danger that the dynamics of class society might once again be forgotten in the attempt to show that policies to increase 'social capital' in neighbourhoods could overcome sharp inequalities in individual living standards (Sloggett and Joshi 1994). To say that structure and agency operate to a large extent in face to face local encounters is one thing, to claim that there are 'area effects' which might attenuate or exacerbate health inequality is quite another. As Curtis and Jones point out, policy implications of such research need to be drawn with great caution. Although the question of social capital, now rising up the health policy agenda, is not directly addressed in this book, the authors of several of the chapters take valuable steps towards clarifying an intellectual context for future work on this topic.

Social and spatial inequalities in health

The second part of this collection assembles a set of empirical studies of health inequality in Britain and the Netherlands at the end of the 20th century. Given the richness of health inequality research at the present time, these inevitably cover only part of the full spectrum. Cameron and Bernardes take a refreshing stance in that they problematise men's, rather than women's health behaviour; a perspective that has been rather lacking given the lower life expectancy of men in most developed industrial societies. Their paper's concern with the barriers to seeking treatment for prostate problems allows them to open up the whole area of 'male embodiment' at a time of rapid change in gender roles, and its implications for health policy.

A gap in the collection might appear to be any essay specifically dealing with policy. However, most of the chapters can clearly be seen to have emerged from policy concerns, even if some of these are at a more 'macro' level than health or social planning in individual nations. At a time of such rapid change, authors seem to have concluded that what is more important is to establish a firm base in terms of theory and observation rather than jump towards policy prescriptions too soon. The contribution of Shaw and her colleagues takes up the call made in some of the theoretical chapters for work on health differences between geographical areas, and shows new data on increases in health inequality. Whereas previous literature has concentrated on increasing differences between officially defined social classes (Drever and Whitehead 1997) or a limited number of areas (McLoone and Boddy 1994, McCarron et al., Phillimore et al. 1994), Shaw et al.' show how mortality differences between more and less disadvantages areas are now at the highest level ever recorded. Once again, the authors relate their findings to policy debate in a thoughtful discussion which sets out their uncertainty as to the interpretation of these findings, and offers suggestions as to how research might address these uncertainties.

Throughout the book, there is an unpacking of traditional social classifications. 'Male gender' is shown by Cameron and Bernardes' rich qualitative material to be many-faceted and to allow a wide variety of responses to the threats posed by chronic illness. Nazroo emphasises the importance of theoretical approaches to the definitions of 'class' and 'ethnicity', and shows the dangers that arise for empirical studies when untheorised definitions are accepted uncritically. He shows how crude and inappropriate measures of inequality can lead to an apparent failure of structural explanations for ethnic differences in health. This, in turn, has led, in some studies, to appeals either to genetic or cultural interpretation of health differences between ethnic groups by a process of elimination. His chapter provides a striking instance of how policy prescriptions based on the use of stereotypical social categories can be seriously misleading. His own development of meaningful categories for the study of health inequality among ethnic minority groups returns to basic considerations of structure and agency, showing that even within the same social classes, members of such groups experienced lower paid, less prestigious and more stressful work, greater job insecurity, and longer periods of unemployment. Both theoretical (Kaufman *et al.* 1997) and empirical (Davey Smith *et al.* 1998) work from the United States has framed questions regarding the association of ethnicity and socioeconomic position in a similar way. The practice of treating class as a 'variable' rather than as part of a set of social relations is increasingly criticised both in the USA (Krieger *et al.* 1997), and in Britain (Higgs and Scambler 1998). Nazroo's paper shows how this results in the failure to capture inequality among ethnic minority citizens, not because the sources of this inequality are genetic or cultural, but because it misrepresents their material situation.

Burrows and Nettleton focus on housing insecurity, an experience which affected people from many different social backgrounds during the 1980s and early 1990s. Their scene-setting, describing the changes in both the labour market and the housing market during the 1980s, forms an invaluable context for all the other papers based on UK data. Their description of mortgage indebtedness as most often a part of a general 'struggle to keep one's health above water' is a striking exemplification of the 'accumulation of risk' theory now growing in importance in health inequality research (Blane *et al.* 1993, Davey Smith 1994, Kreiger 1994, Blane 1995, Wunsch *et al.* 1996). Their qualitative data echo much of what has been discussed in the papers by Wilkinson and Kawachi and Elstad: the importance of social honour and the role played by material goods such as a privately owned house in maintaining this sometimes fragile state. They relate this to questions of identity and biographical disruption (Bury 1982). In this way, an empirical paper adds yet more to the complex picture of the relationships between social forms and individual well-being and sets an example of how to bring general notions about 'social inequality' down to earth in ways that offer plausible pathways to health effects.

Perhaps the most important development in health inequality research in the recent past has been the opening out of a new perspective (though one which was anticipated by mid-century social medicine): the importance of the lifecourse. In 1994 the UK government (then a Conservative one) set up a committee of inquiry into 'social variation in health' (*British Medical Journal* 1994) (the Metters committee) which, in its report, took a quietly revolutionary step. It passed beyond the post-Black report framework of explanations for health inequality, spending little or no time on the discussion of artifact or selection explanations (Variations sub-group 1995). While accepting that the determinants of health inequality arose from the structure of society and its influences on individual lifestyle and quality of life, the Metters Report went on to acknowledge the importance of how these influences work over time.

The Black Report had, of course, itself put emphasis in its policy proposals on improving the circumstances of children, because, as it said, early life 'casts long shadows forward' onto the health of the adult. The founders of the British cohort studies must to some extent have foreseen the importance of early life for adult health. What could not have been foreseen, however, was the extent to which a lifecourse approach would offer the solution to the problem of combining the findings relating to social inequality with those relating to individual living standards and the observed fine grain of health inequality. The more data we have which show, as do those presented here by van de Mheen and her colleagues, how early circumstances contribute to health in later life, the clearer it becomes that 'social class' at any given point is but a very partial indicator of a whole sequence, a 'probabilistic cascade' of events which need to be seen in combination if the effects of social environment on health are to be understood (Blane *et al.* 1996, Davey Smith *et al.* 1997). Different individuals have arrived at any particular level of income, occupational advantage or prestige with different life histories behind them. Variables such as height, education, and ownership of additional consumer goods act as indicators of these past histories. Those with the greatest accumulation of 'bio-material' advantages are likely to have experienced optimal combinations of events from childhood onwards. Hence the fine grain – the two cars and the rather larger house – are serving to indicate that bit more financial security throughout the life of the individual, or in their extended family, as anyone who remembers which students had cars as undergraduates will perhaps recognise. The significance of the degree of inequality in a society is that this indicates how severe the longer term implications of any given adverse event as the life course unfolds is likely to be (unemployment or illness of the bread winner, marital breakdown, periods of under-achievement at school or in the early work career, etc.) and how likely it is to set off a descending spiral of other disadvantages (Power & Matthews 1997; Kuh *et al.* 1997b). In their emphasising on critical theorising, their close coupling of theory with research, and their success in reflecting theoretical advances in new empirical findings, the authors of the papers in this collection have each provided a significant contribution to health inequality research at a crucial time, which will help to stimulate further work in this complex field.

Acknowledgement

Mel Bartley gratefully acknowledges the support of the ESRC (grant nos: L128251012 and L12825001) and the MRC (grant no: G8802774)

References

Barker, D.J.P. (1992) *Fetal and Infant Origins of Adult Disease*. London: British Medical Journal Publishing Group.

Bartley, M. (1991) Health and labour force participation: stress, selection and the reproduction costs of labour power, *Journal of Social Policy*, 21, 327–64.

Bartley, M., Power, C., Blane, D., Davey Smith, G. and Shipley, M. (1994) Birthweight and later social disadvantage: evidence from the 1958 British cohort study, *British Medical Journal*, 309, 1475–8.

Bartley, M., Blane, D. and Montgomery, S. (1997) Health and the life-course: why safety nets matter, *British Medical Journal*, 314, 194–6.

Bartley, M. and Plewis, I. (1997) Does health selective social mobility account for socioeconomic differences in health? Evidence from England and Wales 1971 to 1991, *Journal of Health and Social Behavior*, 38, 376–86.

Blane, D. (1995) Social determinants of health – socioeconomic status, social class and ethnicity, *American Journal of Public Health*, 85, 903–4.

Blane, D., Davey Smith, G. and Bartley, M. (1993) Social selection: what does it contribute to social class differences in health? *Sociology of Health and Illness*, 15, 1–15.

Blane, D., Hart, C.L., Davey Smith, G., Gillis, C.R., Hole, D.J. and Hawthorne, V.M. (1996) Association of cardiovascular disease risk factors with socioeconomic position during childhood and during adulthood, *British Medical Journal*, 313, 1434–8.

Blane, D.B., Bartley, M. and Davey Smith, G. (1997) Disease etiology and material-ist explanations of socio-economic mortality differentials, *European Journal of Public Health*, 7, 385–91.

Bloor, M., Samphier, M. and Prior, L. (1987) Artifact explanations of inequalities in health: an assessment of the evidence, *Sociology of Health and Illness*, 9, 231–64.

British Medical Journal (1994) British government looks at effects of wealth on health, *British Medical Journal*, 308, 1257.

Buchel, F. and Duncan, G.J. (1998) Do parents' social activities promote children's school attainments? Evidence from the German socioeconomic panel, *Journal of Marriage and the Family*, 60, 95–108.

Bury, M.R. (1982) Chronic illness as biographical disruption, *Sociology of Health and Illness*, 4, 2, 167–82.

Clark, T.N. and Lipset, S.M. (1991) Are social classes dying? *International Sociology*, 6, 397–409.

Davey Smith, G. (1996) Income inequality and mortality – why are they related – income inequality goes hand in hand with underinvestment in human-resources, *British Medical Journal*, 312, 987–8.

Davey Smith, G., Shipley, M.J. and Rose, G. (1990) The magnitude and causes of socio-economic differentials in mortality: further evidence from the Whitehall II study, *Journal of Epidemiology and Community Health*, 44, 265–70.

Davey Smith, G., Blane, D. and Bartley, M. (1994) Explanations for socio-economic differentials in mortality: evidence from Britain and elsewhere, *European Journal of Public Health*, 4, 131–44.

Davey Smith, G., Wentworth, D., Neaton, J.D., Stamler, R. and Stamler, J. (1996a) Socioeconomic differentials in mortality risk among men screened for the

Multiple Risk Factor Intervention Trial: II. Black men, *American Journal of Public Health*, 86, 497–504.

Davey Smith, G., Neaton, J.D., Wentworth, D., Stamler, R. and Stamler, J. (1996b) Socioeconomic differentials in mortality risk among men screened for the Multiple Risk Factor Intervention Trial: I, White men, *American Journal of Public Health*, 86, 486–96.

Davey Smith, G., Hart, C., Blane, D., Gillis, C. and Hawthorne, V. (1997) Lifetime socioeconomic position and mortality: prospective observational study, *British Medical Journal*, 314, 547–52.

Davey Smith, G., Neaton, J.D., Wentworth, D. and Stamler, R. (1998) Mortality differences between black and white men in the USA: contribution of income and other risk factors among men screened for the MRFIT, *Lancet*, 351, 934–9.

Deacon, A. (1978) The scrounging controversy: public attitudes towards the unemployed in contemporary Britain, *Social and Economic Administration*, 178, 12–24.

Department of Health and Social Security (1980) *Inequalities in Health: Report of a Working Group*. London: HMSO.

Ditch, J. (1986) The undeserving poor: unemployed people then and now. In Loney, M. (ed) *The State or the Market*. London: Sage.

Douglas, J.D. (1967) *The Social Meaning of Suicide*. Princeton: Princeton University Press.

Drever, F. and Whitehead, M. (1977) *Health Inequalities*. London: HMSO.

Esping-Anderson, F.G. (1990) *Three Worlds of Welfare Capitalism*. Cambridge: Polity Press.

Eyler, J. (1979) *William Farr and Victorian Social Medicine*. Baltimore: Johns Hopkins University Press.

Fox, A.J. and Goldblatt, P. (1982) *Socio-demographic Differentials in Mortality: the OPCS Longitudinal Study*. London: HMSO.

Fox, A.J., Goldblatt, P.O. and Jones, D.R. (1985) Social class mortality differentials – artifact, election or life circumstances? *Journal of Epidemiology and Community Health*, 39, 1–8.

Goldblatt, P. (1990) Mortality and alternative social classifications. In Goldblatt, P. (ed) *Longitudinal Study: Mortality and Social Organization*. London: HMSO.

Hart, C.L., Davey Smith, G. and Blane, D.B. (1998) Social mobility and 21 year mortality in a cohort of Scottish men, *Social Science and Medicine*, in press.

Higgs, P. and Scambler, G. (1998) Explaining health inequalities: how useful are concepts of social class? In Higgs, P. and Scambler, G. (eds) *Modernity, Medicine and Health*. London: Routledge.

Hutton, W. (1996) *The State We're In*. London: Jonathan Cape.

Illsley, R. (1955) Social class, selection and class differences in relation to stillbirths and infant deaths, *British Medical Journal*, ii: 1520–4.

Illsley, R. (1986) Occupational class, selection and inequalities in health, *Quarterly Journal of Social Affairs*, 2, 151–65.

Illsley, R. (1987) Occupational class, selection and ill health: rejoinder, *Quarterly Journal of Social Affairs*, 3, 213–23.

Johnson, N. (1987) The break-up of consensus: competitive policies in a declining economy. In Loney, M. with Bocock, R., Clarke, J., Cochrane, A., Graham, P. and Wilson, M. (eds) *The State or the Market*. London: Sage.

Kaplan, G.A., Pamuk, E.R., Lynch, J.W., Cohen, R.D. and Balfour, J.L. (1996) Inequality in income and mortality in the United States – analysis of mortality and potential pathways, *British Medical Journal*, 312, 999–1003.

Kauffman, J.S., McGee, D.L. and Cooper, R.S. (1997) Socioeconomic status and health in blacks and whites: the problem of residual confounding and the resiliency of race, *Epidemiology*, 8, 621–8.

Kauffman, J.S., Long, A.E., Liao, Y., Cooper, R.S. and McGee, D.L. (1998) The relation between income and mortality in US Blacks and Whites, *Epidemiology*, 9, 147–55.

Kawachi, I. and Kennedy, B.P. (1997) Socioeconomic determinants of health. 2. Health and social cohesion: why care about income inequality? *British Medical Journal*, 314, 1037–40.

Kawachi, I., Kennedy, B.P., Lochner, K. and Prothrow-Stith, D. (1997) Social capital, income inequality, and mortality, *American Journal of Public Health*, 87, 1491–8.

Kennedy, B.P., Kawachi, I. and Prothrow-Stith, D. (1996) Income-distribution and mortality – cross-sectional ecological study of the Robin-Hood index in the United States, *British Medical Journal*, 312, 1004–7.

Kreiger, N. (1994) Epidemiology and the web of causation: has anyone seen the spider? *Social Science and Medicine*, 39, 887–903.

Krieger, N., Williams, D.R. and Moss, N.E. (1997) Measuring social class in US public health research: concepts, methodologies and guidelines, *Annual Review of Public Health*, 18, 341–78.

Kuh, D. and Davey Smith, G. (1993) When is mortality risk determined? Historical insights into a current debate, *Social History of Medicine*, 6, 101–23.

Kuh, D.J.L. and Ben-Shlomo, Y. (1997) *Lifecourse Approach to Chronic Disease Epidemiology*. Oxford: Oxford University Press.

Kuh, D.J.L., Power, C., Blane, D. and Bartley, M. (1997) Social pathways between childhood and adult health. In Kuh, D.J.L. and Ben Shlomo, Y. (eds) *Lifecourse Approach to Chronic Disease Epidemiology*. Oxford: Oxford University Press.

Lee, A.J., Crombie, I.L.K., Smith, W.C.S. and Tunstall-Pedoe, H.D. (1991) Cigarette smoking and employment status, *Social Science and Medicine*, 32, 1309–12.

Macintyre, S. (1997) The Black Report and beyond: what are the issues? *Social Science and Medicine*, 44, 723–45.

Macintyre, S. and West, P. (1991) Lack of class variation in health in adolescence – an artifact of an occupational measure of social class, *Social Science and Medicine*, 32, 395–402.

Marmot, M.G., Davey Smith, G., Stansfeld, S., Patel, C., North, F., Head, J., White, I., Brunner, E. and Feeney, A. (1991) Health inequalities among British civil servants: the Whitehall II study, *Lancet*, 337, 1387–93.

Marmot, M.G. and Wadsworth, M.E.J. (1997) *Fetal and Early Childhood Environment: Long Term Implications*. Edinburgh: Churchill Livingstone.

Marshall, G., Newby, H., Rose, D. and Vogler, C. (1988) *Social Class in Modern Britain*. London: Hutchinson.

McCarron, P.G., Davey Smith, G. and Womersley, J.J. (1994) Deprivation and mortality in Glasgow: changes from 1980 to 1992, *British Medical Journal*, 309, 1481–2.

McLoone, P. and Boddy, A. (1994) Deprivation and mortality in Scotland, 1981 and 1991, *British Medical Journal*, 309, 1465–70.

Messer, J. (1998) Agency, communion, and the formation of social capital, *Nonprofit and Voluntary Sector Quarterly*, 27, 5–12.

Morris, J.N. and Titmuss, R. (1944) Health and social change: recent history of rheumatic heart disease, *The Medical Officer*, 69–71, 77–9, 85–7.

Morris, J.N., Blane, D.B. and White, I.R. (1996) Levels of mortality, education and social conditions in the 107 local education authority areas of England, *Journal of Epidemiology and Community Health*, 50, 15–17.

Moser, C.O.N. (1998) The asset vulnerability framework: reassessing urban poverty reduction strategies, *World Development*, 26, 1–19.

Office of Population Censuses and Surveys (1975) *Cohort Studies: New Developments. Report on Medical and Population Subjects* No. 25. London: HMSO.

Office of Population Censuses and Surveys (1978) *Occupational Mortality: Decennial Supplement for England and Wales 1970–72*. London: HMSO.

Phillimore, P., Beattie, A. and Townsend, P. (1994) Widening inequality of health in northern England, 1981–91, *British Medical Journal*, 308, 1125–8.

Phoenix, A. and Tizard, B. (1996) Thinking through class – the place of social class in the lives of young Londoners, *Feminism and Psychology*, 6, 427–42.

Power, C., Matthews, S. and Manor, O. (1996) Inequalities in self rated health in the 1958 birth cohort – lifetime social circumstances or social mobility, *British Medical Journal*, 313, 449–53.

Power, C. and Matthews, S. (1997) Origins of health inequalities in a national population sample, *Lancet*, 350, 1584–9.

Putnam, R.D., Leonardi, R. and Nanetti, R.Y. (1993) *Making Democracy Work: Civic Tradition in Modern Italy*. Princeton, NJ: Princeton University Press.

Putnam, R.D. (1995) Tuning in, tuning out: the strange disappearance of social capital in America, *Political Science and Politics*, 4, 664–83.

Runciman, W.G. (1966) *Relative Deprivation and Social Justice: a Study of Attitudes to Inequality in 20th Century England*. London: Routledge and Kegan Paul.

Sloggett, A. and Joshi, H. (1994) Higher mortality in deprived areas: community or personal disadvantage? *British Medical Journal*, 309, 1470–4.

Variations Sub-group of the Chief Medical Officer's Health of the Nation Working Group (1995) *Variations in Health: What can the Department of Health and the NHS Do?* London: Department of Health.

Veit Wilson, J. (1992) Muddle or mendacity – the Beveridge Committee and the poverty line, *Journal of Social Policy*, 21, 269–301.

Wadsworth, M.E.J. and Kuh, D.J.L. (1997) Childhood influences on adult health: a review of recent work from the British 1946 national birth cohort study, the MRC National Survey of Health and Development, *Pediatric and Perinatal Epidemiology*, 11, 2–20.

Wilkinson, R.G. (1976) Dear David Ennals, *New Society*, 16 December, 567–8.

Wilkinson, R.G. (1986) Income and mortality. In Wilkinson, R.G. (ed) *Class and Health: Research and Longitudinal Data*. London: Tavistock.

Wilkinson, R.G. (1989) Class mortality differentials, income-distribution and trends in poverty 1921–1981, *Journal of Social Policy*, 18, 307–35.

Wilkinson, R.G. (1990) Income-distribution and mortality – a natural experiment, *Sociology of Health and Illness*, 12, 391–412.

Wilkinson, R.G. (1994) The epidemiological transition – from material scarcity to social disadvantage, *Dædalus*, 123, 61–77.

Wilkinson, R.G. (1996) *Unhealthy Societies: the Afflictions of Inequality*. London: Routledge.

Wilkinson, R.G. (1997a) Comment: income, inequality, and social cohesion, *American Journal of Public Health*, 87, 1504–6.

Wilkinson, R.G. (1997b) Socioeconomic determinants of health – health inequalities: relative or absolute material standards? *British Medical Journal*, 314, 591–5.

Woolcock, M. (1998) Social capital and economic development: toward a theoretical synthesis and policy framework, *Theory and Society*, 27, 151–208.

Wunsch, D., Duchène, J., Thilgès, E. and Salhi, M. (1996) Socio-economic differences in mortality: a lifecourse approach, *European Journal of Population*, 12, 167–85.

I: Understanding the social dynamics if health inequalities

1. Mortality, the social environment, crime and violence

Richard G. Wilkinson, Ichiro Kawachi and Bruce P. Kennedy

Introduction

This chapter uses data on homicide and other categories of crime to explore the nature of the associations between income distribution, mortality and a measure of social cohesion in the United States.

Close associations between income distribution and population mortality rates have now been reported on independent data at least fifteen times (Wilkinson 1996). In different papers the relationship has been shown to withstand controlling for average incomes, expenditure on medical care, poverty, smoking and race (Kennedy *et al.* 1996, Kaplan *et al.* 1996). It has been reported among developed and developing countries and among administrative areas within developed countries (Ben Shlomo *et al.* 1996). Most analyses have used cross-sectional data but the relationship has also been demonstrated using data on changes over time (*e.g.* Wilkinson 1992; Kaplan *et al.* 1996).

When it was believed that the main determinants of health were likely to involve the direct physiological effects of exposure to features of the material environment and to health related behaviour, it was harder to imagine how social relationships of inequality could be strongly associated with mortality. However, the growing body of epidemiological findings suggesting the importance of features of psychosocial life, such as sense of control, social affiliations and support, self-esteem, 'life events' and job security, is now coupled with a clearer understanding of the physiological pathways through which chronic psychosocial stress can have a wide range of health outcomes (Chrousos *et al.* 1995). There is also impressive evidence of the health-related physiological consequences of low social status from studies of non-human primates (Sapolsky 1993, Shively *et al.* 1994, Shively *et al.* 1997).

The difficulty is now more a matter of identifying which are the more important of a wide range of social processes that could plausibly contribute to a relationship between mortality and inequality. Particularly interesting is the question of whether people's health is only affected by income inequality through the impact of their individual relative income on their own health (*i.e.* through things like low self-esteem consequent on low social status, worry over debt, financial insecurity etc.), or whether there are more broadly based social processes which may lead to improvements in health more widely among people living in more egalitarian societies – at least partly independently of their own relative income. On this latter possibility, Kawachi *et al.* (1997) have shown statistical evidence suggesting that the relationship between income inequality and mortality among the states of the USA is mediated by 'social trust' – as measured by the proportion of people in each state agreeing with the statement 'most people would try to take advantage of you if they got the chance'. Similarly, Wilkinson (1996) discussed a number of examples of societies which were both unusually egalitarian and unusually healthy. They all showed a marked tendency to be more socially cohesive. However, not only is it unclear what aspects of social cohesion might be important to health, but it would be possible to argue that rather than income inequality affecting health through social cohesion, the psychosocial effects of low relative income could rebound directly on both health and social cohesion without the latter being a pathway to the former.

In passing, we should mention that it has been suggested (Fiscella and Franks 1997) that the association between income inequality and mortality may reflect a greater incidence of absolute poverty and lower absolute levels of consumption among the less well off in areas of greater inequality. In other words, it has been argued that the relationship of income inequality to mortality simply reflects a compositional effect of more poor people (who are presumably at higher risk of death) residing in areas of high income disparity. We reject this explanation because it has been shown that, of the two variables income distribution and the percentage of households in each state living below the federal poverty threshold, income distribution but not poverty is independently related to mortality. In addition, when the weak relationship between mortality and median state income is controlled for income distribution, rather than the association being strengthened, it disappears altogether and mortality shows no independent relation to median income whatsoever (Kaplan *et al.* 1996, Kennedy *et al.* 1996).

Homicide
One of the intriguing aspects of the relationship between inequality and mortality is that it seems to be mirrored by a relationship between income distribution and homicide. Kaplan *et al.* (1996) reported close correlations between income inequality and both homicide (r = 0.74) and violent crime rates (r = 0.70) among the 50 states of the United States. Kennedy *et al.* (1996) examined the cross-sectional relationship between household income distribution and state-level variations in homicide rates. The greater the disparity in household incomes, the higher was the homicide rate at the state level. Relative deprivation was apparently an even stronger predictor of homicide rates than absolute deprivation. Homicide showed correlations

with income inequality and household poverty rates of 0.74 and 0.53, respectively. Even after adjusting for poverty, income inequality accounted for 52 per cent of the between-state variance in homicide rates. An association between homicide and income inequality has also been found using international data (Messner 1983, Krahn *et al.* 1986). In addition, Wilson and Daly (1997) reported a correlation of 0.88 between homicide and all other causes of death (excluding homicide) among 77 'community areas' in the Chicago region. The link was confirmed in a meta-analysis of some 34 studies (Hsieh and Pugh 1993).

Social disorganisation

There is a substantial body of research which suggests that crime rates reflect 'community social disorganisation'. Social disorganisation theory was originally developed by the Chicago School researchers Clifford Shaw and Henry McKay in their classic work, *Juvenile Delinquency and Urban Areas* (1942). Shaw and McKay demonstrated that the same socioeconomically disadvantaged areas in 21 US cities continued to exhibit high delinquency rates over a span of several decades, despite changes in their racial and ethnic composition, indicating the persistent contextual effects of these communities on crime rates, regardless of what populations experienced them. This observation led them to reject individualistic explanations of delinquency and to focus instead on community processes – like disruption of local community organisation and weak social controls – which led to the apparent trans-generational transmission of criminal behaviour. In general, social disorganisation is defined as the 'inability of a community structure to realise the common values of its residents and maintain effective social controls' (Sampson and Groves 1989). The social organisational approach views local communities and neighbourhoods as complex systems of friendship, kinship, and acquaintanceship networks, as well as formal and informal associational ties rooted in family life and ongoing socialisation processes (Sampson 1995). From the perspective of crime control, a major dimension of social disorganisation is the ability of a community to supervise and control teenage peer groups, especially gangs. Thus Shaw and McKay (1942) argued that residents of cohesive communities were better able to control the youth behaviours that set the context for gang violence. Examples of such controls include: 'the supervision of leisure-time youth activities, intervention in street-corner congregation, and challenging youth "who seem to be up to no good". Socially disorganised communities with extensive street-corner peer groups are also expected to have higher rates of adult violence, especially among younger adults who still have ties to youth gangs' (Sampson 1995).

Recently, social disorganisation theory has been linked to the emerging concept of social capital (Sampson 1995). Social capital has been defined by its principal theorists (Coleman 1990, Putnam 1993) as those features of social organisation, such as networks, norms of reciprocity, and trust in others, that facilitate cooperation between citizens for mutual benefit. Lack of social capital is thus one of the primary features of socially disorganised communities (Sampson 1995). Although the conceptualisation and measurement of social capital are still evolving, two critical features of the concept appear to be the level of trust among citizens and the density and rate of participation in voluntary associations and local organisations (Putnam 1995).

Several empirical studies, reviewed by Sampson (1995), have corroborated the link between low stocks of social capital and high crime rates. Taylor and colleagues (1984) examined violent crimes (such as mugging, assault, murder, rape) across 63 street blocks in Baltimore. Based on interviews with 687 household respondents, Taylor *et al.* constructed block-level measures of the proportion of respondents who belonged to an organisation to which co-residents also belonged, and the proportion of respondents who felt responsible for what happened in the area surrounding their home. Both variables were significantly and negatively associated with rates of violence. Similarly, Sincha-Fagan and Schwartz (1986) collected survey information on 553 residents of 12 neighbourhoods in New York City, and found a significant negative relationship between the rate of self-reported delinquency and rates of organisational participation by local residents. A third set of studies conducted by Sampson and Groves (1989) in Great Britain reported that density of local friendship networks had a significant negative effect on robbery rates, while the level of organisational participation by residents had significant inverse effects on both robbery and stranger violence. Not only does participation in local organisations increase the level of community control, it may facilitate the capacity of communities to obtain extra-local resources – such as police and fire services, as well as block grants – that have indirect consequences for crime control (Burski and Grasmick 1993). In the most convincing demonstration to date of the link between social cohesion and crime, Sampson and colleagues (1997) surveyed 8,782 residents of 343 Chicago neighbourhoods to ask about their perceptions of social cohesion and trust in the neighbourhood. Respondents were asked how strongly they agreed (on a five point scale) that 'people around here are willing to help their neighbors', 'this is a close-knit neighborhood', 'people in this neighborhood can be trusted', 'people in this neighborhood generally don't get along with each other', and 'people in this neighborhood do not share the same values' (the last two items were reverse-coded). The resulting scale was then combined with responses to questions about the level of informal social control (whether neighbours would intervene in situations where children were engaging in delinquent behaviour) to produce a summary index of 'collective efficacy'. Collective efficacy turned out to be significantly ($P < 0.01$) related to organizational participation ($r = 0.45$) and neighbourhood services ($r = 0.21$). In hierarchical statistical models adjusting for individual characteristics (age, socioeconomic status, gender, ethnicity, marital status, home ownership, and years in neighbourhood), the index of collective efficacy was significantly inversely associated with reports of neighbourhood violence, violent victimisation, as well as homicide rates. For example, a two standard deviation elevation in neighbourhood collective efficacy was associated with a 39.7% reduction in the expected homicide rate.

Given these reported links between crime and the nature of the local social environment we decided to use rates of different kinds of crime to re-examine the relationship between income inequality, social trust and mortality which had been identified in previous work (Kawachi *et al.* 1997). Using data for the states of the United States we decided to see whether there were informative differences in the way different kinds of crime fitted into these relationships. Our hope was that they would provide a guide to the social processes which mediate between income distribution and mortality.

Data sources

The social environment

A core feature of 'social capital', as presented by its principal theorists (Coleman 1990, Putnam 1993) consists of levels of interpersonal trust among community members. Following Putnam (1995), we used data from the General Social Surveys (GSS), conducted by the National Opinion Research Center to estimate state variations in levels of interpersonal trust. The GSS is a nationally representative survey of noninstitutionalised adults over 18 years living in the United States. The surveys have been repeated 14 times over the last two decades, and have included a set of questions on interpersonal trust. In the present study, we averaged five years of cumulated data (1986–1990), representing 7,679 individual observations. Of the 50 states, only 39 were sampled in the survey due to the small population of some states (*e.g.* Delaware, Rhode Island); hence, social capital data were not available in these states. Because the sampling design of the GSS was intended to be representative of regions rather than states, we adjusted individual responses using post-stratification weights to reflect the age, race/ethnic, and educational composition of each state. Detailed procedures for the post-stratification weighting are described elsewhere (Kawachi *et al.* 1997).

Our Social Trust variable was assessed from responses to the GSS item that asked: 'Generally speaking, would you say that most people can be trusted, or that you can't be too careful in dealing with people?' For each state, we calculated the percentage of residents who agreed that 'most people cannot be trusted'. Belief in the good will and benign intent of others facilitates collective action and mutual cooperation, and therefore adds to the stock of a community's social capital. In turn, collective action further reinforces community norms of reciprocity.

Based on the well-established association between male youth and violent crime rates, we also obtained Census-derived estimates of the proportion of the population in each state who were males aged 15 to 24 years.

Income measures

Household income data for each state were obtained from the 1990 US Census Summary Tape File STF 3A. The data provide annual household income for 25 income intervals ($0–5,000 at the bottom, and $150,000 or more at the top). To calculate income inequality, counts of the number of households falling into each of the 25 income intervals were obtained for each state. These interval data were converted into income deciles using a programme developed by the US Census Bureau. Our measure of income inequality, the Robin Hood Index (RHI), was estimated for each state from the income decile distribution, which represents the share of total household income in each decile. The RHI is then calculated by summing the excess shares of income for those deciles whose shares of the aggregate income exceed 10 per cent (Atkinson and Micklewright 1992). For example in Massachusetts, the RHI is 30.26 per cent. This represents the share of total income from all households that would have to be transferred from those above the mean to those below the mean in order to achieve a perfectly equal income distribution. The higher the value of RHI, the greater is the degree of income inequality. We also obtained median gross household income for each state.

Mortality and crime rates

Age-adjusted mortality from all-causes and homicide rates were obtained for each state from the Compressed Mortality Files compiled by the National Center for Health Statistics, Center for Disease Control and Prevention (CDC). We subtracted homicide from all-cause mortality to provide two variables – homicide and all-causes mortality excluding homicide – which were entirely separate from each other. Mortality (excluding homicide) was taken for the year 1990, while data for years 1981–1991 were combined to provide more stable estimates of homicide rates.

Incidence rates of other crimes – rape, robbery, aggravated assault, burglary, larceny, and motor vehicle theft – were obtained from the Federal Bureau of Investigation's Uniform Crime Reports (UCR) for the years 1991–1994 (US Department of Justice 1991–1994). These rates are based on the incidents of crime reported to the police, and subsequently to the Federal Bureau of Investigation (FBI) through the crime reporting programme. Incidence data, while subject to various biases related to variations in reporting, are nonetheless considered less susceptible to bias compared to arrest data (Reiss and Roth 1993). Table 1 shows a list of the variables and their definitions. Homicide, rape, robbery and aggravated assault are classified under the broad category of violent crimes, while burglary, larceny, and motor vehicle theft are classified under property crimes.

Table 1 *Definitions of variables used. (Abbreviations used in Table 2 listed in parentheses)*

1. *Males 15–25 yrs* (% 15–24M):
    Percentage of state population who are males 15–24 years old.
2. *Social trust* (SOCTRUST):
    Level of interpersonal trust, measured by percentage of residents in state responding that 'Most people cannot be trusted'.
3. *Income inequality* (ROBINHD):
    The Robin Hood Index of income inequality measures the proportion of income which would need to be redistributed to gain total income equality (see text).
4. *Median income* (MEDINC):
    Median household income in state.
5. *Mortality* (MORTALITY):
    Age-standardised total mortality rate per 100,000 population in each state.
6. *Homicide* (HOMICIDE):
    Age-standardised homicide rate per 100,000 inhabitants in each state.
7. *Aggravated assault* (ASSAULT):
    Reported aggravated assault incidence in state (per 100,000 population). Defined as an unlawful attack by one person upon another for the purpose of inflicting severe or aggravated bodily injury.
8. *Rape* (RAPE):
    Reported rape incidence in state (per 100,000 population).
9. *Robbery* (ROBBERY):
    Reported robbery incidence in state (per 100,000 population). Defined as the taking or attempting to take anything of value from the care, custody, or control of a person or persons by force or threat of force or violence and/or putting the victim in fear.
10. *Burglary* (BURGLARY):
    Reported burglary rate in state (per 100,000 population). Defined as the unlawful entry of a structure to commit a felony or theft.
11. *Larceny* (LARCENY):
    Reported larceny-theft rate in state (per 100,000 population). Defined as the unlawful taking, carrying, leading, or riding away of property from the possession or constructive possession of another. It includes crimes such as shoplifting, pickpocketing, purse-snatching, thefts from motor vehicles, thefts of motor vehicle parts, bicycle thefts, etc., in which no use of force, violence or fraud occurs. This crime category does not include embezzlement, 'con' games, forgery and worthless cheques.
12. *Motor vehicle theft* (MVTHEFT):
    Reported rate of motor vehicle theft in state (per 100,000 population).

Results and discussion

Table 2 shows the correlation matrix between all the variables. Data are presented for the 39 states covered by the General Social Surveys. Strong correlations with mortality in the expected direction are shown with income inequality (r = 0.63), social trust (r = 0.76), and homicide (r = 0.70) (see also Kawachi *et al.* 1997). Much weaker, though still statistically significant, correlations were found with the proportion of males 15–24, median income, and aggravated assault. Correlations between mortality and the other crime variables failed to reach statistical significance: while robbery, burglary and rape showed a weak direct association with mortality, motor vehicle theft showed no association and larceny was inversely correlated with mortality. It could be argued that the differences in the associations between mortality and different categories of crime were simply a reflection of differences in reporting, and that homicide shows a close association because the data are much more accurate. Nevertheless, the statistically significant direct correlations between higher median state income and higher rates of robbery and motor vehicle theft might indicate that some forms of property crime are influenced by the greater opportunities for theft which more prosperous states would provide.

As well as being closely associated with mortality, income inequality is significantly associated with homicide (r = 0.74), social trust (r = 0.73), assault (r = 0.50), burglary (r = 0.44), and robbery (r = 0.36). Inequality's correlations with rape and motor vehicle theft are weakly positive but there is no relationship with larceny.

The fact that violent crime, particularly homicide and aggravated assault, are more closely related both to mortality and to income inequality than are

Table 2 *Correlation matrix for all variables (data for 39 states)*
(Coefficients marked * are significant at P < 0.05)

Variable	% 15–24M	HOMICIDE	MORTALITY	ROBINHD	MEDINC
% 15–24M	1.00	.32*	.37*	.31	−.18
HOMICIDE	.32*	1.00	.70*	.74*	−.24
MORTALITY	.37*	.70*	1.00	.63*	−.38*
ROBINHD	.31	.74*	.63*	1.00	−.47*
MEDINC	−.18	−.24*	−.38*	−.47*	1.00
SOCTRUST	.32*	.82*	.76*	.73*	−.24
RAPE	.14	.38*	.13	.13	−.07
ROBBERY	−.04	.63*	.23	.36*	.38*
ASSAULT	.19	.73*	.35*	.50*	−.01
BURGLARY	.13	.67*	.17	.44*	−.04
LARCENY	−.07	.26	−.31	−.04	.12
MVTHEFT	−.05	.39*	−.01	.24	.54*

property crimes, may tell us something of the nature of the relationship between mortality and income inequality. If we assume that violent crime is indicative of some aspect of the social fabric, how does this factor fit into the relationship between mortality and both income inequality and social trust?

Regressing mortality simultaneously on income inequality and homicide shows that income inequality is not related to mortality independently of homicide ($p = 0.76$), though homicide is strongly related to mortality independently of income inequality ($p = 0.0002$). Regressing mortality against homicide and social trust shows that social trust is related significantly to mortality independently of homicide ($p = 0.005$), but the relationship between mortality and homicide independent of social trust fails to reach significance ($p = 0.19$).

What these results suggest is that the social conditions which produce homicide are near the heart of the relationships we want to understand between income distribution and mortality. The social conditions which produce homicide are also very closely related to social trust (the simple correlation between homicide and social trust is 0.82) but homicide does not wholly account for the relationship between social trust and mortality. Other forms of crime have either no relationship or a weaker relationship to this pattern. It would appear that homicide and larceny (or motor vehicle theft) – the most and least violent crimes – are at opposite extremes in how they are related to income distribution and mortality, with assault, burglary and robbery taking up intermediate positions. The associations with assault are most like those with homicide, so adding to the impression that we are dealing with a distinction between social conditions which lead to increased violence and those which lead to increased property crime. Rape, as a violent crime which lacks strong associations with income distribution or social

SOCTRUST	RAPE	ROBBERY	ASSAULT	BURGLARY	LARCENY	MVTHEFT
.32*	.14	−.04	.19	.13	−.07	−.05
.82*	.38*	.63*	.73*	.67*	.26	.39*
.76*	.13	.23	.35*	.17	−.31	−.01
.73*	.13	.36*	.50*	.44*	−.04	−.24
−.07	.38*	−.01	−.04	.12	.54*	
1.00	.17	.45*	.61*	.54*	.01	.31
.17	1.00	.19	.43*	.53*	.57*	.20
.45*	.19	1.00	.64*	.49*	.29	.77*
.61*	.43*	.65*	1.00	.74*	.45*	.56*
.54*	.53*	.49*	.74*	1.00	.63*	.55*
.01	.57*	.29	.45*	.63*	1.00	.32*
.31	.20	.77*	.56*	.55*	.32*	1.00

trust, appears to be an exception to this pattern, but as rape statistics are notoriously affected by differences in reporting, it may be unwise to read much into this.

We are inclined to take the differences in the associational patterns of violence and property crime seriously partly because they echo earlier findings. In an analysis of data for 27 countries, Krohn (1976) found statistically significant relationship between higher homicide and greater income inequality which remained after controlling for GNPpc. However, he found the relationship with property crime was, if anything, the other way round. A number of other pieces of research also reveal a sharp distinction between violence and property crime. Field (1990) analyses fluctuations in crime in Britain in relation to the business cycle and shows sharply differing patterns: property crime is negatively related to changes in consumer's expenditure per capita while violence is positively related. He suggests that property crime is a result of relative deprivation, whereas violence occurs more frequently when there are more people on the street and alcohol consumption is higher. Hennigan et al. (1982) examined the effects of the introduction of television in different parts of the United States in the 1950s and '60s on the rates of violent crime, burglary, auto theft and larceny. They found no effect on violence, burglary or auto theft, but a consistent association between the spread of television and rises in larceny.

What then are the differences between the social conditions conducive to homicide and those conducive to property crime, and what can the difference tell us about the way the social environment associated with greater income inequality affects health? We conjecture that one of the salient characteristics of social environments marked by wide income disparities is that they generate invidious social comparisons, which in turn engender a sense of exclusion and alienation among vulnerable individuals. Under such conditions, violent behaviour may be seen as an expression of the quest for respect from others. To shore up these arguments, we turn to evidence of a different nature, viz. narrative histories of violent individuals describing their quest for respect. In the section to follow, we move purposely from community-level analysis (the inter-relationships among income inequality, social cohesion, and mortality) toward an individual-level description of the relationship between the psychological sense of exclusion and the expression of violent behaviour. The reason for making this macro-to-micro transition is to attempt to link the social environment (income inequality) to individual health outcomes, via intervening psychological variables, including the lack of self-esteem and the sense of not being respected.

Antecedents of violence

Few authorities can match James Gilligan's detailed personal knowledge of men imprisoned for violence. He worked for 25 years as a psychiatrist in American prisons talking daily to violent offenders (Gilligan 1996). As a former director of the Centre for the Study of Violence at Harvard Medical School, he regards his book, *Violence*, as a contribution to public health and we shall quote from it extensively. Gilligan says:–

> . . . the prison inmates I work with have told me repeatedly, when I asked them why they had assaulted someone, that it was because 'he disrespected me', or 'he disrespected my visit' (meaning /visitor'). The word 'disrespect' is central in the vocabulary, moral value system, and psychodynamics of these chronically violent men that they have abbreviated it into the slang term, 'he dis'ed me'. (1996: 106)

The challenge 'Are you dis'in' me?' has now also become the standard way young people on the streets of Britain threaten belligerence.

Gilligan continues:–

> I have yet to see a serious act of violence that was not provoked by the experience of feeling shamed and humiliated, disrespected and ridiculed, and that did not represent the attempt to prevent or undo this 'loss of face' – no matter how severe the punishment, even if it includes death (1996: 110)

Describing one prisoner, he says

> a very angry and violent inmate in his thirties, in prison for armed robbery, was referred to me because he had been yelling at, insulting, threatening, and assaulting another inmate. He had been doing this kind of thing for the past several weeks, and, off and on, for years . . . (and I had little) success in persuading him to stop his endlessly self-defeating power struggles with everyone around him, which inevitably resulted in his being punished more severely.
>
> In an attempt to break through that vicious cycle with this man, I finally asked him 'What do you want so badly that you would sacrifice everything else in order to get it?' And he . . . replied with calm assurance, with perfect coherence and even a kind of eloquence: 'Pride. Dignity. Self-esteem.' And then he went on to say, again more clearly than before: 'And I'll kill every mother-fucker in that cell block if I have to in order to get it! My life ain't worth nothin' if I take somebody disrespectin' me and callin' me punk asshole faggot and goin' Ha, Ha! at me. Life ain't worth livin' if there ain't nothin' worth dyin' for. If you ain't got pride, you got nothin'. That's all you got! I've already got my pride'. He explained that the other prisoner was 'tryin' to take that away from me. I'm not a total idiot. I'm not a coward. There ain't nothin I can do except snuff him. I'll throw gasoline on him and light him'. (1996: 106)

About the use of violence in robbery, Gilligan says:–

> Some people think that armed robbers commit their crime in order to get money. And of course, sometimes that is the way they rationalize their

behavior. But when you sit down and talk with people who repeatedly commit such crimes, what you hear is, 'I never got so much respect before in my life as I did when I first pointed a gun at somebody', or 'You wouldn't believe how much respect you get when you have a gun pointed at some dude's face'. For men who have lived for a lifetime on a diet of contempt and disdain, the temptation to gain instant respect in this way can be worth far more than the cost of going to prison, or even dying. (1996: 109)

Discussing the kind of events which can trigger violence, Gilligan says:–

... it is well known to anyone who reads the newspapers that people often seem to become seriously violent, even homicidal, over what are patently trivial events. (1996: 12)

It is the very triviality of the incidents that precipitate violence, the kinds of things that provoke homicide and sometimes suicide, whether in family quarrels or those that occur among friends and lovers on the street or in barrooms, that has often been commented on, with surprise and perplexity – being given a 'dirty look', having one's new shoes stepped on, being called a demeaning name, having a spouse or lover flirt with someone else, being shoved by someone at a bar, having someone take food off one's plate, or refuse to move a car that is blocking one's drive-way ... (1996: 133)

Everyone has experienced 'trivial' insults that rankle. A child is teased for a difficult word mispronounced, a professional woman is asked to get the coffee. If these small incidents rankle people with power, prestige, and status, imagine their effect on people who don't have these advantages ... (1996: 134)

... events that are utterly trivial from any moral or legal point of view may be of the very greatest importance and significance from a ... psychological perspective. (1996: 135)

This view from a prison psychiatrist accords well with Jimmy Boyle's descriptions of himself. Once known as 'the most violent man in Scotland', Boyle wrote his autobiography in the 10th year of a sentence for manslaughter (Boyle 1977). Violence as a means of gaining status and respect is equally clear in his account.

There is no doubt that when I was sober, alone and faced with reality I hated myself ... there was just this completely lost feeling ... Yet ... when I was with my pals, there was this feeling that it was okay and that having attacked a gang single handed the previous night, I had in some way proved myself and gained enough confidence to fight alongside them. I had this hunger to be recognised, to establish a reputation for myself and it acted as an incentive being with the top guys in the district at sixteen. There was this inner compulsion for me to win recognition amongst them. (1977: 79)

Talking of one spell in Barlinnie Prison: ' . . . each of us had reputations, there had never been this sort of gathering of guys in the criminal element in Glasgow ever before. Although we were inside this was still the great motivating force – our reputation' (1977: 131).

Of a period of fundamental self-examination, Boyle said 'For the first time in my life, I was having to think very deeply about violence and other methods of gaining status' (1977: 240).

The contribution of low socio-economic status to the need to earn respect through violence is shown not only in the association between homicide and income distribution, but also in the frequency with which Boyle mentions that fellow prisoners were also from the Gorbals (then the poorest slum area of Glasgow) and had sometimes even been to the same school as himself.

Given that violence is a defence of status among those who have few sources of status and self-esteem, Gilligan suggests that there are three factors which make the difference between people who are violent and others. First, he says,

Many of the violent criminals who fill our maximum security prisons . . . desperately want to feel that they are big, tough, independent, self-assertive, self-reliant men, so as not to feel needy, helpless, frightened, inadequate, unskilled, incompetent, and often illiterate. . . . For we will never understand violence and violent criminals until we see through what is, in truth, a defensive disguise . . . (1996: 127)

He continues:

The second precondition for violence is met when these men perceive themselves as having no non-violent means of warding off or diminishing their feelings of shame or low self-esteem – such as socially rewarding economic or cultural achievement, or high social status, position or prestige. Violence is a 'last resort', a strategy they will use only when no other alternatives appear possible. (1996: 112)

On the third precondition for violence, Gilligan says

What is startling about the most violent people is how incapable they are, at least at the time they commit their violence, of feeling love, guilt, or fear. The person who is overwhelmed by feelings of shame is by definition experiencing a psychically life-threatening lack of love . . . (1996: 113)

This accords well with Jimmy Boyle's statement (above) that in the cold light of day he hated himself. It is tempting to see this in the context of his description of the lack of physical affection in his family life. He says:

for some strange reason or other, actual physical contact in families that I knew was very limited. I would never think of coming into the house after all this long absence (on release from several years in prison) and cuddling my Ma or giving her a kiss or for that matter shaking my brothers by the hand or embracing them; these things just weren't done. That was sissy stuff, therefore not for us. (1977: 113)

We are left then with a strong impression that homicide and violence are so closely related to income inequality because they come out of an extreme sensitivity to issues of personal social status to which people are particularly vulnerable when excluded from many of the usual sources of status. Although we have quoted material relating to violent offenders, it is clear that the same relationships hold in society more widely. The pervasive discrimination and exclusion of African-Americans from mainstream American society has been postulated to be the phenomenological explanation for younger blacks' preoccupation with respect (readers are referred, for example, to the eloquent qualitative work by American scholars like Elijah Anderson (1990) and Bourgois (1995)). The *Washington Post* reporter, Nathan McCall, who grew up in a poverty-stricken neighbourhood in Virginia and served time in prison for violent crime, says in his autobiography:–

For as long as I can remember, black folks have had a serious thing about respect. I guess it's because white people disrespected them so blatantly for so long that blacks viciously protected what little morsels of self-respect they thought they had left. Some of the most brutal battles I saw in the streets stemmed from seemingly petty stuff . . . But the underlying issue was always respect. You could ask a guy, 'Damn, man, why did you bust that dude in the head with a pipe?'
    And he might say, 'The motherfucka disrespected me!'
    That was explanation enough. It wasn't even necessary to explain how the guy had disrespected him. It was universally understood that if a dude got disrespected, he had to do what he had to do. It's still that way today. Young dudes nowadays call it 'dissin''. They'll kill a nigger for dissin' them. Won't touch a white person, but they'll kill a brother in a heartbeat over a perceived slight. This irony was that white folks constantly disrespected us in ways seen and unseen, and we tolerated it. Most blacks understood that the repercussions were more severe for retaliating against whites than for doing each other in. It was as if black folks were saying, 'I can't do much to keep whites from dissin' me, but I damn sure can keep black folks from doing it'. (McCall 1994: 52)

Property crime
What then of property crime – larceny and motor vehicle theft? The indications of the social milieu in which it is most common are less clear. While

there have been several papers (cited above) which testify to a sharp distinction between patterns of violence and theft, there is little work which explores the differences in the social environment from which these crimes come. The finding that property crime increases in economic recessions (Field 1990), and that it also rose in response to the spread of television in the United States (Hennigan *et al.* 1982) both suggest that it is a response to relative deprivation. However, the broad pattern of correlations in Table 2 (above) shows that it is not even weakly related to income distribution. More surprising still is that larceny's weak association with mortality is an inverse association (Table 2), and that motor vehicle theft shows a significant positive relation with median income ($r = 0.54$) and no relation with mortality.

Using the World Values Survey (WVS) and the International Crime Victim Surveys, Halpern (1996) found that 'although moral values have little or no relationship with the covariants of crime and cannot therefore "explain" it, a specific sub-set of items tapping "self-interest" do covary (with crime) and therefore offer some explanations ' (1996: 5). The WVS covered 50 countries, and common groupings of values were picked out using factor analysis before the factors were related to crime victimisation rates. In a subsequent more detailed analysis Halpern (personal communication) reported a correlation of 0.5 between international crime victimisation rates and the 'self-interest' factor. Although these results come from data which make no distinction between kinds of crime, as theft is the most common form of crime in most countries, the patterns which emerge are likely to reflect its distribution.

Given that in our data larceny and motor vehicle theft are unrelated to income distribution and tend, if anything, to be more prevalent where median income is higher and mortality lower, one might then speculate – as Halpern (1996) indeed does – that theft arises from values rooted in something closer to self-interest and individualism, fuelled perhaps as much by the habit of consumption as by deprivation. Our data did not include fraud which is clearly a form of property crime not involving violence. Traditionally regarded as a 'white collar crime', fraud is likely to have even less association with deprivation than larceny and its inclusion would have led to an even sharper distinction between the pattern of violence and property crime.

Indeed, a limitation of our study is the lack of data addressing a broader conceptualisation of violence and property crime. Thus the routine reporting of violent *crime* ignores the many other forms of institutionalised violence in society: (a) those which are perpetrated by the State and its personnel (armed forces, warfare, police, and prisons); (b) those to which the State turns a blind eye (domestic violence, firearm ownership, motor vehicle violence – 'road rage', speeding, and drunk driving); as well as (c) those which are professionalised, rarely apprehended, and a necessary part of illegal business activity (illegal drugs, loan sharking, prostitution, protection). Similarly, a broader definition of property crime (*e.g.* extraction of surplus value, tax evasion, fraud and white collar crime) would have sharpened the distinctions we are trying to draw. Additionally, the usual caveats apply in attempting to interpret findings based on crime *statistics*, which are mediated via processes of report, arrest, charge, and trial; and are consequently biased against the poor, the inarticulate, and those with low social status.

Conclusions

Our argument is not that the number of homicide victims account for the relationship between health and income distribution. It is that the violence associated with income inequality serves as an indicator of the psychosocial impact of wider income differences. What we can take away from this discussion is that the most pressing aspect of relative deprivation and low relative income is less the shortage of the material goods which others have, as the low social status and the desperate lack of sources of self-esteem which usually goes with it. If social cohesion matters to health, then perhaps the component of it which matters most is that people have positions and roles in society which accord them dignity and respect. We infer this from the fact that it is violence rather than property crime which varies so closely with income distribution, social trust and mortality. Unlike theft, which is in a sense a relationship with property, violence is a much more intensely social crime and seems above all to express a lack of adequate internal and external sources of self-esteem, dignity and social status.

As Miller and Ferroggiaro (1996) have pointed out 'Respect and self-respect are central components of an enlarged concept of citizenship . . . Respect affects how we are treated, what help from others is likely, what economic arrangements others are willing to engage in with us, when reciprocity is to be expected'. Respect acts as a resource for individuals, and should be considered a component of the norms of reciprocity, trust, and social obligation that are essential for minimising the risks of poor physical, psychological, or social health (Aday 1994). Indeed, mutual respect and the avoidance of inflicting humiliation on people is the central concept of Margalit's 'decent society' (Margalit 1996). As he says, a decent society 'does not injure the civic honour of those belonging to it' (1996: 151). That honour and shame are so crucial to human social relations and may often become issues of life and death has long been recognised by social anthropologists (Peristiany 1965).

The impressive body of work on the physiological effects of the chronic stress experienced by low status baboons and macaques (Sapolsky 1993, Shively *et al.* 1994, Shively *et al.* 1997) suggests that there may be a number of health effects which spring directly from low social status among humans, and some of the same physiological effects of low social status have been found among humans as among these non-human primates (Brunner 1997). However, if issues round shame, respect, self-esteem, are how we conceptualise the most powerful psychosocial impact of low social status, then it is still difficult to distinguish between the individual and social effects of inequality on health status. As Pitt-Rivers (1965) says, 'Honour is the value of a person in his own eyes, but also in the eyes of society. It is his estimation of his own worth, his claim to pride, but it is also the acknowledgement of that claim . . . by society' (1965: 21).

Considerable research has already documented the contribution to the social gradient in health attributable to factors such as unemployment, job insecurity, sense of control and other sources of difficulty associated with disadvantage. Perhaps more attention should now be given to the psychosocial effects most directly inherent in low social status itself.

Acknowledgements

Richard Wilkinson is supported by the Paul Hamlyn Foundation; Ichiro Kawachi and Bruce Kennedy are recipients of the Robert Wood Johnson Foundation Investigator Awards in Health Care Policy. The authors wish to thank two anonymous reviewers for their helpful comments made on an earlier version of this manuscript.

References

Aday, L.A. (1994) Health status of vulnerable populations, *Annual Review of Public Health*, 15, 487–509.

Anderson, E. (1990) *Streetwise: Race, Class, and Change in an Urban Community*. Chicago: Chicago University Press.

Atkinson, A.B. and Micklewright, J. (1992) *Economic Transformation in Eastern Europe and the Distribution of Income*. Cambridge: Cambridge University Press.

Ben-Shlomo, Y., White, I.R. and Marmot, M. (1996) Does the variation in the socioeconomic characteristics of an area affect mortality? *British Medical Journal*, 312, 1013–14.

Bourgois, P.L. (1995) *In Search of Respect: Selling Crack in El Barrio*. Cambridge, New York: Cambridge University Press.

Boyle, J. (1977) *A Sense of Freedom*. London: Pan Books.

Burski, R.J. Jr. and Grasmick, H. (1993) *Neighborhoods and Crime: the Dimensions of Effective Community Control*. New York: Lexington.

Brunner, E. (1997) Stress and the biology of inequality, *British Medical Journal*, 314, 1472–6.

Chrousos, G.P., McCarty, R., Pacak, K., Cizza, G., Sternbery, E., Gold, P.W. and Kvetnansky, R. (eds) (1995) *Stress: Basic Mechanisms and Clinical Implications*.

Annals of the New York Academy of Sciences, Vol. 771. New York: The New York Academy of Sciences.

Coleman, J.S. (1990) *The Foundations of Social Theory*. Cambridge, MA: Harvard University Press.

Field, S. (1990) *Trends in Crime and their Interpretation*. Home Office Research and Planning Unit Report. London: HMSO.

Fiscella, K. and Franks, P. (1997) Poverty or income inequality as predictors of mortality: longitudinal cohort study, *British Medical Journal*, 314, 1724–8.

Gilligan, J. (1996) *Violence: our Deadly Epidemic and its Causes*. New York: G.P. Putnam.

Halpern, D. (1996) Changes in moral concepts and values: can values explain crime? Royal Society of Edinburgh. Causes of Crime Symposium, 5 June 1996.

Hennigan, K.M., Heath, L., Wharton, J.D., Del Rosario, M.L., Cook, T.D. and Calder, B.J. (1982) Impact of the introduction of television on crime in the United States: empirical findings and theoretical implications, *Journal of Personality and Social Psychology*, 42, 461–77.

Hsieh, C.C. and Pugh, M.D. (1993) Poverty, income inequalites and violent crime: a meta-analysis, *Criminal Justice Review*, 18, 182–202.

Kaplan, G.A., Pamuk, E., Lynch, J.W., Cohen, R.D. and Balfour, J.L. (1996) Inequality in income and mortality in the United States: analysis of mortality and potential pathways, *British Medical Journal*, 312, 999–1003.

Kawachi, I., Kennedy, B.P., Lochner, K. and Prothrow-Stith, D. (1997) Social capital, income inequality and mortality, *American Journal of Public Health*, 87, 1491–8.

Kennedy, B.P., Kawachi, I. and Prothrow-Stith, D. (1996) Income distribution and mortality: cross sectional ecological study of the Robin Hood index in the United States, *British Medical Journal*, 312, 1004–7.

Krahn, H., Hartnagel, T.F. and Gartrell, J.W. (1986) Income inequality and homicide rates: cross-national data and criminological theories, *Criminology*, 24, 269–95.

Krohn, M.D. (1976) Inequality, unemployment and crime, *Sociological Quarterly*, 17, 303–13.

Margalit, A. (1966) *The Decent Society*. Harvard: Harvard University Press.

McCall, N. (1994) *Makes Me Wanna Holler. A Young Black Man in America*. New York: Random House.

Messner, S.E. (1982) Societal development, social equality and homicide, *Social Forces*, 61, 225–40.

Miller, S.M. and Ferroggiaro, K.M. (1996) Respect, *Poverty and Race*, 5, 1, 1–14.

Peristiany, J.G. (ed) (1965) *Honour and Shame: the Values of Mediterranean Society*. London: Weidenfeld and Nicolson.

Pitt-Rivers, J. (1965) Honour and social status. In Peristiany, J.G. (ed) *Honour and Shame: the Values of Mediterranean Society*. London: Weidenfeld and Nicolson.

Putnam, R.D. (1993) *Making Democracy Work. Civic Traditions in Modern Italy*. Princeton, NJ: Princeton University Press.

Putnam, R.D. (1995) Bowling alone: America's declining social capital, *Journal of Democracy*, 6, 65–78.

Reiss, A.J. and Roth, J.A. (eds) (1993) *Understanding and Preventing Violence*. Washington DC: National Academy Press.

Sampson, R.J. (1987) Urban black violence: the effect of male joblessness and family disruption, *American Journal of Sociology*, 93, 348–82.

Sampson, R.J. (1995) The community. In James, Q., Wilson, and Petersilia, J. (eds) *Crime*. San Francisco: Institute for Contemporary Studies.

Sampson, R.J., Raudenbush, S.W. and Earls, F. (1997) Neighborhoods and violent crime: a multilevel study of collective efficacy, *Science*, 277, 918–24.

Sampson, R.J. and Groves, W.R. (1989) Community structure and crime: testing social-disorganization theory, *American Journal of Sociology*, 94, 774–802.

Sapolsky, R.M. (1993) Endocrinology alfresco: psychoendocrine studies of wild baboons, *Recent Progress in Hormone Research*, 48, 437–68.

Shaw, C. and Mckay, H. (1942) *Juvenile Delinquency and Urban Areas*. Chicago: University of Chicago Press.

Shively, C.A. and Clarkson, T.B. (1994) Social status and coronary artery atherosclerosis in female monkeys, *Arteriosclerosis and Thrombosis*, 14, 721–6.

Shively, C.A., Laird, K.L. and Anton, R.F. (1997) The behavior and physiology of social stress and depression in female cynomolgus monkeys, *Biological Psychiatry*, 41, 871–82.

Simcha-Fagan, O. and Schwartz, J. (1986) Neighborhood and delinquency: an assessment of contextual effects, *Criminology*, 24, 667–704.

Skogan, W. (1991) *Disorder and Decline*. New York: Free Press.

Taylor, R., Gottfredson, S. and Brower, S. (1984) Block crime and fear: defensible space, local social ties, and territorial functioning, *Journal of Research in Crime and Delinquency*, 21, 303–31.

US Department of Justice, Federal Bureau of Investigation (1991–1994) *Crime in the United States, 1991–1994*, Uniform Crime Reports. Washington DC: Federal Bureau of Investigation, US Department of Justice.

Wacquant, L.J.D. and Wilson, W.J. (1989) The cost of racial and class exclusion in the inner city, *Annals of the American Academy of Political and Social Science*, 501, 8–25.

Wilkinson, R.G. (1992) Income distribution and life expectancy, *British Medical Journal*, 304, 165–8.

Wilkinson, R.G. (1996) *Unhealthy Societies. The Afflictions of Inequality*. London: Routledge.

Wilson, M. and Daly, M. (1997) Life expectancy, economic inequality, homicide, and reproductive timing in Chicago neighbourhoods, *British Medical Journal*, 314, 1271–4.

2. The psycho-social perspective on social inequalities in health

Jon Ivar Elstad

Introduction

Recent debates indicate that most researchers believe that genetics, social selection, and access to health services explain only minor parts of current social inequalities in health (Blane *et al.* 1996, Carroll *et al.* 1996, Evans 1994, Evans and Stoddart 1994, Tarlov 1996, Vågerö and Illsley 1995, Wilkinson 1996b: 53–71, Baird 1994, Blane *et al.* 1993). This renders the social causation explanation more plausible. However, even the two main approaches within social causation, focusing on health-related behaviour and material standard of living, seem insufficient.

Health-damaging behaviour, such as smoking, unhealthy diets, and accident-prone behaviour, is usually overrepresented among lower social strata. This accounts, however, for only some part of current health variations (Marmot 1986, Blane *et al.* 1996: 5–7, Carroll *et al.* 1996: 29, Evans 1994, Wilkinson 1996b: 63–6). Moreover, as health-related behaviour is seldom chosen 'freely', but is heavily influenced by social status and cultural milieus, health-related behaviour can hardly be regarded as the basic cause of health inequalities.

Social medicine has primarily explained health variations by harmful physical factors in the environment, such as poor nutrition or polluted and hazardous workplaces. Scepticism has, however, grown as to the explanatory power of material explanations in contemporary Western societies. If material shortages were the major determinant of ill-health, one would expect that social inequalities in health would diminish as post-war improvements in standard of living raised the majority above certain threshold levels (Kadushin 1964, Blane *et al.* 1996: 3). But although life expectancy has increased, social inequalities in health have persisted (Carroll *et al.* 1996, Dahl and Kjærsgaard 1993, Link and Phelan 1995). If population health is determined by economic level, one would predict that each country's life expectancy would correspond to its international economic ranking. But Wilkinson's research (1990, 1994, 1996b: 72–109, 1997) indicates that life expectancy in affluent countries is associated with *income equality* rather than with average level of income, and his findings are echoed by others (Wennemo 1993, Kaplan *et al.* 1996, Kennedy *et al.* 1996, Waldmann 1992, Kawachi and Kennedy 1997). The so-called 'challenge of the gradient' (Adler *et al.* 1994) is another aspect of the puzzle, illustrated by findings of the Whitehall studies that not only low-level employees, but even civil servants close to the top, had worse health than the top category (Marmot 1986, Marmot 1994). Differences in current material standards could hardly account for these mortality differentials, as these two occupational groupings are both favourably placed in the income hierarchy.

The psycho-social perspective: towards a paradigm shift?

Thus, established explanations are challenged, and alternative interpretations have gained support, in a manner resembling Kuhn's thesis of scientific revolutions (1970). One emerging perspective has been proclaimed a 'paradigm shift' (Evans *et al.* 1994a: ix) that will become 'enormously important' and 'destined to transform social and economic policy' (Wilkinson 1996b: 5, ix). It employs the familiar social causation type of explanation, assuming that the roots of social inequalities in health are found in the varying environment of social positions. But instead of material shortages and negligent behaviour, focus is now on psychological stress, relative deprivation, and the psycho-social injuries of inequality structures.

To give an overview of this *psycho-social perspective* is the purpose of this chapter. The term 'perspective' is chosen because I consider it a set of related approaches rather than a unified theory. It can, however, be identified by three core assumptions: (1) the distribution of psychological stress is an important determinant of health inequalities in present-day affluent societies, (2) psychological stress is strongly influenced by the quality of social and interpersonal relations, and (3) the latter are determined to a large extent by the magnitude of society's inequalities. First, I will make some remarks on the aetiological basis. Then follows a presentation of what I consider the four main sources of the perspective: the *social stress* approach, the related *self-efficacy* approach, the newer *sociology of emotion*, and the *social cohesion* approach. I will highlight elements which I believe are of particular interest for the study of health inequalities. Through this, I also intend to contribute to the construction of this perspective; although there are many controversial issues, I believe it has many promising aspects. In the last section I will however question the 'paradigm shift' thesis: could the psycho-social perspective more properly be described as an enrichment of existing perspectives?

Aetiology

Any explanation of social inequalities in health must combine a general understanding of what causes health and illness with analyses of particular societies. This combination is often what makes the study of health inequalities fruitful, both for medicine and sociology. If current ideas about illness causation seem insufficient to account for observed health inequalities, other aetiological notions are required; attempts to explain health inequalities may on the other hand direct attention to previously neglected aspects of the workings of society.

The psycho-social perspective is a case in point. That grief, loneliness, and similar distressed feelings can impair health, have been part of lay notions of illness for centuries. Since the 1960s a growing number of academic studies have also addressed this topic. Accumulating doubts about the material deprivation explanation for health inequalities has further stimulated interest in the psycho-social environment. The aetiological basis for the psycho-social perspective is the health-damaging potential of psychological stress. Two somewhat different pathways from stress to poor health are proposed: a *direct* effect on disease development, and an *indirect* route, when stress is expressed by health-damaging behaviour.

The indirect pathway implies that people react to adverse circumstances by excessive alcohol use, smoking, accident-prone behaviour, etc., sometimes as conscious or subconscious self-destructive acts, sometimes more 'innocently' in order to alleviate stress. That health can suffer from such behaviour is well documented – and sometimes self-evident, as in the case of violence and homicide.

More controversial is the direct pathway – not as regards mental illness, but as regards somatic disease: can it occur because of psychological stress? Generally, this implies that experiences transmitted by the central nervous system provoke changes in other human organs in a way that threatens health (Kelly *et al.* 1997). Many recent reviews are in favour of this view (see for instance Maes *et al.* 1987, Thoits 1995, Uchino *et al.* 1996, Cohen and Herbert 1996). Evans *et al.* state that 'There is now no longer room for doubt as to the existence of a complex web of linkages, having important implications for health, between the nervous system and other body systems' (1994b: 182). Others are not so sure (see, for instance, Davey Smith and Egger 1996). Despite a rapidly increasing number of studies, reflecting the expansion of fields such as psychoneuroimmunology and psychoneuroendrocrinology, uncertainty remains.

The question is not whether *some* health-related bodily changes may follow from mental appreciations of external circumstances. Recent reviews leave few doubts that psychological stress, generated by despairing circumstances, unsurmountable tasks, or lack of social support, can influence disease-related parameters. Examples are found as regards the cardiovascular system (*e.g.* systolic/diastolic blood pressure), the endocrine system (*e.g.* secretion of catecholamine and cortisol), and the immune system (*e.g.* number of T-cells and Natural Killer cells) (Uchino *et al.* 1996, Cohen and Herbert 1996, Kelly *et al.* 1997, Kiecolt-Glaser and Glaser 1995). The roblem is, however, to demonstrate that such changes are large enough and longterm enough to affect health in a significant way. In other words: is the onset of somatic disease, its course, and recovery from it, influenced by psychological stress in a way that makes a difference?

For practical, not to mention ethical, reasons it is difficult to answer this question. A number of observational studies, laboratory experiments, and interventions provide strong indications (see Uchino *et al.* 1996), but most studies utilise only a limited set of variables, and the observed effects of psycho-social factors may sometimes include unmeasured effects of other factors as well. Sufficiently longitudinal approaches are still rare (but see Kelly *et al.* 1997: 438). Laboratory experiments, intervention studies, and animal studies (as regards the latter, see Evans *et al.* 1994b, Wilkinson 1996b; 193pp) have produced suggestive evidence, but under conditions that deviate considerably from 'real' human life. Accordingly, strong conclusions are difficult to draw, not only because of the above-mentioned reasons, but also because diverging findings occur (for instance Carroll *et al.* 1995).

How to conceptualise the role of psychological stress in aetiological processes is moreover a disputed topic. That social inequalities are found for a wide range of diseases has been interpreted to indicate that stress has a general negative effect on health (Syme and Berkman 1976, Wilkinson 1996b: 71). If so, the mechanisms can be understood in different ways. Stress can be seen as a specific causal factor in the various chains of events which lead to particular diseases (see Uchino *et al.* 1996). Alternatively, stress could influence the body's general capacity for homeostasis, by conditioning 'biological responses . . . in ways that lead to systematic differences in resilience and vulnerability to disease' (Kelly *et al.* 1997: 438). Thus, Kiecolt-Glaser and Glaser (1995) found evidence that cancer, infections, and disorders associated with ageing share the same type of psycho-socially mediated immuno-suppressive mechanisms. Notions of stress-related *general susceptibility* is often part of the aetiological understanding of the psycho-social perspective. Challenges to traditional concepts of disease entities are also raised: Evans suggests that specific diseases should not primarily be understood as endpoints, but rather as alternative pathways from stressful circumstances to illness (1994: 7).

In summary, the aetiological basis for the psycho-social perspective is complex. That psychological stress may contribute to mental illness and health-damaging behaviour is usually agreed; the direct link to specific somatic diseases, or to somatic disease in general, is more contested. One objection to the psycho-social view is that disease aetiology, even in the most affluent societies, cannot be constructed solely in terms of psychological stress. Both the psycho-social *and* the physical environment, and their interaction and interpenetration over time, are perhaps imperative elements of any convincing aetiology, and correspondingly the key to understand

health inequalities. I will leave these questions here, and pr
'medical' aspects of the psycho-social perspective to its
through what kind of processes does psychological stress e
are they related to society's social inequalities?

The social stress approach

The social stress approach developed especially from Hans Selye's investigations, during the 1940s and 1950s, of physiological responses to external exi-
gencies (see Polloci 1988: 384). In this tradition, stress was defined as 'a state
of arousal resulting either from the presence of socioenvironmental
demands that tax the ordinary adaptive capacity . . . or from the absence of
the means to attain sought-after ends' (Aneshensel 1992: 16). Thus, socioenvironmental demands – stressors – engender psychological stress, *i.e.* a troubled state of the mind which can surface in many ways, as anxiety, fear,
hopelessness, or anger.

Stress research is extremely multifaceted (see, for instance, Thoits 1995).
Two main tendencies, one more medically, the other more sociologically,
oriented, can be distinguished (Aneshensel 1992, Aneshensel *et al.* 1991,
Pearlin 1989). While the former is primarily concerned with consequences of
stress in terms of ill health, the latter focuses on the social origins of stress,
and includes social inequalities and the stratification system in its models.
The two tendencies utilise social variables differently: medically oriented
researchers employ information on social background as controls in order
to accentuate the links from stressors to stress reactivity, while sociologically oriented researchers focus on how the distribution of stressors depends
on people's location within social structures.

The sociologically oriented tendency within stress research can be
regarded as the original source of the psycho-social perspective. To explain
social inequalities in health has always been part of its agenda. Since the
1960s, various developments have further underlined how people's location
in the social structure could result in health differences. What I have in
mind are four reorientations: from *any* type of stressors to *negative* stressors; from the 'objective' features of a situation to the 'subjective' impact;
the substitution of chronic strain for life events; and the focus on buffers
which could reduce the health-damaging potential of stressors.

Stress research started out with the assumption that any kind of event
was a potential threat to health (Pearlin *et al.* 1981: 339). This was in line
with Selye's preoccupation with reactions to change itself (see Oatley and
Jenkins 1992: 72). Thus, not only divorces and deaths, but also marriages
and births, could constitute health-damaging experiences, given that the
event required overburdening adaption. Poor empirical evidence for this
'neutral' attitude to stressors led to a focus on negative stressors: stressors

racterised as unfortunate and unwelcome. As there was little doubt that less privileged social strata tend to face negative circumstances more frequently than those more favourably located in society, the connection between stress processes and the social gradients in health was underscored.

Second, when negative events were highlighted, the subjective impact of events came into focus, because the definition of 'negative' could hardly exclude subjective evaluations. Attention was directed away from the 'objective' characteristics of stressors, towards the way they were appraised by those afflicted (see, for instance, Lazarus 1993). This development put the social environment on the agenda. Appraisals could hardly be seen as isolated individual judgements, but rather as constructed judgements within a social setting. Prevailing norms, types of classifications, and systems of labelling would influence the subjective impact. If events led to social isolation, loss of respect, or other distressing interpersonal relations, the subjective impact would make matters worse. Less exclusionary attitudes towards 'deviants' and more supporting practices towards those who were hit by misfortunes would alleviate the subjective impact. This directed attention to the quality of society's social relations and networks, the cultural representations it favoured, and furthermore towards how such attributes were related to the material differences in society.

Third, findings indicated that the 'deleterious health effects of life changes are of consistently modest magnitude' (Aneshensel 1992: 17). Thus, the one-sided focus upon short-term, abrupt events, as compared with more long-standing stressors – 'enduring problems, conflicts and threats that many people face in their daily lives' (Pearlin 1989: 245) – was criticised. Chronic strain was given a more prominent place in stress research (see, for instance, Turner *et al.* 1995). When stressors were conceptualised as enduring life problems, the association between stress experiences and location in the social structure became more marked, as longstanding economic problems, difficulties related to subordinate positions in the workplace, and the burden of poor neighbourhoods were typical examples.

A fourth reorientation was to focus on vulnerability, *i.e.* why the impact of similar adverse circumstances differed between individuals. One answer was the existence of buffers. Coping resources of diverse types could help people master and overcome adverse circumstances without suffering health setbacks (Maes *et al.* 1987). Social support is the main example, but almost any type of resource connected to personality, social background, education, and financial resources, has been proposed as a moderator of the harmful effects of stressors. Access to buffering factors is related both to the supportiveness of the social environment, and to a person's location in the social structure. Thus, the connection between social position and the circumstances that influence psychological stress was underlined even more.

In this way, the social stress approach explains how social inequalities in health arise. Stressors, particularly long term, chronic stressors, are unevenly distributed in society, basically in line with its structural inequalities. The impact of stressors depends on their subjective appraisal, which follows not only from stressors' factual character, but also from the distribution of buffering resources. Accordingly, psychological stress could be expected to vary with social position and to result in social variations in health. The other approaches outlined below build in many ways on this social stress model, but they also develop particular points and introduce new aspects, thereby contributing to a more comprehensive understanding.

Developing the social stress model: the self-efficacy approach

Social stress research has brought forward a multitude of concepts and hypotheses, addressing topics such as the types of external circumstances that provoke psychological stress, the types of mechanisms that connect circumstances to stress, and the contextual and buffering factors that will influence this process (see, for instance, Maes *et al.* 1987, Pollock 1988, Thoits 1995, Pearlin 1989). In spite of this diversity, it can be argued that stress research has been biased in two respects. It had tended to view people as *passive recipients* of external circumstances, and it has tended to focus solely on *health deterioration*. Moreover, although the emphasis on chronic strain introduces a more longitudinal view, it could be argued that the social stress approach has often avoided a lifecourse perspective on health.

The *self-efficacy approach* (see Aneshensel 1992: 27–30) can be considered a development of the social stress model which counters all these drawbacks. It addresses the first of these tendencies by pointing to capabilities and power as crucial stress-protecting factors. Humans are conceptualised as acting subjects and not only as being governed by external and structural forces. By emphasising human agency, connections to fundamental theoretical debates in sociology are made. In addition, the self-efficacy approach also opens up for a life-time perspective and for notions about growth in health.

Self-efficacy can be defined as a 'cognitive orientation attributing outcomes such as success and failure to personal attributes, such as ability and effort' (Aneshensel 1992: 27). Mirowsky and Ross (1984) observe that its meaning is virtually synonymous with other frequently employed terms within stress research, such as mastery, internal locus of control, personal control, perceived control of the environment, and instrumentalism. Opposite concepts are fatalism, external locus of control, powerlessness, and learned helplessness. Whatever the term used, the kernel is 'the extent to which people see themselves as being in control of the forces that importantly affect their lives' (Pearlin *et al.* 1981: 339). Self-efficacy is linked to various other phenomena often studied by stress researchers, such as self-esteem, self-concept, social support, and coping style. To emphasise self-efficacy, instead of other related concepts, is therefore somewhat arbitrary. These phenomena are all correlated, and the division of them into separate units, each with a special term, may be artificial, as the sense of support, mastery, self-esteem, and similar traits within an individual is often a tightly connected bundle.

The feeling of mastery, self-efficacy, and being in control, can be assumed a health-promoting factor by itself, as it goes together with a balanced, non-stressed, state of mind. However, it is more common to regard it as a buffer which protects against the damaging effects of adverse external circumstances. Self-efficacy maintains the belief that one can influence one's lot, and this constitutes a defence against feelings of frustration and hopelessness. Thus, self-efficacy makes people less vulnerable to external stressors, and it can be equated with a kind of mental strength which maintains self-esteem and protects against distress.

What generates self-efficacy? The characteristics of the social environment, and social location, seem to be two important factors. Satisfying interpersonal relations will support and enhance self-efficacy. But this is probably also associated with placement in the social structure. Gecas and Schwalbe suggest that the formation of self-esteem is heavily influenced by 'the possibilities that social structures afford for individuals to engage in efficacious action' (1983: 82). Thoits summarises that '[p]erceived control over life circumstances is inversely distributed by social status' (1995: 60). Thus, the formation of self-efficacy is rooted in the structural features of society, including its system of material inequalities, but also in the supportiveness of the social environment.

The contribution of the self-efficacy approach to the psycho-social perspective is particularly, therefore, that it specifies *mechanisms* involved in the stress process, and that it takes into account the active, participating, actor. It is moreover closely linked to studies which examine the relationship between work organisations and health. Karasek's hypothesis, made credible by many empirical studies, that work-related stress is not dependent on job demands in themselves, but on the combination of a low level of decision latitude with large job demands (see Peterson 1994), points to the significance of having the capability to influence circumstances. Thus, self-efficacy could be importantly involved in the processes whereby health inequalities are formed by hierarchical work organisations.

Furthermore, the notion that health develops over the lifecourse can be viewed as part of the self-efficacy approach. Thus, is parallels the expanding lifecourse perspective on health inequalities (see, for instance, Carroll *et al.* 1996, Davey Smith *et al.* 1997, Wunsch *et al.* 1996). Self-efficacy is commonly seen as a result of a lifetime development. The importance of early life is not only emphasised by biomedically oriented researchers, but also by researchers who focus on psycho-social circumstances. Attachment theory, for instance, argues that inner feelings of security, with important consequences for stress resistance, result from the characteristics of social relations in infancy and childhood (Fonagy 1996). The notion of a life-span development of one's health potential is a prominent part of Antonovsky's concept 'sense of coherence' (1987: 89–127). The principal components of this concept are that the external world is experienced as comprehensible, manageable, and meaningful (1987: 16–19). Given a strong sense of coherence, resistance against deleterious effects of stress, as well as against physical risk factors, is enhanced. Social variations in health are related to the way the sense of coherence is formed. It is no short-time personal characteristic, but develops through life, influenced by placement in the social structure and the availability of resources.

Moreover, Antonovsky's variant of the self-efficacy approach entails a particular view on health evolution. He argues that a sense of coherence can be a salutogenic factor, *i.e.* a contributor to better health. Often, good health is regarded as a kind of 'natural condition', which prevails as long as the environment does not frustrate it; accordingly, poor health is a negative deviation from the 'natural'. In contrast, Antonovsky's writings imply the plasticity of human health, entailing the notion that health may strengthen and grow, as well as deteriorate. It may develop towards more mental and physical strength and towards a longer life, or in the opposite direction. Correspondingly, Wadsworth sees health in terms of a capital analogy: one may 'add interests to' or 'deplete' one's health capital (1996: 159). Such attempts to theorise health are obviously relevant in view of the remarkable growth in life expectancy during this century, and suggest explanations for variations in life expectancy changes, for instance between social classes or between different countries.

The sociology of emotions: filling black boxes

Emotions are studied in their own right (see, for instance, Collins 1981, Thoits 1989, Kemper 1990, Oatley and Jenkins 1992), but many have also pointed out their relevance for an understanding of health and illness (Freund 1990, James and Gabe 1996, Williams and Bendelow 1996). The structural resemblance between the social stress model and the standard approach of sociologists of emotions is easily recognised. The former addresses the link between social position, stressors, psychological stress, and health outcomes; the latter examines how the social world is experienced in emotionally loaded categories which have bodily correlates: blushing cheeks when feeling shame, muscular tension when angry, throwing up when feeling disgust, etc. Thus, the link between a person's social, subjective, and corporal existence is emphasised by the sociology of emotions. Accordingly, dichotomies such as mind/body, culture/nature, and society/biology are challenged, because such mutually excluding concepts block the understanding of their inner connections (Williams and Bendelow 1996: 28).

In the context of this chapter, I will argue that the study of emotions contributes to the psycho-social perspective by addressing certain unclear aspects of the social stress model. Put simply, an awkward problem for the social stress approach is why experiences, which could be regarded as nothing but perceptions of the external world, could possibly be fateful to health. Why aren't they simply mental reflections arousing no more excitement than a dull TV commercial? The general reason is that significant experiences are emotionally loaded. Lots of experiences are irrelevant. Those which have an important meaning also engender emotional responses. Oatley and Jenkins maintain that 'emotions are usually elicited by evaluating events that concern a person's important needs or goals' (1992: 60). As Lazarus puts it: 'there is a world of difference between a non-emotional and an emotional event' (1993: 11). In general, we would expect that emotional experiences have an impact both on mental and physiological processes, while perceptions without this quality would hardly effectuate significant alterations, neither in behaviour nor in physiological functioning.

Psychological stress should accordingly 'be considered part of a larger topic, the emotions' (Lazarus 1993: 10). Stress is a subset of negative emotions, and the study of psychological stress is a special branch within a more general study of emotions. Thus, the question about how emotions emerge encompasses the more specific inquiry into the origins of psychological stress. Attempted solutions to this question range from social construction approaches at one end of the scale, to positivistic theories at the other end, with (symbolic) interaction theory somewhere in between (Thoits 1989: 319, William and Bendelow 1996: 30). The quality of interpersonal relations is often at the centre of interest. Thus, Burkitt emphasises the relational background to the formation of emotional dispositions (1997); while Lazarus's 'cognitive-motivational-relational theory of emotion' addresses how processes of appraisal attribute meanings to social encounters, accompanied by various types of emotions (1993).

Such approaches underline the social 'nature' of emotions. However, in order to be relevant for the psycho-social perspective, not only a focus on the micro-world of social relations is required, but also a connection to inequality structures at the macro level. The 'positivist' Kemper is more explicit in this respect: he argues that emotions like security, guilt and fear-anxiety arise from social relations formed by dimensions of power and status (Kemper 1979, see also Thoits 1989: 325, Hochschild 1981). Highly relevant, furthermore, is the existential-phenomenological approach of Freund (1988, 1990), who argues that people exhibit 'emotional modes of being' strongly influenced by their positions in social hierarchies, and that these modes become embodied and expressed through various bodily states, including illness.

In order to support the psycho-social perspective, empirical studies should indicate increasing experiences of negative emotions the further 'down' the social ladder people are located. That the frequency of social disadvantages increases in lower social positions is hardly contested, but are they correspondingly associated with emotional responses of a negative character? One alternative hypothesis could be that negative experiences lose their subjective impact when they are common. Based on historical evidence, Lofland (1985) argues that grief will vary according to the degree of infant mortality: the higher the child mortality, the lower the emotional investment in children, so that shorter and less intense grief follows a child's death. Thus, devastating social circumstances could also produce defence mechanisms against negative emotions. On the other hand, one may conjecture that the information supply in modern Western societies implies that people's standards and expectations are usually formed with reference to a national level, maybe even to the international level. People will therefore not compare their fates only with common life situations within their own social milieus, but will refer to wider circumstances. Thus, the idea that disadvantaged social groupings become 'emotionally immune' against their misfortunes because they know of nothing else, is perhaps less viable in present-day Western societies.

To clarify such topics is a challenge for the sociology of emotions, but also of considerable interest for the further development of the psycho-social perspective on health inequalities. It can be added that investigations of the social distribution of negative emotions present many methodological difficulties. Not only are emotions subjective, but they are often partly subconscious and even prelinguistic. Standard research techniques based on verbal responses may therefore miss the target, and this difficulty is an obstacle to empirical studies of how negative emotions are involved in the generation of health inequalities.

The social cohesion approach

The current interest in psycho-social explanations of social inequalities in health has been spurred on not least by the research of Richard G. Wilkinson (1986, 1990, 1992, 1993, 1994, 1996a, 1996b, 1997). Paradoxically, his interest in psycho-social explanations followed from empirical studies using an indicator of material circumstances, income, as the principal independent variable. His findings, now widely diffused, indicate that in present-day affluent societies, the absolute level of income is no straightforward determinant of health. As absolute deprivation is reduced, health variations become more linked to relative deprivation (or relative income or relative poverty), and life expectancy is influenced by the magnitude of society's income inequalities.

The use of the concept relative deprivation invites some comments. It originated in social psychology around 1940s, as a hypothesis that 'people take the standards of significant others as a basis for self-appraisal and evaluation' (Merton 1967: 40). Contrary to commonsense notions that self-appraisals were linked to absolute standards, it was claimed that people evaluate their situation according to how it compares with others. How people came to choose reference groups, how the processes of social comparisons took place, and what kind of norms of fairness were involved, were central topics of these studies. If people were denied the standards of their reference group, a feeling of deprivation was supposed to follow, i.e. disappointment, frustration, and similar distressed feelings because one experienced a standard below what one felt entitled to. This 'classic' relative deprivation model has been applied to the study of mental health (Wagner 1993, Sheeran et al. 1995), as well as topics such as migration, absenteeism, criminality, subjective well-being, and especially political attitudes (see Runciman 1966).[1]

This model of relative deprivation, involving reference groups, norms of fairness, and social comparison processes, has however seldom been utilised in its stringent form by researchers of health inequalities. The concept is often introduced without definitions (cf. Hasan 1989: 384, Marmot 1994, Wennemo 1993) and used more or less as a shorthand for the view that material standards probably do not damage health directly; nevertheless people's health will vary inversely to their position in society's hierarchical order due to various 'psycho-social processes'.

With Wilkinson's more recent writings (see especially 1996b), a more general framework which addresses the transforming of social inequalities into health inequalities has been suggested. The kernel is that social inequalities, i.e. not only income inequalities, but also power inequalities (for instance, authoritarian hierarchies and non-democratic social organisations) and status inequalities (for instance, as between the two genders, or between ethnic groups), have a fundamental influence on the content of social relations and interactions. The greater the social inequalities (longer distances from top to bottom of the income scale, more authoritarian patterns in families, schools, etc.), the more will the quality of social relations suffer. Inequalities will tend to produce anger, frustration, hostility, fear, insecurity, and other negative emotions. Material inequalities will often go together with fear of, or the actual distressing experience of, failures to secure a socially acceptable material standard of living. Authoritarian power patterns engender feelings of hostility and anger. Differences in status produce contempt from those above and fright and insecurity among those below. Thus, an overall association is assumed to exist between the amount of inequalities in society and the amount of negative feelings and emotions signifying psychological stress. From this, health problems would follow, along both the direct and indirect pathway as described above in the section on aetiology. Smaller social inequalities are, on the other hand, associated with better social relations, *i.e.* more trust, more security, more social support, more self-esteem and self-respect, and more sense of belonging; and also with less financial insecurity and fewer feelings of being materially disadvantaged. Democratic, participatory styles in social organisations, from the family to the political system, ensure self-respect and feelings of being appreciated by one's surroundings, and have therefore additional health-enhancing effects.

Wilkinson substantiates his view both by studies of stress and by accounts of actual societies (1996b: 113–36). He points out, for example, that the low death rate of Roseto (a small US town), which has astonished researchers, could be related to its egalitarian ethos; that variations in infant mortality between Italian regions depend on the degree of 'civic community' which in its turn is associated with the magnitude of social inequalities; and that the remarkable increase in longevity in Japan should be explained not only by economic progress but also by the increased sense of community and the reduced rigidity of the stratificational order developing since 1945.

Social cohesion is accordingly a key concept. It implies a *Durkheimian* view (Durkheim 1964) that 'social facts', *i.e.* societal and collective traits, are more than the sum of individual attributes, and that individuals cannot be understood without grasping the collectivities they are part of. This contrasts with the approaches discussed above, which are mainly individualistic in focus. Wilkinson not only asks questions relating to individual variations in health, but also addresses macro health profiles such as population health and average life expectancy. Instead of analysing individual health as functions of individual variations in income and health behaviour, Wilkinson advances the importance of global characteristics of social life, for instance in terms of the amount of social capital. This has been defined as 'networks, norms and trust . . . that enable participants to act together more effectively to pursue shared objectives' (Wilkinson 1996b: 221, quoting Putnam 1995: 664–5). The underlying hypothesis is that the degree of social inequalities is highly influential on the formation or deformation of social capital, which is, in its turn, significant for people's health. This theme has also been dealt with by several newer studies, for instance a study of 39 American states (Kawachi *et al.* 1997) which found associations between average mortality, levels of trust, density of group memberships, and income inequality.

Critical views have been raised. There are methodological objections to the studies finding associations between income inequality and population mortality (Judge 1995, but see also Kawachi and Kennedy 1997); and West has maintained that the evidence has 'striking gaps' (1997). The association between population mortality and social inequality is suggestive; nevertheless, this does not release one from examining why the level of individual (or household) income is still closely related to mortality risk within most present-day affluent societies (see, for instance, Davey Smith *et al.* 1996). The hypothesis that material circumstances are without significant influence after certain threshold levels are surpassed, is not necessarily true, and increasing material wealth could have a positive health effect also on higher levels than has often been assumed. Or could it be that the focus on current income is irrelevant, compared with accumulated material disadvantages over the lifecourse (Davey Smith 1996, Bartley *et al.* 1997)? Moreover, Wilkinson's underlying social theory is not always convincing. At the base of the social cohesion approach is the idea that the larger the material inequalities, the more will social environments that lack social support prevail. Thus, it is assumed that social life is more or less directly determined by material structures, which arguably is a much too uncomplicated answer to the perennial question about the relationship between society's material, social, and cultural structures.

In my view, the main contribution of the social cohesion approach to the psycho-social perspective is that it takes components of individual-centred approaches and develops them at the macro level. Wilkinson shows that individual attributes are closely related to collective characteristics. Individual experiences of hostility and social support parallel, on the level of society, the overall occurrence of altruism, trust, and generosity. Individual traits correspond to collective phenomena, and individual processes are insufficiently understood when it is overlooked that individuals are to a large degree formed by the social facts of society, its inequality structures, and its social capital.

Concluding remarks

The psycho-social perspective is a striking and promising attempt to comprehend crucial questions asked by contemporary research regarding, for instance, the persistence of social inequalities in health even in the most affluent societies, the 'challenge of the gradient', and why the growth in life expectancy varies considerably between countries. The social stress approach, especially through its reorientations since the 1960s, provides an overall understanding of why health inequalities mirror social inequalities, in terms of the social distribution of psychological stress. By emphasising the role of human agency, the self-efficacy approach makes up for previous theoretical deficits, and advances the significance of developments over the lifecourse. The sociology of emotions refines the understanding of how external circumstances are transformed into troubling mental states, and the social cohesion approach raises these themes from an individual-centred view to the macro level. Various pieces of the puzzle seem to fall into place when integrating the four approaches, and an encompassing view on health, health inequalities, and its determinants is constructed, based on aetiological notions about the significance of the psycho-social environment and its repercussions in terms of psychological stress. Noteworthy, moreover, is its potential for addressing not only socio-economic differentials but also health differences related to other dividing lines in society such as gender and ethnicity. In addition, it unites health sciences and social studies to a higher degree than has been usual, since its basic theme is the *social* determination of health and illness.

But does it signal a coming paradigm shift? A paradigm can be viewed as an inclusive set of related propositions which contrasts other understandings and can even replace them, and which is based – at least to a considerable degree – on empirical evidence. Various features of the psycho-social perspective correspond to this: it is comprehensive, consists of several strategies which share, more or less, key concepts, and is informed by numerous empirical studies. Furthermore, it may aim at reinterpreting not only present, but even past health inequalities. A logical next step would be to ask whether psycho-social deprivation has been a major cause all the time, even in the early days of industrialisation, but overlooked by investigators both because material inequality was overwhelming and because natural science has been more prestigious.

Nevertheless, the paradigm metaphor is perhaps too demanding. West (1997) argues that although impressive, the psycho-social perspective does certainly not nullify findings of other perspectives. Many of its suppositions are in need of clarification, for instance the assumption that the distribution of psychological stress reflects, more or less directly, society's inequality structures. The focus on psycho-social environments is certainly justified, as many bits of evidence point to their contribution. But there is a difference between 'contribute' and 'determine', and current research has not provided evidence that multifactor aetiology, including both psycho-social *and* physical environments, should be succeeded by a one-sided emphasis on psychological stress. Social classes differ also as to their physical milieus, even in the most affluent parts of the world, and the extent to which this has direct repercussions on the body's well-being as well as being mediated by the central nervous system, throughout people's biographies, should be further examined.

Lastly, the claim that the psycho-social perspective will revolutionise our ideas should not hinder us from acknowledging that there are also similarities between the psycho-social perspective and a material deprivation perspective. Both would support Wilkinson's statement that 'the extent of material inequality is a major determinant of population health' (1996b: 9); thus, both would tend to support policies addressing equity questions. They differ as regards the relative weight of the psycho-social and the material pathway from social structure to health inequalities. The most 'extreme' point of view is that psycho-social pathways are decisively most important in present-day societies (see, for instance, Wilkinson 1996b: 4), but there are also less drastic possibilities, allowing for the relevance of psycho-social links without claiming that this implies that direct consequences of material deprivation are eliminated. Thus, one may suggest that the role of the psychosocial perspective will perhaps not be to institute a paradigm shift, but rather to extend and enrich the social causation explanation of health inequalities.

Acknowledgements

The author thanks two anonymous referees for valuable criticism of a previous draft.

Note

1   Another example is the relative deprivation approach to the study of poverty (Townsend 1979), which can be regarded as a more sociological application of the concept. Here, relative deprivation (*i.e.* relative poverty) is considered to be an *objective state*, which occurs when people's level of resources makes them unable to take part in the customs and activities considered normal in their society. Relative poverty implies a withdrawal from normal social life, which occurs when access to resources drops below a critical point. Thus, this concept of relative deprivation does not exclude the feeling of deprivation, but emphasises in particular ways of life characterised by social isolation and non-participation. It could be added that the relative deprivation theory stands in contrast, in some respects, to the theory of cognitive dissonance (Festinger 1957), which claims that a typical reaction to distressing circumstances is to adjust aspirations in order to reconcile them with actual circumstances. The cognitive dissonance pattern modifies reference points in order to diminish the gap between reality and aspirations, while relative deprivation would occur when expectations are relatively inflexible.

References

Adler, N.E., Boyce, T., Chesney, M.A., Cohen, S., Folkman, S., Kahn, R.I. and Syme, S.L. (1994) Socioeconomic status and health: the challenge of the gradient, *American Psychologist*, 49, 1, 15–24.

Aneshensel, C.S. (1992) Social stress: theory and research, *Annual Review of Sociology*, 18, 15–38.

Aneshensel, C.S., Rutter, C.M. and Lachenbruch, P.A. (1991) Social structure, stress, and mental health: competing conceptual and analytic models, *American Sociological Review*, 56, 166–78.

Antonovsky, A. (1987) *Unraveling the Mystery of Health. How People Manage Stress and Stay Well*. San Francisco: Jossey-Bass Publishers.

Baird, P.A. (1994) The role of genetics in population health. In Evans, R.G., Barer, M.L. and Marmor, T.R. (eds) *Why are Some People Healthy and Others not? The Determinants of Health of Populations?* Berlin/New York: de Gruyter.

Bartley, M., Blane, D. and Montgomery, S. (1997) Socioeconomic determinants of health. Health and the life course: why safety nets matter, *British Medical Journal*, 314, 1194–6.

Blane, D., Davey Smith, G., and Bartley, M. (1993) Social selection: what does it contribute to social class differences in health? *Sociology of Health and Illness*, 15, 1–15.

Blane, D., Brunner, E. and Wilkinson, R.G. (1996) The evolution of public health policy: an anglocentric view of the last fifty years. In Blane, D., Brunner, E. and Wilkinson, R.G. (eds) *Health and Social Organization. Towards a Health Policy for the 21st Century*. London and New York: Routledge.

Burkitt, I. (1997) Social relationships and emotions, *Sociology*, 31, 37–55.

Carroll, D., Davey Smith, G., Sheffield, D., Shipley, M.J. and Marmot, M.G. (1995) Pressor reactions to psychological stress and prediction of future blood pressure: data from Whitehall II study, *British Medical Journal*, 310, 771–6.

Carroll, D., Davey Smith, G. and Bennett, P. (1996) Some observations on health and socio-economic status, *Journal of Health Psychology*, 1, 1, 23–39.

Cohen, S. and Herbert, T.B. (1996) Health psychology – psychological factors and physical disease from the perspective of human psychoneuroimmunology, *Annual Review of Psychology*, 47, 113–42.

Collins, R. (1981) On the microfoundations of macrosociology, *American Journal of Sociology*, 86, 984–1014.

Dahl, E. and Kjærsgaard, P. (1993) Trends in socioeconomic mortality differentials in post-war Norway – evidence and interpretations, *Sociology of Health and Illness*, 15, 447–71.

Davey Smith, G. (1996) Income inequality and mortality: why are they related? *British Medical Journal*, 312, 987–8.

Davey Smith, G., Neaton, J.D., Wentworth, D., Stamler, R. and Stamler, J. (1996) Socioeconomic differentials in mortality risk among men screened for the Multiple Risk Factor Intervention Trial: I. white men, *American Journal of Public Health*, 86, 4, 486–96.

Davey Smith, G. and Egger, M. (1996) Commentary: understanding it all – health, meta-theories, and mortality trends, *British Medical Journal*, 313, 1584–5.

Davey Smith, G., Hart, C., Blane, D., Gillis, C. and Hawthorne, V. (1997) Lifetime socioeconomic position and mortality – prospective observational study, *British Medical Journal*, 314, 547–52.

Durkheim, E. (1964 [1895]) *The Rules of Sociological Method*. New York: Free Press.

Evans, R.G. (1994) Introduction. In Evans, R.G., Barer, M.L. and Marmor, T.R. (eds) *Why are Some People Healthy and Others not? The Determinants of Health of Populations?* Berlin/New York: de Gruyter.

Evans, R.G., Barer, M.L. and Marmor, T.R. (1994a) Preface. In Evans, R.G., Barer, M.L. and Marmor, T.R. (eds) *Why are Some People Healthy and Others not? The Determinants of Health of Populations?* Berlin/New York: de Gruyter.

Evans, R.G., Hodge, M. and Pless, I.B. (1994b) If not genetics, then what? Biological pathways and population health. In Evans, R.G., Barer, M.L. and Marmor, T.R. (eds) *Why are Some People Healthy and Others not? The Determinants of Health of Populations?* Berlin/New York: de Gruyter, 161–88.

Evans, R.G. and Stoddart, G.L. (1994) Producing health, consuming health care. In Evans, R.G., Barer, M.L. and Marmor, T.R. (eds) *Why are Some People Healthy*

Vågerö, D. and Illsley, R. (1995) Explaining health inequalities: beyond Black and Barker. A discussion of some issues emerging in the decade following the Black Report, *European Sociological Review*, 11, 3, 219–41.

Wadsworth, M. (1996) Family and education as determinants of health. In Blane, D., Brunner, E. and Wilkinson, R.G. (eds) *Health and Social Organization. Towards a Health Policy for the 21st Century*. London and New York: Routledge.

Wagner, R.M. (1993) Psycho-social adjustments during the 1st year of single parenthood – a comparison of Mexican-American and Anglo women, *Journal of Divorce and Remarriage*, 19, 1–2, 121–42.

Waldmann, R.J. (1992) Income distribution and infant mortality, *Quarterly Journal of Economics*, 107, 1283–302.

Wennemo, I. (1993) Infant mortality, public policy and inequality – a comparison of 18 industrialized countries 1950–85, *Sociology of Health and Illness*, 15, 4, 429–46.

West, P. (1997) (Book Review) Wilkinson, R.G., Unhealthy societies: the afflictions of inequality, *Sociology of Health and Illness*, 19, 5, 668–70.

Wilkinson, R.G. (1986) Income and mortality. In Wilkinson, R.G. (ed) *Class and Health. Research and Longitudinal Data*. London and New York: Tavistock Publications.

Wilkinson, R.G. (1990) Income distribution and mortality: a natural experiment, *Sociology of Health and Illness*, 12, 4, 391–412.

Wilkinson, R.G. (1992) Income distribution and life expectancy, *British Medical Journal*, 308, 1113–14.

Wilkinson, R.G. (1993) The impact of income inequality on life expectancy. In Platt, Stephen, Thomas, Hilary, Scott, Sue and Williams, Gareth (eds) *Locating Health. Sociological and Historical Explorations*. Aldershot: Avebury.

Wilkinson, R.G. (1994) The epidemiological transition: from material scarcity to social disadvantage, *Dædalus*, 123, 4, 61–77.

Wilkinson, R.G. (1996a) How can secular improvements in life expectancy be explained? In Blane, D., Brunner, E. and Wilkinson, R. (eds) *Health and Social Organization. Towards a Health Policy for the 21st Century*. London and New York: Routledge.

Wilkinson, R.G. (1996b) *Unhealthy Societies. The Afflictions of Inequality*. London and New York: Routledge.

Wilkinson, R.G. (1997) Health inequalities: relative or absolute material standards? *British Medical Journal*, 314, 22, 591–8.

Williams, S.J. and Bendelow, G. (1996) Emotions, health and illness: the 'missing link' in medical sociology? In James, V. and Gabe, J. (eds) *Health and Sociology of Emotions*. Oxford: Blackwell Publishers, Sociology of Health and Illness Monograph Series.

Wunsch, G., Duchêne, J., Thiltgès, E. and Salhi, M. (1996) Socio-economic differences in mortality. A life course approach, *European Journal of Population*, 12, 167–85.

3. Theorising inequalities in health: the place of lay knowledge

Jennie Popay, Gareth Williams, Carol Thomas and Anthony Gatrell

Introduction

This chapter seeks to contribute to the development of a more adequate theoretical framework for future research on social inequalities in health. It begins by exploring some of the limitations in the existing largely quantitative research in this field, pointing in particular to the failure of this work adequately to address the relationship between human agency and social structure. We then explore at a conceptual level the contribution which lay knowledge – in its narrative form – may make to understanding this relationship.

We are not the first to have begun a discussion of research on health inequalities by highlighting the limits of existing research. However, our position is somewhat different from that of other critics. First, the ideas we describe below form the theoretical basis of a piece of empirical research.[1] This chapter is unashamedly critical and conceptual in content, but empirical exploration and testing of the ideas we develop is under way and will form the basis for further papers. Second, our focus on the centrality of lay knowledge in the search for a better understanding of inequalities in health is unusual. Third, our critique of current research into inequalities in health is linked to the changing context in which theory, research and policy are being developed. At the level of social theory, the process of reflexive modernisation is creating growing pressure for greater dialogue between 'experts' – be they scientists, civil servants or social theorists – and lay publics – be they patients, members of self-help groups or community and neighbourhood pressure groups (Giddens 1991). At the level of research, it is increasingly apparent that many stakeholders need to be brought into the processes whereby findings about public health are generated and then fed through into policy and practice in health and welfare. At the level of national policy there is a renewed interest, across Western Europe at least, in the development of interventions which might reduce, if not remove, inequalities in health – though there are those who remain understandably sceptical of the motives underlying recent 'political transformations' of the inequalities debate (Wainwright 1996).

It can be argued, therefore, that this is a particularly significant time for the development of theory and research on inequalities in health. We would also argue that this fertile ground will only yield new fruits if researchers are prepared to embrace the need for different frameworks of understanding as well as different research methods; and are willing to use these frameworks in the context of a genuine dialogue across disciplines. It is an unfortunate outcome of the tendency to work within narrow disciplinary or sub-disciplinary boundaries, and the limited view of 'science' that often accompanies this, that historical, anthropological and philosophical literatures on the nature of class, identity, social action, and well-being have rarely informed epidemiological or empirical social research on inequalities in health. Much of this latter work has focused on the categories of 'social class' (occupation) and health (mortality and morbidity), but has tended to regard health, implicitly if not explicitly, as a category of the phenomenal world that is ontologically detachable from both power and experience. In contrast, we suggest there is much to be gained from adopting an historico-sociological perspective which defines inequalities in health neither as a category nor a structure but as ' . . . an *historical* phenomenon . . . something which in fact happens (and can be shown to have happened) in human relationships' (Thompson 1963: 9). On this basis, occupational social class is not necessarily the determining factor in the picture of inequalities in health.

We begin with a brief overview of conventional approaches to describing and explaining inequalities in health. We then consider some of the main criticisms of these approaches. Finally, building on recent studies which focus on 'place' as a way of better understanding how structural inequalities work their way out in people's everyday lives, and drawing on recent developments in social theory, we explore – at a conceptual level – the role lay knowledge may play in mediating the relationship between structural inequalities, individual or group action and health status. In so doing we develop two linked but separate arguments. The first and main point is that 'lay knowledge', rooted in the places that people spend their lives, has theoretical significance for our understanding of the causes of health inequalities. The second, essentially political, argument is that lay knowledge represents a 'privileged' form of expertise about inequalities in health which may pose a challenge to those who claim the status of either research or policy expert in this field.

Existing approaches to studying health inequalities

Whitehead (1995; see also Dahlgren and Whitehead 1991) has constructed a graphical model attempting to capture the relationship between different modes of explanation in the inequalities field (Figure 1). Notwithstanding the criticisms of this model as a basis for action (Wainwright, 1996), it pro-

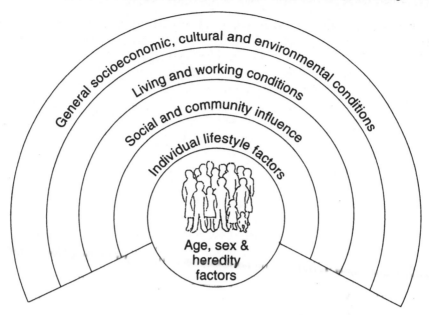

Figure 1: *The Whitehead/Dahlgren model (source: Dahlgren and Whitehead 1991)*

vides a convenient framework within which to discuss existing approaches to the study of these inequalities.

At the heart of the Whitehead/Dahlgren model are the 'biological givens'; not only our sex and age, but also what is given to us by our biological parents. These are factors over which the individual has no control and include the environmental influences that shaped our parents' health when they were conceiving us, or, indeed, when they themselves were conceived. These factors have been the focus of considerable research effort and there is now a substantial body of evidence, much of which derives from the work of David Barker and colleagues at Southampton University (see, for example, Barker 1991, 1992, 1994). This suggests that experiences (such as nutrition), *in utero* determine or 'programme' our risk of developing diseases later in life. Barker has, for example, demonstrated that mortality from cardiovascular disease is elevated among men whose birthweight was low or who were particularly thin.

Surrounding these biological determinants in the Whitehead/Dahlgren model, are a set of factors that are theorised to impact upon our likelihood of developing disease, or dying prematurely. These factors, that may be labelled 'lifestyle', embrace behaviours over which we may be said – though not without considerable argument – to have some degree of control. They include smoking, alcohol consumption, eating patterns, and propensity to exercise. Some of these are theorised to have direct effects on health outcome, while others are seen to operate indirectly. By far the most numerous of the studies directed at understanding inequalities in health have been focused on exploring the role of risk factors such as these. This body of work is widely referred to as 'risk factor epidemiology'.

Much current epidemiological research has come in for criticism from those who see the outer layers of the Whitehead/Dahlgren model – the population level and the wider social context of individuals – as having more explanatory power than this body of research appears to allow. Such criticism includes that from social epidemiologists themselves (Syme 1996, Shy 1997). For example, Syme has noted that ' . . . epidemiologists tend to study individuals in order to find causes of disease even though it is clear that this will not be helpful in understanding the distribution of disease in the population'. He continues: ' . . . almost all epidemiologists study large numbers of individuals in communities. This is not epidemiology. It is clinical medicine in large groups' (1996: 22, 23).

Syme's own solution to this problem is to address the social context of individuals through the set of factors identified in the second and third layer of the model – 'social and community influences' and 'living and working conditions'. (It is important to note that whilst these factors can be conceptualised as enveloping the lifestyle factors, they too operate at the individual level.) Syme gives prominence to the health implications of 'control over one's destiny'. This has been explored in considerable detail in relation to the workplace by Karasek and others who have developed and operationalised the notion of 'job decision latitude' (Karasek and Theorell 1990). Those working in occupations where there is the flexibility to structure one's own working day have been shown to suffer fewer health problems than those whose working practices are tightly defined and who have little or no discretion to influence the shape, schedule and content of their work.

A particularly important body of epidemiological work, which seeks to incorporate the social context of individual risks as well as aspects of individual lifestyle, has emanated from the Whitehall I and II studies (Marmot et al. 1978). These studies have demonstrated clear gradients in mortality across the fine and distinct grades of employment amongst English civil servants. The differences in mortality identified between the various grades mirror national differences between social classes except that they are even more marked: a greater than threefold difference in mortality being reported between the lowest and highest grades in the civil service.

The Whitehall studies have been important in drawing attention to the possibility that excess mortality is not just a matter of the cumulative effect of conventional risk factors. For example, they have shown that variations in risk factors (exercise, obesity, smoking and blood pressure) can 'explain' only about a third of the variation among employment grades – although this approach to interpreting statistical findings has recently been criticised as misrepresenting the cumulative impact of risk factors (Peckham 1997). The Whitehall Studies have also sought to incorporate psychosocial factors within and outside the world of work into the analysis (Marmot *et al.* 1991). Additionally, they have enabled Marmot and his colleagues to go beyond the presentation of aggregate, cross-sectional data and explore, in a 'captive population', changes in mortality over time.

A considerable body of research, beside the Whitehall Studies, supports the view that the structure, and especially quality, of social relations (layer two in the model) impacts on health and health inequalities. For example, a wide-ranging review of work on social ties and health (Seeman 1996) suggests that social integration reduces the risk of mortality and leads to better mental health. Similarly, Oakley's (1992) review of research on the links between social support and motherhood, points to many positive health outcomes related to social relationships. However, these reviews, and other work (Williams *et al.* 1998, Hall and Wellman 1995) also point to negative health outcomes associated with social relationships.

The outermost level of the Whitehead/Dahlgren model represent the material aspects of the context within which individual and population health is located – aspects which are largely determined by national and international forces. Low income, poor housing and unemployment, for example, have been shown to be determinants of health inequalities. Research has demonstrated this relationship at an aggregate level, for example by taking small area data on ill-health and attempting to account for variations using measures of material deprivation (Townsend *et al.* 1988). Townsend's composite index, including Census-based measures of car ownership, overcrowding, household tenure, and unemployment, has been used on numerous occasions as a predictor of mortality and limiting long-term illness.

More recently, researchers have begun to explore the relationship between patterns of mortality and morbidity and the macro socio-economic environment, focusing in particular on the role of relative deprivation. This work has also begun to link different parts of the Whitehead/Dahlgren model – macro socio-economic circumstances and the nature and quality of social relationships, for example. Wilkinson (1996) has assembled a body of evidence, involving international comparisons, to demonstrate correlations between income inequality (as measured, for example, by the percentage of household income received by the least well-off households) and mortality and life expectancy. Others have pursued these associations at a national and small area level (Kaplan *et al.* 1996, Kennedy *et al.* 1996, Ben-Shlomo *et al.* 1996, Boyle *et al.* 1997).

Wilkinson's explanation for this link between ill-health and relative deprivation extends the interest in the role of social relationships, drawing on work on the structure of civic society in Italy. He argues that involvement in community life (as measured, for example, by voting turnout and membership of local clubs and organisations) generates 'social capital' that is conducive to good health. In effect, Wilkinson is suggesting an interaction between income inequalities, manifested in the outermost layer of the Whitehead/Dahlgren model and psychosocial factors operating within the second ring.

The potential theoretical leverage of the notion of social capital is generating growing research interest. It is, for example, prominent in the recently published research strategy for the English Health Education Authority (Health Education Authority 1996). A related, but now neglected concept is that of the 'social wage' prominent in social welfare research in the 1960s. This was developed in an attempt to capture the improved quality of life (in material and social terms) accruing to individuals and households as a result of public spending on common services – such as education, health, housing and transport. Research has demonstrated that at some points during the postwar period the social wage was redistributive downwards to those living in poorer material circumstances, and over these periods there were major improvements in life expectancy (Charlton *et al.* 1997). Ultimately, however, the main beneficiaries of welfare spending were the middle classes (Titmuss 1958, Glennnester 1983).

The concept of a 'social wage' is more materialist in its formulation, and less psychological and relational than social capital. Although it may sound rather unfashionable in the wake of the 1980s and 90s critique of public welfare spending, it has not lost its salience for those concerned with understanding inequalities in health and the policies which might reduce these. Concepts such as 'social capital' and the 'social wage' may together have an important contribution to make to research in the health inequalities field. However, despite some empirical work seeking to operationalise them, these concepts remain somewhat ill-defined, and further work is required in order to demonstrate how these phenomena may impact upon health.

The final research tradition within the inequalities in health field we wish to highlight is that concerned with lifecourse or life-histories. There has been increasing academic interest in this approach in recent years, partly in response to the dominance of risk-factor epidemiology. For example, Power and colleagues (1996) have criticised Barker's work as being a narrow biologically deterministic explanation of potential health inequalities. They argue instead for an approach that recognises that birthweight is itself influenced by socioeconomic circumstances (of the parents), and that socioeconomic experiences of individuals as they mature into and continue through adulthood are also crucial in drawing the contours of the relative risk of disease in later life. For instance, work using longitudinal data (Bartley *et al.* 1994) has shown that males of low birthweight are more likely to live, as children and adolescents, in poorer quality housing.

Although a lifecourse approach to inequalities research is sometimes presented as a recent methodological innovation, it actually has a long and honourable history. As reviews of this field have documented (Wadsworth 1991, 1997), early and pathbreaking lifecourse work was begun in the 1940s in the field of social medicine and sociology at the MRC Sociology Unit in Aberdeen (Illsley 1955). This has been followed up in the decades since, as in the programme of work begun in the early 1980s at the MRC Medical Sociology Unit in Glasgow, Scotland.

The recent burgeoning of work using a lifecourse approach has been fuelled by the availability of new longitudinal datasets – such as the OPCS/ONS Longitudinal Study linking census data with mortality information over time for a 1% sample of the population of England and Wales – and the maturing of the samples involved in the national Cohort Studies begun in the 1940s, 50s and 70s. This type of research has also been stimulated by developments in computer hardware and statistical techniques, which have allowed for the easier handling of these complex longitudinal datasets. Wadsworth summarises the value of this type of research thus:

> The overwhelming strengths of prospective studies are their information on the sequence and timing of events, and the opportunities they offer to study not only, in the conventional way, the relative predictive strengths of precursors of an outcome, but also the range of outcomes associated with a presumed risk factor or combination of risk factors which may either co-occur or be related sequentially or synergistically. (Wadsworth 1997: 860)

Recognising these strengths of the lifecourse approach, Bartley and her colleagues have pointed to its significance for better targeting of policies to reduce inequalities:

> . . . a life course approach . . . is needed in order to take into account the complex ways in which biological risk interacts with economic, social and psychological factors in the development of chronic disease. Such an approach reveals biological and social 'critical periods' during which social policies that will defend individuals against an accumulation of risk are particularly important. (Bartley *et al.* 1997: 1194)

However, whilst lifecourse approaches to understanding inequalities in health have undoubted advantages they are also characterised by many of the limitations of much other research in the inequalities field.

Critiques of conventional inequalities in health research

Having reviewed the dominant research approaches within the health inequalities field, we want now to examine some of the existing critiques of this work. We draw particularly, but not exclusively, on Kathryn Dean's critique of population health research in general (1993), Keith Paterson's critique of epidemiology (1981), Mike Kelly and Bruce Charlton's (1995) critique of the knowledge base of health promotion and Sally Macintyre's (1997) recent discussion of polarisation in explanatory modes in health inequalities research.

Three main linked points emerge from these and other critiques. First, existing theoretical frameworks (and by implication much empirical research) fail to capture the complexity of causal explanation in the health inequalities field. In particular, these writers point to the inadequate attention paid to the role of social organisations, processes and relationships at a macro level in the generation of inequalities. Second, and linked to the first point, there has been a lack of attention to the development of concepts which will help explain why individuals and groups behave in the way they do in the context of wider social structures – to link agency and structure to use the sociological language. Third, the importance of developing work on the re-conceptualisation of the notion of 'place' within explanatory models of inequalities in health is highlighted alongside the neglect of a robust historical perspective. We discuss these points in more detail below.

Missing complexity
Dean (1993), Paterson (1981) and Macintyre (1997), in different ways, criticise much existing research on inequalities in health for failing to allow for the likely complexity of explanations. In her review of quantitative population health research, Kathryn Dean (1993) locates the difficulties in understanding the causal processes shaping health and illness in the failure of both epidemiology and social survey research to break free from positivistic philosophical foundations and empiricist methods. The problem, as Dean sees it, is that existing methods are simply not up to grasping the complexity inherent in the processes which shape health and illness: as she argues, health is ' . . . among the most complex of all dynamic systems' (1993: 26).

Dean traces the roots of this inadequacy back to the attempts made in both disciplines in the 1960s to overcome the acknowledged limitations of logical positivism. In resolving some of the methodological problems, she argues that these disciplines nevertheless remained wedded to positivism's empiricist tenets through the refinement of 'single factor' studies and experimental design:

> In spite of debates about empiricism and the limits of positivism, pressure grew in both fields for research approaches and methods which seek to predict the impact of specific factors on specific outcomes – factors separated from confounding influences by experimental design or its approximations. (1993: 21)

As we indicated in the last section, in epidemiology and social survey health research, the 'risk factor' approach became, and remains, supreme and, to a large extent, continues its quest to isolate risk factors – carefully considering each in turn. Whilst there has been a clear move to incorporate aspects of social relationships in this type of work, the danger is that it simply adds another possible risk factor to the existing set, ignoring the complexity involved. Put crudely, social support, for example, becomes another covariate to enter into a regression model, after adjustment for other risk factors. This atomistic approach disconnects individuals from their social context, and destroys the structure of the social network within which they are embedded (Hall and Wellman, 1985). As Dean argues:

> risk factor methods have severe limitations for uncovering multicausal mechanisms . . . This is because health and the influences that lead to its deterioration are multifaceted . . . and accumulate over the life course. (1993: 17).

Dean goes on to argue that whilst social survey researchers have gone some way to overcoming the 'factors' approach by developing techniques in causal modelling they, too, exhibit a strong tendency to fall back into the search for single causes. One recent summary of the state of the epidemiological art illustrates the continuing dominance of positivist thinking in this field:

> . . . the aim of epidemiology is to decipher nature with respect to human health and disease. (Trichopoulos, 1996: 436)

For many of those working within conventional positivist epidemiology, the idea developed within modern philosophy that knowledge cannot simply be a 'mirror of nature' (Rorty 1980) – that there is no easy correspondence between what we know and what exists – is a challenge that has yet to be faced.

Dean suggests that the solution for quantitative population health researchers lies in the transfer to health research of some of the breakthroughs in knowledge in other scientific fields. In particular, she believes that theoretical developments in the study of dynamic systems, involving chaos and complexity theory, offer hope of new ways of thinking which could facilitate an understanding of the interplay of influences and processes shaping health and illness. Of key significance for Dean is the requirement for theory and empirical work to become more intimately related.

In his earlier critique, Keith Paterson (1981) also highlighted the lack of sophistication in epidemiological research in particular. However, unlike Dean he was explicitly concerned with the neglect of structural issues, and his work is a critique of what might be called the political ontology of epidemiology. In his writing he attempts to counterpoise a 'materialist epidemiology' to the dominant positivistic one. Because they are embedded in a biological conception of disease, he argues, epidemiologists' empirical investigations of aetiological factors have left them dealing with surface appearances only – the result of an ideological stance which leaves the aetiological role of the social structure unquestioned. By giving primacy to the observable, privileging orthodox statistical techniques, and limiting its gaze to the 'host', the 'agent' and a limited number of environmental factors, he suggests, epidemiology fails to see the social relationships within which these factors are embedded:

> By its focus on disease as a problem of incidence, conceived of as a product of a number of mechanically related risk factors, epidemiology denies that the structure of social relationships in society also has a primary determining role . . . (1981: 26)

In contrast, for Paterson a materialist epidemiology would:

> . . . focus on these underlying structures and relationships and consider that the purpose of theory is to describe the fundamental processes that actually explain the observable regularities. Thus the aim of a materialist epidemiology would not be to deny the observed relationships between various diseases and different facets of the 'host', 'agent' and environment, but rather, to penetrate beneath the surface appearances described in statistical associations to the underlying socio-economic and historical context in which these associations are located. (1981: 27)

However, whilst a strong materialist/ structural research tradition did develop in the health inequalities field through the 1980s and into the 1990s, in the wake of the Black Report (DHSS 1980), this tended to be empiricist in nature, simply adding more social variables to an increasingly long list of risk factors. The more wide-ranging critique of positivism was largely lost until writers like Dean (1993) returned to theoretical matters. Today, a great deal of epidemiology and social survey work in the inequalities in health field remains profoundly non-social – in the sense that it does not explore the complex interactive relationship between individual experience, social action and the way in which societies are organised at a macro level.

Macintyre's critique of current research on inequalities in health provides a different, but related, perspective on the neglect of complexity – one focusing on the extent and nature of dualism in explanatory models in this field. In a recent research review (1997) she traces the continuities in modes of explanation of health determination and class differences in the patterning of death over the last 140 years in Britain. However, rather than focusing on positivism or the neglect of individual experience, as key elements of these continuities, Macintyre explores explanatory discourses in their historical and political context and argues that, for largely political and rhetorical reasons, explanations for inequalities in health have become unhelpfully polarised.

Of most significance for our purposes is the polarisation in explanatory approaches over the last 17 years along the lines of what Macintyre calls the 'hard' versions of the four main categories of explanation for socio-economic mortality differentials considered in the Black Report (DHSS 1980): artifact explanations; theories of natural and social selection; materialist/structural explanations; and cultural/behavioural explanations. She argues that in research following the Black Report, there was:

> . . . the sense that there were two or more opposing or polarised views, with proponents of each trying to convince the others, and an audience, of the correctness of their views. (Macintyre 1997: 731)

According to Macintyre, the proponents tended to adopt the position that explanatory approaches were mutually exclusive, setting up false antitheses: 'selection versus causation', 'artifact versus real differences' and 'behaviour versus material circumstances' (1997: 740). She suggests that in more recent research the tendency to polarise positions has continued noting, for example that:

> in the reaction to Barker's work (1991; 1994) on 'early life programming' the 'continued social disadvantage' theorists have rejected the former approach in its entirety; within the materialist/structural explanatory approach there has been a dichotomising into 'material' and 'psychosocial' factors such that these two components are seen to constitute competing and mutually exclusive explanations. (1997: 737)

Macintyre argues that health inequalities research now requires a move beyond this binary opposition so that a ' . . . more micro-level examination of the pathways by which social structure actually influences mental and physical health and functioning and life expectancy' (1997: 736–7) becomes possible. This, she suggests, would mean adopting a 'more fine grained' approach (1997: 740) which explores not only the relative importance of categories of factors 'but also their possible interactions or additive effects' (1997: 740). Importantly, she notes that:

> . . . the social context needs continually to be taken into account and is likely to result in more differentiated models (there is no a priori reason to suppose that the processes generating inequalities are the same at the top as at the bottom of the social scale, among men as compared with women, or in Northern Europe as compared with Mediterranean countries, the USA, or the Far East). (1997: 740)

Individuals and social structure
Neither Dean nor Macintyre explicitly address the neglect of individual agency within health inequalities research. It certainly does not figure in Macintyre's list of future research priorities. Paterson somewhat unusually does point to the potential theoretical significance of subjectivity, suggesting that, by restricting science only to observables, positivism:

> . . . specifically excludes any account of the experiences, perceptions, feelings and other subjective states of individuals . . . [whereas . . . a materialist epidemiology would] . . . give consideration to subjective states and meanings. (1981: 26 and 28)

However, this is not a central issue in Paterson's work, nor does he explore the epistemological and methodological implications of this comment in detail. In contrast, recent sociological critiques of the conceptual foundations of health promotion (see, for example, Bunton *et al.* 1995) are centrally concerned with the neglect of the subjective – of individual lived experience – in much recent research and practice. Alongside Foucauldian analyses of epidemiology (Armstrong 1983, 1993), these critiques suggest that the conceptualisation of the determinants of health found in health promotion, as in conventional epidemiology, are fundamentally modernist. Kelly and Charlton (1995) have argued, for instance, that despite being a product of postmodernism, health promotion's attachment to a social model of health does not signify a break with the tenets of 'normal science'. Rather:

> the social model of health is, in this regard, no different to the medical model. In the medical model the pathogens are microbes, viruses or malfunctioning cellular reproduction. In the social model they are poor housing, poverty, unemployment and powerlessness. The discourse may be different but the epistemology is the same. (1995: 82)

This argument echoes that of Dean and Paterson. From a sociological perspective, however, Kelly and Charlton are concerned to point to a different set of problems which flow from a deterministic and dualistic stance:

> Unemployment causes ill health. Deprivation causes disease. Society (the biggest system of all) is held to be at fault . . . The individual is relegated to being nothing more than a system outcome, not a thinking and acting human being. (1995: 83)

Pointing to Giddens' structuration theory, they argue that developments in modern social theory may assist in resolving some of the difficulties in reconciling free will and determinism. In this body of work, they suggest, there may be concepts, or ways of thinking, which can help to enhance understanding of the interaction between the experience and action of individual human beings – seen potentially at least, as creative agents acting on and shaping the world around them – and the structures of power and control within which they are embedded. As Kelly and Charlton note:

> Such dynamic and reciprocal analysis of the individual set into context ought to be at the heart of health promotion . . . Developing this, and making it work, is the task ahead. (1995: 90)

This task, daunting as it may be, is equally salient to health inequalities research in general.

'Place' and time in current inequalities research

Our earlier description of research within the inequalities field included a brief reference to studies which looked at the association between geographical area and patterns of mortality and morbidity. Much of this research has reproduced the same epistemological assumptions and methodological strategies evident in population health research. There has, for example, been relatively little work investigating the relationship between mortality and morbidity and the socio-economic or cultural features of areas (Macintyre *et al.* 1993). Nor is there much research which conceptualises 'place' as the primary site for the impact of macro social structures to be played out in the daily lives of individuals.

In a recent review, Macintyre and colleagues (1993) divide existing research on place and health into two types: studies which focus on specific aspects of the physical environment and are concerned to provide information about the genesis of specific diseases; and those which use area level aggregate data to study the relationship between deprivation and mortality and/or morbidity. Focusing on these latter studies, Macintyre has further argued that whilst asset-based measures based on individuals, such as the car and home ownership variables used by Townsend and others in Britain, may do a good job of describing the social composition of an area, they do not describe other features of the area that may be health-promoting or health-damaging (1997: 173).

Phillimore (1993) similarly stresses the important conceptual and analytical distinction between characteristics of people and places, noting that:

> the characteristics of places may be as important as the characteristics of people for an understanding of particular patterns of health. (1993: 176)

As Jones and Moon argue in relation to research in the field of medical geography:

> Seldom . . . does location itself play a real part in the analysis; it is the canvas on which events happen, but the nature of the locality and its role in structuring health status and health related behaviour is neglected. (1993: 515)

The need for a re-conceptualisation of the notion of 'place' is re-inforced by recent work demonstrating that places with similar socio-economic profiles can have very different population health profiles (Phillmore and Morris 1991, Phillimore 1993, Barker and Osmond 1987). Similarly, Blaxter (1990) has noted that while men and women in manual occupations have worse health than those in non-manual occupations, the differences between them seem to be greater in 'good' residential areas and industrial areas than in rural or resort areas. To understand these variations we need a richer description of access to opportunity structures (good recreational and transport facilities, for example, as well as data on levels of crime and vandalism) that more adequately reflect an impoverished social topography (Macintyre *et al.* 1993).

More profoundly, however, in re-conceptualising 'place' it will be important to bring individuals into the analysis. What, for example, are the health consequences of being a materially deprived individual in a relatively prosperous place? How do individuals living in the most materially disadvantaged areas of societies make sense of and act upon their environments, with what consequences for their health and those they care for? What is the relationship between material risk, individual experience and action at the individual or group level? Much of this remains contested ground (see, for example, Sloggett and Joshi 1994). Additionally, while new statistical techniques, such as multi-level modelling, may be brought to bear on such questions, the extent to which they offer good explanations, as opposed to good statistical descriptions, is a matter for theoretical debate.

There is some indication that research into health and place is beginning to include a focus on the experience and perspective of the people who live in the places being studied. In their recent research, for example, Macintyre and colleagues have given prominence to the importance of people's experience (Macintyre *et al.* 1993). Sooman and Macintyre (1995) studied residents' perceptions of their local environment in four socially contrasting neighbourhoods in Glasgow. Six aspects of the areas – local amenities, local problems, area reputation, neighbourliness, fear of crime and general satisfaction – differed significantly between the neighbourhoods. They also found significant difference in levels of anxiety and depression and self assessed health. The multivariate analysis they performed suggested that perceptions of the area acted independently of social class in influencing health differences between neighbourhoods. However, the quantitative, structured nature of this type of work means that it cannot explore the subjective – in the sense of capturing the meanings people themselves attach to experiences. In the words of Phillimore and Moffatt:

> Whatever the methodological challenges involved, the voices of those living in local communities most at risk from possible environmental hazards must be heard. (1994: 150)

Any re-conceptualisation of 'place' in health research must also pay more attention to the significance of time – both historical and biographical. The historical dimensions of 'place' have been shown to be important in the work of Barker and Osmond (1987) exploring health variation in three Lancashire towns. This work highlights the significance of the socio-economic history of 'places', pointing, in particular, to the contemporary health legacy of public housing initiatives begun at the end of the last century. Similarly, in his comparative work in Middlesborough and Sunderland, Phillimore (1993) has considered the role of a range of area characteristics, including economic/industrial history, pollution and cultural factors, in explaining area differences in patterns of mortality and morbidity. In the main, however, the historical dimension of 'places' has been largely neglected in health inequalities research to date. As Mills (1959) argued: 'Every social science – or better, every well considered social study – requires an historical scope of conception and a full use of historical material' (1959: 145).

The theoretical significance of 'place' and 'lay knowledge' in inequalities research

It is clear from the literature discussed so far that there is an urgent need for future research on inequalities in health to be more strongly informed by theory. We have also argued that the theoretical framework shaping future research in this field should give greater prominence than has hitherto been the case to the relationship between individual human agency and wider social structures. While the distinction between the layers of the Whitehead/Dahlgren model is a convenient one, these layers have thin membranes, and interact in complex ways. As Tarlov has it:

> the rings are porous . . . [the model] . . . is not like a game of pool wherein a ball in the outer ring strikes a stationary ball in the intermediate ring which in turn collides with a resting ball in the inner ring . . . [a]ll of the balls are in motion most of the time. (1996: 83)

This interaction, or 'porosity' between different layers of explanation is central to the work of social theorists such as Giddens (1984, 1991) and Bourdieu (1977, 1990). Both argue in effect for approaches to explanation in the social sphere that give due consideration to the combined effect of social structures and individual human agency. This argument is particularly relevant to future research on inequalities in health.

In this final section we suggest that two key developments are necessary to produce a richer and more dynamic framework for understanding the relationship between individual human agency, social structures and health inequalities. The first is to explore the conceptualisation and measurement of 'place' within a historical context as the location in which macro social structures impact on individual lives. The second is to consider how 'places', conceptualised in this way, are understood within lay experience of 'the everyday life-world'. In doing this we would be consciously exploring the connections between the sub-universes which people directly experience and the wider world which shapes those sub-universes (Schutz 1962).

Reconceptualising place

The writings of social reformers in the last century provide fine detailed analyses of the relationship between health, wellbeing and 'place' (broadly defined). The work of people like Engels, exploring the 'ruinous and filthy districts' of Salford and Manchester in 1842 (Engels 1969: 94), and of Mayhew (quoted in Hardy 1993), revealing the places of work of the nineteenth century London labour force, is alluring because it focuses on particular features of the places in which people lived and worked: the effects of working in this occupation rather than that, or of living in this group of streets as compared with those half a mile away. In the absence of any theoretically sophisticated analysis of class and health, neighbourhoods and places were the natural focus for early public health analysis and, in any event, epidemic infectious diseases did seem to strike particular localities, streets, and even households (Hardy 1993 Chadwick 1842).

Recent developments in research looking at place and health, briefly discussed above, suggest that a reconceptualisation of 'place' is possible, recapturing and moving beyond the richness of this earlier work. There are, however, dangers in the seemingly innocent anthropological fascination with the particularities of places. It can, for instance, too readily lead to the stigmatising of neighbourhoods. Work on the 'fear of crime', for example, shows that people's perceptions of personal safety in different neighbourhoods vary dramatically regardless of the 'actual' differences in the likelihood of being mugged or burgled (Taylor *et al.* 1996). Particular areas of large cities, such as Moss Side in Manchester (Fraser 1997) seem to retain a 'reputation' long after the circumstances which gave rise to that reputation have changed. Research needs to be sensitive to these 'labelling' processes.

These caveats notwithstanding, a refocusing on place in inequalities research may allow us to understand the dynamics of social class during a period when traditional class categorisations based on men's positions in the labour market are arguably less relevant than they have ever been. By looking at places with different social geographies and histories we may be able to understand the 'hidden injuries of class' (Sennett and Cobb 1977), as well as their hidden sources of benefit, in a more sophisticated way than occupational classifications have allowed. The study of the places people inhabit may still allow us to explore the way in which structures work themselves through into the dynamics of everyday life. Places can be conceptualised as the locations for 'structuration' – the interrelationship of the conscious intentions and actions of individuals and groups and the 'environment' of cultural, social and economic forces in which people exist. Indeed, although the new interest in place can deflect attention from the continuing impact of the major social divisions of gender, class and ethnicity – encouraging the victim-blaming of particular working class households in places with 'bad reputations' – it could equally provide a better context for exploring the dynamics of class in the context of the history and urban or rural geography of particular places.

In conventional studies of class and health, class is something that has become 'taken-for-granted' both theoretically and in the methods that are used to measure it. As Macintyre and her colleagues (1993) indicate, one of the implications of comparing places is that it allows for a much broader area-based definition of class. In addition to looking at the personal charac-teristics of individuals in households – income, occupation, and housing tenure – it is possible also to explore availability and price of good foods, recreational and sporting facilities, public transport, local health services and the safety and security of the local environment. In theorising 'place' we can gain much from looking at the writings of contemporary geographers and planners as they grapple with alternative notions of space and how we might collect information about 'place' conceptualised in Aristotelian rather than Newtonian or Leibnizian terms (Curry 1996). These approaches might allow for a theoretically and empirically more sophisticated approach to the operationalisation of concepts such as social capital and the social wage.

It is also necessary to develop a conception of both places, and individu-als in places, that takes history and biography into account. Places have dif-ferent histories and the history, and the present, of a neighbourhood or locality will mean different things to individual people who have their own temporal and historical associations with the area. People's relationships to places will be variable and diverse. For some people there will be one domi-nant 'place' in which they spend much of their time. For others paid employment or education might involve extensive travel – and their rela-tionship with the different 'places' they inhabit might be more or less intense. The individual experience of place can be expected to be structured by gender, age, ethnicity, and other social factors – but individuals will be differentially and multiply positioned in relation to these aspects of social structures. Whilst some research has considered these issues in a spatial and quantitative way – mapping people's movement across physical space, time and social networks for example – there is little if any work exploring the meanings people attach to their travels, nor how these meanings change over time.

Lay knowledge, narratives and social action
Places have histories and people have biographies which they articulate through stories or narratives. The history of sociology is replete with attempts to theorise this macro-micro link, to look at the intersection of his-tory and biography, but the theoretical directions suggested by this work have rarely been taken up in empirical research on inequalities in health. Attention to the meanings people attach to their experience of places and how this shapes social action could provide a missing link in our understanding of the causes of inequalities in health. In particular, the

articulation of these meanings – which we refer to as lay knowledge – in narrative form could provide invaluable insights into the dynamic relationships between human agency and wider social structures that underpin inequalities in health. As with the notion of place, however, the notion of 'lay knowledge' requires re-conceptualisation if it is to fulfil this potential. Recent developments in social theory and research, outwith the inequalities in health field, point to possible directions for this reconceptualisation.

Williams and Popay (1998 forthcoming) have recently drawn a useful distinction between concepts which may help to link agency and structure and those which may link individuals to their capacity to act. In their discussion of a number of 'mediating concepts' they also point to the substantive and methodological importance of narrative accounts of experience. In relation to the connection between structure and agency, for instance, Williams and Popay highlight the work of Janet Finch (1989). They discuss, in particular, the concepts of 'normative guidelines and timescales' which Finch develops out of people's narrative accounts of care-giving within families, to help explain the non-material factors that shape people's action and how these change over time. Finch argues that these guidelines represent the 'proper thing to do' but not in any simple way. Social norms and obligations shape individual behaviour but, in acting to 'mobilise obligations' for example, people reproduce and mould these same norms and obligations in specific ways. In discussing the notion of 'purposeful action', Finch points to the formative role of people's explanations for action:

> People need to, and are able to, explain what they have done and why they have done it and this in itself forms part of the action. (Finch, 1989: 88)

In a similar way, developing the concept of 'narrative reconstruction' as a means of understanding lay experiences of chronic illness, Williams (1984) has explored the way in which people living with chronic illness use this narrative knowledge, actively interpreting existing social norms and cultural values in order to pursue a virtuous course of action in response to the consequences of the illness (Williams 1993).

In exploring ways in which individuals may be linked to their capacity for purposeful action, Williams and Popay (1998), point to the mediating potential of concepts such as autonomy, control and identity and to the central role of narratives in the 'construction' of self-identity:

> An engagement with the understanding and structuring of self identity is, according to Giddens, a characteristic of contemporary social life, not as a given but is something which individuals create and sustain through their own accounts (or narratives) of their life experience . . . New circumstances, new risks, new identities (for example created through divorce . . .) mean that people need to reassess the 'proper thing to do' and one way they may

do this is by recalling their experience and reconstructing their identities. (1998 forthcoming)

Williams and Popay (1998) further suggest that the concept of discourse, alongside that of identity, may also perform a bridging function because 'it enables us to consider the structural and ideological influences upon people's lives in one frame' (1998: 16). To illustrate this they refer to research by Duncan and Edwards (1996) which explores the respective influence of discourses around motherhood and work on lone mothers' decisions about employment, compared to neo-liberal discourses around costs and benefits. In this work too the link between lone mothers' decision-making and discursive practices was drawn out from women's narrative accounts of their experiences.

Linking narratives and place

Until recently much of the work on people's narratives and stories has been empirical, but there has been a growing body of work at a theoretical level (see, for example, Hatch and Wisniewski 1995, Hinchman and Hinchman 1997, Somers 1994). Somers' work is particularly interesting from the perspective of this chapter as it serves to link at a conceptual level lay knowledge in the form of narratives with our discussion above of 'place' as the location for structuration.

Somers argues that recent research is revealing the substance of narratives as central to our understanding of social action:

> namely that social life is storied and that narrative is an ontological condition of social life . . . showing us that stories guide action; that people construct identities (however multiple and changing) by locating themselves or being located within a repertoire of emplotted stories: that 'experience' is constituted through narratives; that people make sense of what has happened and is happening to them by attempting to assemble or in some way to integrate these happenings within one or more narratives; and that people are guided to act in certain ways and not others on the basis of the projections, expectations and memories derived from a multiplicity but ultimately limited repertoire of available social, public and cultural narratives. (Somers 1994: 614)

Narrative understanding, Somers argues, develops by connecting experience to structure in terms of a personal understanding of episodes rather than an abstract conceptualisation of events. Somers identifies four dimensions of narrative: ontological, public, conceptual, and 'meta'. Ontological narratives, she argues, are used to define who we are and are the basis for knowing what to do – akin to Finch's normative guidelines. It is through these that apparently disconnected sets of events are turned into meaningful episodes. Public narratives are those attached to cultural or institutional formations, such as families or workplaces, often by the mass media that transcend the individual. They often provide the legitimating context for ontological narratives. Metanarratives are 'master' narratives of progress, decline, crisis which transcend the immediate context and are often used politically to construct a particular ideological position. Conceptual narratives are those which researchers construct, using concepts that lie outside both ontological and public narratives, drawing on them both but introducing concepts such as social class, behaviour-change, mortality rate and so on which might not be found in either ontological or public narratives.

For Somers, the analytical challenge is 'to develop concepts which will allow us to capture the narrativity through which agency is negotiated, identities are constructed and social action mediated' (1994: 620). She suggests that two central components here are narrative identity and relational settings – the latter being relations between people, narratives and institutions. These notions, she suggests, provide a conceptual bridge to (re)-introduce time, space, relationships and cultural practices into the process whereby people are categorised in research. In applying her arguments to an analysis of the relationship between social class and political action in the turbulent 18th century, Somers concludes that:

> From the narrative identity perspective, these same working classes would be seen as *members* of political cultures whose symbolic and relational *places* in a matrix of narratives and relationships are better indicators of action than their categorical classifications.

This approach holds out the possibility of a deeper understanding of why different groups within the same class or social position can and do respond differently across the social and geographical landscape. Somers concludes her paper by arguing that as social scientists:

> We need concepts that will enable us to plot over time and space the ontological narratives of historical actors, the public and cultural narratives that inform their lives, as well as the relevant range of other social forces – from politics to demographics – that configure together to shape history and social action. (Somers 1994: 625)

The importance of seeing lay knowledge in its narrative form in this way is that it provides a different perspective on the relationship between individuals and the places, or 'relational settings' in which they live. This perspective makes 'place' more than a set of static environmental deficits or provisions, no matter how imaginatively these are operationalised, and it makes the 'lifecourse' more than a biological trajectory during which the individual is inertly exposed to various accumulating risks or benefits. It highlights the need to look not just at the statistical associations between significant events in people's lives as defined by researchers, but at the meanings people give to the relationship between these events – how they translate events into meaningful episodes. In the context of inequalities in health it provides a strong case for looking at people's perceptions of 'episodes' in their lives and the ways in which these may orientate or fail to orientate action at the individual or collective level. While narratives express a knowledge of the relationship between episodes over time, the relational settings which shape these narratives (and are shaped by them) also have a history and need to be explored in 'place' and time.

Conclusion

Within the health inequalities field there is a widespread acceptance of the need for a deeper understanding of the relationship between the individual and their social context. What we are proposing here is a way in which the theoretical framework underpinning much of this work could be developed to provide this understanding. We have argued that the study of lay knowledge in the context of 'place' and time should be central to this framework. It is the medium through which our understanding of the relationship between health and the 'places' we inhabit is expressed. It is the means by which we locate ourselves within these 'places' and determine how to act within and upon them. These places, in turn, are the site in which macro social structures impact upon individual lives. However, there are major barriers to the developments in inequalities research which would flow from this analysis.

First, major barriers flow from the way in which lay knowledge finds expression. Lay knowledge differs from expert knowledge in the sense that it has an ontological purpose, orientating behaviour in terms of an understanding to the individual's place in their life-world. It is, as we have argued, expressed in narrative form. This form is antithetical to traditional models of cause and effect, such as those given prominence within the inequalities research literature. Second, insofar as such narratives draw on or relate to wider public narratives (or discourses) they may also constitute a form of knowledge that challenges that of experts. Lay knowledge may stand not just as a different kind of knowledge but as knowledge which takes issue with the way in which media or experts characterise the relationships between events or the nature or needs and/or identity – on occasions forming what Nancy Fraser (1989) has described as 'oppositional discourses'. This challenge may hinder the developments in inequalities research we have argued for.

There is an on-going and welcome debate about the need for different and better research methods and techniques in the inequalities field, and for greater collaboration between disciplines. However, to date this has largely failed to address the implications for future research which arise from the very different frameworks of understanding we have been discussing here.

What we are suggesting – to coin an old-fashioned phrase – is that people make their own history (and future) – but not always in conditions that they have themselves chosen. In order to further our understanding of the causes of health variations we need to study directly the experiences of individuals and their biographies, and link these to the social organisation of places and their histories. This analysis requires, in turn, an awareness of the influence of national and global socio-economic change. We would argue that this cannot be done without profound reconsideration of the scope and conception of social scientific investigations in the field of inequalities in health and its relationship to the work of other disciplines. What it means in practice is that the kind of social science we do should have four characteristics: it should ask questions about social structures and processes situated concretely in time and space; it should address processes over time and examine temporal sequences; it should look at the interplay of meaningful actions and social contexts; and it should highlight the particular and varying features of specific structures and patterns (Skocpol 1984).

Note

1   This study is part of the ESRC's programme on social inequalities in health. Contract number L 128 25 1020.

References

Armstrong, D. (1983) *Political Anatomy of the Body: Medical Knowledge in Britain in the Twentieth Century*. Cambridge: Cambridge University Press.

Armstrong, D. (1993) Public health spaces and the fabrication of identity, *Sociology*, 27, 3, 393–410.

Barker, D.J.P. (1991) The foetal and infant origins of inequalities in health in Britain, *Journal of Public Health Medicine*, 13, 64–8.

Barker, D.J.P. (ed) (1992) Fetal and infant origins of adult disease, London: British Medical Journal.

Barker, D.J.P. (1994) Mothers, babies and disease in later life. London: British Medical Journal Publications.

Barker, D.J.P. and Osmond, C. (1987) Inequalities in health in Britain: specific explanations in three Lancashire towns, *British Medical Journal*, 294, 749–52.

Bartley, M., Power, C., Blane, D. and Davey Smith, G. (1994) Birthweight and later socio-economic disadvantage: evidence from the 1958 British cohort study, *British Medical Journal*, 309, 1475–8.

Bartley, M., Blane, S. and Montgomery, S. (1997) Health and the life course: why safety nets matter, *British Medical Journal*, 314, 1194.

Ben-Shlomo, Y., White, I.R. and Marmot, M. (1996) Does the variation in the socioeconomic characteristics of an area affect mortality? *British Medical Journal*, 312, 1013–14.

Blaxter, M. (1990) *Health and Lifestyles*. London: Routledge.

Bourdieu, P. (1977) *Outline of a Theory of Practice*. Cambridge: Cambridge University Press.

Bourdieu, P. (1990) *The Logic of Practice*. Cambridge: Polity Press.

Boyle, P.J., Gatrell, A.C. and Duke-Williams, O. (1997) Self-Reported Limiting Long-Term Illness and Variations in Population Change within and in Neighbouring Small Areas. Unpublished paper.

Bunton, R., Nettleton, S. and Burrows, R. (1995) *The Sociology of Health Promotion: Critical Analyses of Consumption, Lifestyle and Rick*. London: Routledge.

Chadwick, E. (1842) *Report of an Enquiry into the Sanitary Conditions of the Labouring Population of Great Britain*. London: Poor Law Commission.

Charlton, D. and Murphy, M. (eds) (1997) *Adult Health: Historical Aspects 1850–1980*. London: HMSO.

Curry, M. (1996) Space and place in geographic decision-making. In *Technical Expertise and Public Decisions*, Conference Proceedings, Princeton University, USA, 311–18.

Dahlgren, G. and Whitehead, M. (1991) *Policies and Strategies to Promote Social Equity in Health*. Stockholm: Institute for Futures Studies.

Dean, K. (1993) Integrating theory and methods in population health research. In Dean, K. (ed) *Population Health Research: Linking Theory and Methods*. London: Sage.

Department of Health and Social Security (1980) *Inequalities in Health: Report of a Working Group Chaired by Sir Douglas Black*. London: DHSS.

Duncan, S. and Edwards, R. (1996) Lone mothers and paid work. In *Social Politics. International Studies of Gender, State and Society*, 13, 2/31 95–222.

Engels, F. (1969) *The Condition of the Working Class in England: from Personal Observation and Authentic Sources*. London: Panther.

Fraser (1998) Unruly Practices: *Power, Discourse and Gender in Contemporary Social Theory*. Cambridge: Polity Press.

Finch, J. (1989) *Family Obligation and Social Change*. Cambridge: Polity Press.

Giddens, A. (1984) *The Constitution of Society*. Cambridge: Polity Press.

Giddens, A. (1991) *Modernity and Self-Identity*. Cambridge: Polity Press.

Glennester, H. (1983) *The Future of the Welfare State: Remaking Social Policy*. London: Fabian Society.

Hall, A. and Wellman, B. (1985) Social networks and social support. In Cohen, S. and Syme, S.L. (eds) *Social Support and Health*. London: Academic Press.

Hardy, A. (1993) *The Epidemic Streets: Infectious Disease and the Rise of Preventive Medicine, 1856–1900*. Oxford: Clarendon Press.

Hatch, J.A. and Wisniewski, R. (1995) *Life History and Narrative*. London: The Falmer Press.

Health Education Authority (1996) *Annual Report*. London.

Hinchman, L.P. and Hinchman, S.K. (1997) *Memory, Identity, Community: the Idea of Narrative in the Human Sciences*. New York: State University of New York Press.

Illsley, R. (1955) Social class selection and class differences in relation to stillbirth and infant deaths, *British Medical Journal*, 2, 1520–4.

Jones, K., Moon, G. (1993) Medical geography: taking space seriously, *Progress in Human Geography*, 17, 515–24.

Kaplan, G.A., Pamuk, E.R., Lynch, J.W., Cohen, R.D. and Balfour, J.L. (1996)

Inequality in income and mortality in the United States: analysis of mortality and potential pathways, *British Medical Journal*, 312, 999–1003.

Karasek, R. and Theorell, T. (1990) *Healthy Work: Stress, Productivity, and the Reconstruction of Working Life*. New York: Basic Books.

Kelly, M. and Charlton, B. (1995) The modern and the postmodern in health promotion. In Burrows, R., Nettleton, S., and Burrows, R. (eds) *The Sociology of Health Promotion*. London: Routledge.

Kennedy, B.P., Kawachi, I. and Prothrow-Stith, D. (1996) Income distribution and mortality: cross-sectional ecological study of the Robin Hood index in the United States, *British Medical Journal*, 312, 1003–7.

Macintyre, S. (1997) The Black Report and beyond: what are the issues? *Social Science and Medicine*, 44, 6, 723–45.

Macintyre, S., MacIver, S. and Sooman, A. (1993) Area, class and health: should we be focusing on places or people? *Journal of Social Policy*, 22, 213–34.

Marmot, M.G., Rose, G., Shipley, M. and Hamilton, P.J.S. (1978) Employment grade and coronary heart disease in British civil servants, *Journal of Epidemiology and Community Health*, 3, 244–9.

Marmot, M.G., Davey Smith, G., Stansfield, S., Patel, C., North, F., Head, J., White, L., Brunner, E. and Feeney, A. (1991) Health inequalities among British civil servants: the Whitehall II study, *Lancet*, 337, 1387–93.

Mills, C.W. (1959), *The Sociological Imagination*. New York: Oxford University Press.

Oakley, A. (1992) *Social Support and Motherhood: the Natural History of a Research Project*. Oxford: Basil Blackstone.

Paterson, K. (1981) Theoretical perspectives in epidemiology – a critical appraisal, *Radical Community Medicine*, Autumn, 23–34.

Peckham (1997) *The Guardian* newspaper, July 1997.

Phillimore, P. (1993) How do places shape health? Rethinking locality and lifestyle in North East England. In Platt, S., Thomas, H., Scott, S. and Williams, G. (eds) *Locating Health: Sociological and Historical Explorations*. Aldershot: Avebury.

Phillimore, P. and Moffatt, S. (1994) Discounted knowledge: local experience, environmental pollution and health. In Popay, J. and Williams, G. (eds) *Researching the People's Health*. London: Routledge.

Phillimore, P. and Morris, D. (1991) Discrepant legacies: premature mortality in two industrial towns, *Social Science and Medicine*, 33, 2, 139–52.

Power, C., Bartley, M., Davey Smith, G. and Blane, D. (1996) Transmission of social and biological risk across the life course. In Blane, D., Brunner, E. and Wilkinson, R. (eds) *Health and Social Organisation*. London: Routledge.

Rorty, R. (1980) *Philosophy and the Mirror of Nature*. Oxford: Blackwell.

Schutz, A. (1962) *Collected Papers*. The Hague: Nijhoff.

Seeman, T.E. (1996) Social ties and health – the benefits of social integration, *Annals of Epidemiology*, 6, 442–51.

Sennett, R. and Cobb, J. (1977) *The Hidden Injuries of Class*. Cambridge: Cambridge University Press.

Shy, C.M. (1997) The failure of academic epidemiology: witness for the prosecution, *American Journal of Epidemiology*, 145, 479–87.

Skocpol, T. (ed) (1984) *Vision and Method in Historical Sociology*. Cambridge: Cambridge University Press.

Sloggett, A. and Joshi, H. (1994) Higher mortality in deprived areas: community or personal disadvantage? *British Medical Journal*, 309, 1470–4.

Somers, M.R. (1994) The narrative constitution of identity: a relational and network approach, *Theory and Society*, 23, 605–49.

Sooman, A. and Macintyre, S. (1995) Health and perceptions of the local environment in socially contrasting neighbourhoods in Glasgow, *Health and Place*, 1, 1, 15–26.

Syme, S.L. (1996) To prevent disease: the need for a new approach. In Blane, D., Brunner, E. and Wilkinson, R. (eds) *Health and Social Organisation*. London: Routledge.

Tarlov, A. (1996) Social determinants of health: the sociobiological translation. In Blane, D., Brunner, E. and Wilkinson, R. (eds) *Health and Social Organisation*. London: Routledge.

Taylor, I., Evans, K. and Fraser, P. (1996) *A Tale of Two Cities*. London: Routledge.

Thompson, E.P. (1963) *The Making of the English Working Class*. Harmondsworth: Penguin.

Titmuss, R.M. (1958) *Essays on the Welfare State*. London: Unwin.

Townsend, P., Phillimore, P. and Beattie, A. (1988) *Health and Deprivation: Inequality and the North*. London: Croom Helm.

Trichopoulos, D. (1996) The future of epidemiology, *British Medical Journal*, 313, 436–7.

Wadsworth, M. (1991) *The Imprint of Time: Childhood, History and Adult Life*. Oxford: Oxford University Press.

Wadsworth, M.E. (1997) Health-inequalities in the life course perspective, *Social Science Medicine*, 44, 6, 859–69.

Wainwright, D. (1996) The political transformation of the health inequalities debate, *Critical Social Policy*, 49, 16, 67–82.

Whitehead, M. (1995) Tackling inequalities: a review of policy initiatives. In Benzeval, M., Judge, K. and Whitehead, M. (eds) *Tackling Inequalities in Health*. London: The King's Fund.

Whitehead, M. and Dahlgren, G. (1991) What can be done about inequalities in health? *Lancet*, 338, 1059–63.

Wilkinson, R.G. (1996) *Unhealthy Societies: the Afflictions of Inequality*. London: Routledge.

Williams, F. and Popay, J. (forthcoming 1998) Developing a new framework for welfare research. In Williams, F., Popay, J. and Oakley, A. (eds). London: University College Press.

Williams, F., Popay, J. and Oakley, A. (eds) (1998 forthcoming) *'Welfare Research: A Critical Review*. London: University College Press.

Williams, G.H. (1984) The genesis of chronic illness: narrative reconstruction, *Sociology of Health and Illness*, 6, 175–200.

Williams, G.H. (1993) Chronic illness and the pursuit of virtue in everyday life. In Radley, A. (ed) *Worlds of Illness: Cultural and Biographical Perspectives on Health and Disease*. London: Routledge.

4. Is there a place for geography in the analysis of health inequality?

Sarah Curtis and Ian Rees Jones

Introduction

Health data for geographical areas are frequently used to demonstrate health inequality. However, the interpretation of such data on geographical variation in health is often equivocal. Some authors tend to down-play the significance of places for health difference, arguing that processes operating at the individual level are far more important for our understanding of health inequality. Others suggest that processes influencing individual health experience may operate differently in different places. This debate is important for many disciplines concerned to comprehend health inequalities and act to reduce health variation. It is of fundamental interest for geographers interested in health.

This chapter considers how ideas about space and place are used in discourses relating to health variation and discusses some of the theory which might illuminate the possible impact of place on health inequalities. In the light of this theoretical debate, we review the empirical evidence concerning place as a contributor to health inequalities. The discussion here focuses particularly on research on geographical health variation among British populations. We have not extended the discussion to consider the equally interesting issues of geographical health differences at the international level between countries.

Ideas of space and place in the geography of health

A discussion of the geography of health involves ideas of both space and place. A complex set of concepts is encompassed in these two terms. Kearns and Joseph (1993) and Jones and Moon (1993) have drawn attention to the need to develop our understanding of how health differences may relate to aspects of space and place.

Space denotes a dimension in which phenomena are distributed. Conventionally it has been viewed as orthodox geometric space, quantifiable in terms of Euclidean distance. Alternative, relative concepts of space might be determined by the degree of linkage in spatial networks (Chorley and Haggett 1974), or even by hyperspaces, created by cybernetic systems.

Kearns and Joseph (1993), are among those who argue that space can also be seen as both the medium and outcome of social relations. Space therefore has social significance and is socially constructed. Groups in society which are most socially separate are quite often most spatially distant, especially in their residential distribution. Smith (1994) and Sibley (1995) stress the ways that space is implicated in social exclusion, whether this be rigid social exclusions, such as those of prisons and asylums, or the more complex partial social exclusions of segregation in residential space. Moral beliefs, according to Smith (1994), are also closely related to local cultures, and one's sense of moral responsibility for others tends to decay the more one is separated from them by distance.

The idea of *place* is more specific and idiosyncratic. In some respects, it has an older pedigree in geographies which aim to provide accounts of the peculiar social and physical attributes of particular regions. A place may be thought of as a *location*. For example, in geometric space it may be identified by means of grid coordinates denoting a certain position. It may also be positioned in a system of spatial organisation, such as a district situated in the administrative geography of a country. Other conceptualisations of place include the idea of *locale*; a specific setting in which social relations are constituted. (This concept is considered in more detail below with reference to the work of Giddens 1984, 1991.) There has also been considerable discussion in geography (for example, *Environment and Planning* A, 1991) of the related idea of *locality*, which again denotes a particular area or region (usually of sub-national scale) in which various social and economic processes come together in combinations which may be specific to the place and may themselves be influenced by the conditions prevailing in the locality. We may also consider a *sense of place* (the meaning, intention, felt value and significance that individuals or groups give to particular places). This perspective is often emphasised in cultural and and humanistic approaches in geography (*e.g.* Yi Fu Tuan 1974a and b, Jackson 1991, Gesler 1992).

The link between space, place and time is also significant. Thrift (1992) points out that geographical perspectives view human interaction in time-space. Hagerstrand (1982) has used analysis of time-space paths to show the constraints operating on individual human action. Spatial networks may be measured in terms of the time needed to travel between points in space. The differential health trends of populations in different places over time may help us to understand the processes which contribute to health variation. The time-space perspective is emphasised, for example, in studies of disease diffusion, which aim to describe, simulate and predict population health change (*e.g.* Haggett 1994). Also, inequalities in health which are persistent or widening over time are often of particular concern. Smith (1994: 29) cites Young's (1990) comment that, for issues of social justice and social inequality: ' . . . what is important is not the particular pattern of distribution at a particular moment but rather the reproduction of a regular distributive pattern over time'.

Health variation in the UK space: compositional and contextual interpretations

There is a long tradition of studying health inequalities by examining how the health of populations varies in space, and of making comparative studies of population health in particular places. This has produced a large literature on social and geographical differences in the health of resident populations in different parts of Britain. For example, see reviews by Britton (1990), Townsend et al. (1988a), Benzeval et al. (1995).

Spatial variations in health may be interpreted in different ways, and some authors (e.g. Duncan et al. 1993, Duncan and Jones 1995, Macintyre et al. 1993) have suggested that we need to distinguish both conceptually and empirically between compositional effects and contextual effects. Compositional effects arise from the varying distribution of types of people whose individual characteristics influence their health. A purely compositional interpretation of geographical health variation might imply that similar types of people will have similar health experience, no matter where they live. The problem of the ecological fallacy is often emphasised, whereby characteristics of aggregated regional populations might be used to generate inaccurate assumptions about individuals in the population (Susser 1994, Schwartz 1994). Because of this problem, some researchers accord less value to ecological studies than to studies based on individual data. Research on population health differences between areas is seen either as a way of developing preliminary hypotheses about health difference, to be tested more rigorously on individuals, or as a substitute for data on individuals when these are unavailable.

However, ecological research might also allow for some impact of the aggregated effect of individual characteristics. Susser (1994) points out that the effects of aggregation in an area may mediate the effects on health of individual level variables, and stresses the significance of the effects of collective attributes of populations. For example, individual ethnicity may relate to health differently when it constitutes a minority state from when it denotes membership of a majority group in the local population. Also, the association between individual deprivation and health might vary in relation to the aggregated socio-economic profile of the population of which the individual forms a part. This broader interpretation of compositional effects would suggest that ecological studies of health variation have special value in their potential to capture these effects of aggregation. An over-emphasis on individuals as the most useful unit of analysis may result in problems associated with the atomistic fallacy, whereby one may overlook or misinterpret effects which can better be understood at the level of households, neighbour-hoods or regions. Schwartz (1994) points out that research needs to consider ecological variables in order to understand the structural, contextual and sociological effects on public health.

Such a view leads towards the analysis of contextual effects, which oper-ate where the health experience of an individual depends partly on the social and physical environment in the area where they live. This type of effect would cause people with similar individual attributes to have different health status from one part of the country to another.

The extent to which compositional and contextual effects are clearly distinguishable seems open to some debate. For example, do we interpret ethnic concentration as an essentially compositional attribute resulting from aggregation, or is it a contextual effect of the social environment? Nevertheless, the discussion about these effects does suggest that ecological information is important to our understanding of health variation, not merely as a substitute for individual data, but also as a means of testing for the combined effects of compositional and contextual influences.

This debate about individual and contextual dimensions of health varia-tion is important for the way that we understand risk to health and develop policies to address health inequalities. Castel (1991) discusses the shift in emphasis in preventive strategies, away from the 'dangerousness' of specific health hazards and towards a consideration of health risk in populations (Jones and Curtis 1997). Bauman (1995) has argued that there is a tendency to view health risk individually and to emphasise individual responsibility for reducing health risks. Beck (1992) points out that risks today are multi-ple and complex in their effects on different social groups and individuals. Some can have selective impact, others can affect populations more widely, and risks may be difficult to observe and quantify. It may be appropriate to think of population risk in compositional terms (resulting from the aggrega-tion of individual risk factors) and also in contextual terms (arising from factors which are external to individuals and which operate on groups of people in particular settings).

Empirical research using a variety of methods to explore the existence or the relative importance of contextual effects has produced results which are not always consistent. This inconsistency may arise partly from the different data and methods which have been used. It also seems likely that we have not yet fully and adequately theorised how contextual or environmental effects may occur; this may have implications for the design and the inter-pretation of empirical studies. The first part of this paper considers some of the theoretical bases which might help to illuminate ecological studies of health variation from this point of view. The second part of the discussion below focuses on the different empirical approaches used to examine the importance of place and of contextual effects in health variation, and con-siders them in the light of theory.

There are also, of course, empirical and theoretical controversies as to the nature of individual effects on health, which may also be important for our understanding of the geography of health. One example is the debate over the relative importance of material deprivation or of health selection in bringing about health differences (West 1991). We do not propose to discuss these in any detail here, since they are covered by other chapters in this book.

Theoretical accounts of contextual health effects

There is an extensive body of theory which would seem to support the argument that contextual health effects associated with place and space may contribute to health variation. However, our understanding of the ways that place may interact with health remains 'under theorised' in the sense that different parts of the body of theory are not very well integrated, and some parts are relatively undeveloped.

At least three types of theoretical framework seem to support the concept of contextual effects, and may be useful to organise ideas about how contextual effects may operate on health risks and on associated health variation in populations. The first type of interpretation relates to the spatial patterning and diffusion of physical and biological risk factors. The second perspective emphasises the role of space and place in social relations important for health. Finally, the landscapes which are envisaged in terms of senses of place may help us to understand the significance of place for health inequalities.

Spatial patterning and diffusion of physical and biological risk factors

Various authors have sought to explain contextual variation in health in terms of the 'ecological landscape' and its importance for varying exposure to health risks due to factors such as environmental pollution, climate, risk of accidental injury or death, or housing quality. Theories of this type have been used in medical geography to explain the spatial patterning of particular diseases in human population (reviewed, for example, by Meade *et al.* 1988, Learmonth 1988). Meade *et al.* make the point that problems of environmental change and the 'pollution syndrome' call for new approaches to the science of ecology and ecological systems which will help us to understand technologically created hazards to health as well as natural physical hazards.

A detailed discussion of theories about health inequalities based on environmental and biomedical sciences are outside the scope of this chapter. However, it is relevant to note that research on socio-economic inequalities in health often invokes exposure to physical and biological risks as part of their explanatory theory. Also, the interaction between socio-economic and physical and biological processes influencing health risk is of fundamental importance. Phillimore and Morris (1991) and Phillimore (1993), for example, suggest that different exposure to industrial pollution might explain the discrepant legacies of population health they discovered in two industrial towns, leading them to review the economic geography of the two settlements as it had evolved over time. The regional heart study (*e.g.* Shaper 1984) has sought to clarify how far socio-economic and physical environmental factors might explain the differences in heart disease between regional populations of Britain. Though not based on British research, a study by Dunn *et al.* (1994), showed that perceptions of physical environmental hazard differed between those living in the affected area and observers from outside. This suggests that the psycho-social impacts of pollution, as well as the physical health outcomes, may depend on the community context, and that social construction of hazard may be significant to interpretation of physical environmental risk.

Models of spatial diffusion of contagious diseases in human populations also contribute to our understanding of health risk from an epidemiological perspective. These draw on theories concerning the method and rate of disease transmission, the statistical probability of contact and the likelihood of transmission over varying distances. Geographers (*e.g.* Cliff and Haggett 1988, Gould 1993, Loytonen 1991, Pyle 1969, 1980) are among those who stress that the geographical dimensions of these models are not limited to information about Euclidean distances between susceptible individuals. Research on communicable diseases such as cholera, influenza or measles or (more recently) on the spread of HIV and AIDS, has often demonstrated that the probability of transmission over a given distance depends on the variable concentration of populations in space and variation in the speed and rate of communication between places. Thus epidemiological theory is usefully informed by geographical theories about the structure of settlement hierarchies and variations in 'friction of distance' associated with communication networks.

The role of space and place in social relations
Dear and Wolch (1987) argue that the social relations relevant to health variations are *constituted, constrained* and *mediated* through space, and Jones and Moon (1987) argue for a realist approach to the study of geographical health variation which would consider underlying social structures as well as individual human agency. Place interacts in complex ways with social processes. An interesting example is provided by geographical studies of disability. Social and political structures marginalise people with physical impairments and generate built forms which further exacerbate both the disablement and the social exclusion associated with impairment (Golledge 1993, Imrie 1996, Levy 1997, Smith 1997). This research also clearly shows that the impact of place is variable, depending on individual attributes.

Social theory gives a variety of perspectives on the social relevance of the material landscape which are pertinent to these aspects of our understanding. These include theories concerned with structuration (especially as postulated by Giddens), theories of the geographies of consumption and lifestyle (particularly the idea of *habitus* put forward by Bourdieu) and theories of social control and territoriality.

Theoretical debates within human geography have been marked by a concern for structures and human agency and the work of Giddens has had an important influence. Giddens's theory of structuration, involves a strong engagement with the ideas of time-space geography. The *durée* of daily life involves actions that have intended and *unintended consequences* (Giddens 1984). People act out their lives in a variety of hierarchical settings for interactions which Giddens refers to as *locales*. It is possible to identify certain dominant locales such as home, work and school. These locales 'structure people's life paths in class-specific ways' and are the context for daily routines, socialisation, interaction, exclusion and conflict (Thrift 1992). An analysis of inequalities in health may also be informed by insights of structuration theory, although Giddens does not see structuration theory as something that can be tested empirically (Pinch 1997). The relationship between knowledge, risk and behaviour can therefore be thought of as a complex interaction between structure, agency, beliefs, accounts and action. An investigation of the differences in the ways in which individuals manage their diabetes, for example, could be informed by looking at the different constraints on their lives in different locales (school, office, factory) at different times (youth, middle age, retirement). Equally, a materialist approach to social class and risk factors, using oral histories to collect life-cycle data such as that outlined by Blane (1987), could include an interrogation of the experience of dominant locales over the lifecourse.

Williams (1995) has considered the work of Bourdieu as a perspective on class, health and lifestyles. Bourdieu's approach to agency sees the logic of practice as being located in time and space. That practice itself is not wholly consciously organised, but may be 'taken for granted' or 'routinized' in daily life (Bourdieu 1990). Bourdieu constructs a mediating concept between structure and agency which he calls *habitus*. This is a structure made up of perceptions and dispositions that reproduce social structure and yet is limited by the conditions of its production. It only exists in and through individual practices and interactions. In this schema society is seen as a network of semi-autonomous 'fields' each with a particular habitus. A field is a space for struggles concerning unequal relations; a structured system of people in different social positions, competing over access to goods and resources manifest in different forms of capital. This can be economic, cultural, social, symbolic or physical capital (*i.e.* the body and health status). An analysis of the space in which struggles over these different forms of capital take place may help us understand how choices concerning health and lifestyles are constrained. For Bourdieu consumption patterns are fields of struggle in a 'game' in which rules are forever changing. The rich have power to bestow value on certain forms of lifestyles thus placing limits on the ability of the working class to convert from one form of capital to another (Bourdieu 1984). Such forms have a strong spatial component, leading to ideas of *landscapes of consumption*. For example, the locations for upper class recreation (exclusive gyms, restaurants, sports holidays) can be contrasted with working class locations (streets, pubs, recreation grounds). The locational patterns of consumption associated with food, alcohol and drug use could be interpreted in a similar way (see, for example, Bell and Valentine 1997). Bourdieu's work emphasises the importance of cultural consumption in defining and appropriating social space and has profound implications for our understanding of geographical and social aspects of health.

Authors such as Dandeker (1990) and Sack (1986) have explored theories concerning landscapes of *territoriality* and *surveillance*, drawing on Foucault's (1977) work. They argue that the welfare state, in its surveillance and disciplinary activities, interacts with the everyday lives of actors in time and space. We are thus led to think about locales as power containers and sites for social control. Such an approach allows us to consider the degree of individual autonomy a person has in the home, workplace, or the hospital and can lead to explorations of the conflicts between hegemony and resistance. This type of perspective may be useful in understanding health-related behaviour since it provides a framework for considering the degree of empowerment and scope for initiative experienced by different social groups. It can also inform analysis of medicine as an institution of social control which is resisted by consumers and users. Gesler (1992) cites the hydrotherapy movement in USA in 19th century spas as an example of this. Such hegemonic struggles can also be viewed through the concept of territoriality that is manifested in struggles for beds between different specialties and struggles for contracting markets between London hospitals. This perspective could assist in an analysis of inequalities in the supply of health-care resources.

These theories suggest that health and health behaviour interact with structural material landscapes, landscapes of consumption, and landscapes of surveillance and control, and that these landscapes are often determined by the most influential and privileged groups in society and are of greatest benefit for them. These perspectives can also illuminate the ways that we think about health risk. Wright (1995) argues that people who belong to marginalised groups are not valued by capitalist society. They also have worse health risks and experience more ill health. Higgs (1998) argues that while governments take some responsibility, through regulatory measures, for contextual risks (*e.g.* environmental public health hazards), there is an inequality of exposure and inequality of protest and protection. For example, Dolk *et al.* (1995) showed that poorer populations are more likely to live close to waste incineration plants. They are therefore more at risk of any health hazards from these plants, but confounding with socio-economic variables makes it epidemiologically more difficult to determine whether such hazards are significant for health. Thus for the populations involved, their weak political power to contest these plant locations is further undermined by lack of epidemiological evidence. Governments also seem unable, or unwilling, to intervene effectively to reduce compositional risks that result from the cumulative impact of individual behaviour on population health. While society tends to place equal responsibility on individuals for 'compositional' health risks, it offers inequality in the means to deal with them. Deviant behaviour is only regulated under certain conditions or in certain settings. This may be achieved by enclosing spaces, reifying them as 'containers' within which individual behaviour is partially regulated and controlled. Outside such protected areas, individuals are still subject to health risks. Office workers seen smoking at the entrance to their office buildings, which are controlled as non-smoking places, exemplify the spatial exclusion involved. This type of regulation is of most benefit to non-smokers (already at low risk) as it protects them from the risk of passive smoking. Smokers (already at higher risk) are excluded and marginalised, but their individual behaviour is not much modified. Thus, the individual with 'deviant' (risky) health behaviour becomes interpreted as the 'risk' itself. Policies excluding individual deviances, are then able to be developed in ways that allow the material constraints on individual lives to be forgotten.

Landscapes and sense of place

A humanist approach to landscapes emphasises meaning, *verstehen*, hermeneutics and subjectivity but, most importantly, the notion of a *sense of place*. Yi Fu Tuan (1974b) developed the idea of *topophilia* (the affective bonds individuals develop with places) and drew a distinction between places as public symbols (having a strong visual element and held in awe) and places as fields of care (appealing to other senses and affection). The cultural turn in geography has further explored the philosophies of meaning, understanding, beliefs and the importance of the lifeworld. This type of perspective has implications for the ways that we study health variation. It involves interpreting subjective experiences and eliciting private accounts (Cornwell 1984) to explore communicative practices and power relations, metaphors, myths, stories and narrative accounts.

Authors such as Kearns (1991) and Joseph (1993) consider the ways that certain cultures imbue particular places with special meanings from the point of view of health. Holistic approaches to understanding varying experiences of health and illness may encourage a consideration of how mental and physical wellbeing interact and how mental state is associated with sense of place.

Gesler (1992) describes the focus of the new cultural geography on cultural landscapes, adopting such concepts as: sense of place, landscape as text, symbolic landscapes, negotiated reality, as well as contrasting hegemony with resistance and legitimisation with marginalisation. Gesler shows how landscapes are ambiguous, multiple and pluralistic; products of human minds as well as material circumstances. The ideas of *therapeutic landscapes* and of healing places (*e.g.* Gesler *et al.* 1997) provide accounts of how healing occurs in particular places and milieux. There is scope for research examining the extent of unequal opportunities or predispositions to experience therapeutic settings and how these may relate to health inequalities.

Bringing together theories of space and place in accounts of health inequality
Attempts to bring together empirical observation with relevant theories concerning health and place can provide accounts of health inequalities which incorporate explanations for contextual effects. These may be seen to be drawing on more than one of the theoretical frameworks discussed above. Table 1, shows how different theoretical accounts may focus on alternative landscape perspectives.

Thus, instead of searching for a single grand theory to explain the role of place in inequalities in health, it may be that we should utilise complementary and interconnected theoretical approaches. Some authors have explicitly set out such theoretical frameworks to account for contextual effects.

For example, one account of the role of place in health variation is offered by Macintyre *et al.* (1993) who propose broad types of socioenvironmental influences of place upon health (listed in Table 2), in order to account for their observations of health inequalities, as exemplified in their research on different areas in Scotland. Macintyre and Soomans (1995) have also used survey information to show that residents' perceptions of some of these dimensions of place are associated with self-reported health in ways which are not explained by individuals' age, sex or class.

It may be possible to map their analyses onto some of the alternative theoretical frameworks which are listed in Table 1. Thus, for example, in hypothesising the significance of the physical environment for health difference, one may invoke ecological and epidemiological theories relating to the ecological landscape to account for the impact of pollution. Accounts of

Table 1 *Alternative theoretical perspectives on health and space*

Theoretical framework	Focus on landscapes
ecological/epidemiological theories	ecological landscapes
structuration theory	materialist landscapes
theory of habitus, consumption and lifestyle	landscapes of consumption
theory of surveillance and territoriality	landscapes of social control
humanist theories of sense of place	therapeutic landscapes

Table 2 *Influences of place on health*
(Macintyre et al. 1993)

Physical environment
Availability of health/unhealthy environments
Services provided
Socio-cultural factors of neighbourhood or locale
Representation of neighbourhood
Lay systems of beliefs and behaviours
Labour markets

---

service provision may also draw on social relations of the material land-scape and landscapes of consumption. The notion of neighbourhood repre-sentation may combine theories of landscapes of consumption with ideas concerning sense of place.

Another explicit attempt to bring theory to bear on observed health inequality is provided by Dear and Wolch (1987), who examine the experi-ence of community care for mentally ill people and present a model of the development of the 'service-dependent ghetto' in American cities which may also have relevance for Britain. They show how the social polarisation of different parts of the city is associated with a tendency for people with men-tal illness to congregate in inner urban areas where provision of community services is concentrated, while being excluded from suburban areas by the negative, 'NIMBY' attitudes of wealthier and more influential residents toward living near facilities for mentally ill people. The processes are self-reinforcing. Marginalised mentally ill people tend to gravitate towards com-munities which include other people like themselves, and thus find themselves further segregated and marginalised from other parts of society. Health professionals find it more necessary to concentrate effort and resources where the needs are seen to be greatest, and this leads to further influx of mentally ill people and increased pressure on the service in the service-dependent ghetto. Outside the ghetto, lack of contact with mentally ill people fosters prejudicial attitudes against them in suburban areas. The influence of structuration theory can be seen in this account and also theo-ries concerning landscapes of surveillance and social control.

Wallace (1990) and Wallace *et al.* (1994) also put forward arguments con-cerning the public health effects of 'urban desertification' of the inner areas of American cities, which they claim will also have relevance in countries such as Britain. They argue that inner areas of cities like New York have been socially and economically weakened by industrial restructuring and that degeneration of the social and physical fabric of these areas has been encouraged by the withdrawal of key public services, such as fire fighting services. This is seen to be part of a policy of 'planned shrinkage', exercised

by powerful political groups to undermine the concentrations of poor, predominantly black voters in particular parts of the city. Physical destruction,
especially by uncontrolled fires, has led to social disintegration of residential
neighbourhoods, leaving only residual populations of highly marginalised
people with particularly high risks of contracting infections such as the
virus causing AIDS. Wallace *et al.* (1994) argue that these concentrations of
very vulnerable populations pose a public health threat not only locally but
throughout the urban region, because of the tendency for communication
and transmission throughout the urban hierarchy. Their account therefore
invokes elements of theories of structuration, habitus, spatial epidemiology
and landscapes of social control.

Empirical evidence for contextual effects on health variation

Having briefly described some of the theoretical frameworks which may help
us to explain the effect of geographical settings on health difference, we now
turn to a consideration of the empirical observations of health inequality
which have explored these effects. These include both extensive statistical
analyses and qualitative, intensive research. The results do not always seem
consistent. This may partly be because of differences in the theoretical frameworks on which research is based (which are sometimes implied rather than
clearly stated), leading to differences in research design. Also, the following
review demonstrates a considerable diversity of methods, some of which are
better suited to the exploration of contextual effects than others. We consider both intensive and extensive studies, which complement each other in
terms of our overall understanding of how place relates to health variation.

Intensive qualitative research on health and place

A number of studies have used qualitative and intensive approaches to
examine how place and space figure in discourses about health variation
and health experience at the individual level. Qualitative studies have the
potential to explore in depth the possible causes of the findings of statistical
analysis, which are often essentially descriptions of the statistical associations between a limited set of measurable indicators. Intensive and qualitative research provides 'insider' knowledge and understanding about health
in the holistic context of individual experience. Brown (1995), for example,
contrasts ethnographic research on HIV and AIDS with other epidemiological and geographical research which tends to distance itself from the people
affected because it is hooked on mapping the *virus* not *people*. Similar criticisms could be aimed at other research focusing on statistical inequalities of
other medically defined morbidity indicators in the population.

One of the important contributions of qualitative analysis is its emphasis
on the need to be constantly reflexive. It raises questions about how 'objec-

tive' and neutral it is possible to be in one's approach to research, even when using a positive paradigm. Some intensive research, discussed in the conclusion to this paper focuses on how contextual effects are perceived by policy makers and the impact that this can have on policy relating to health inequalities. It is probably impossible for the researcher as 'outsider' fully to comprehend the insider view. As Williams (1995) points out, any research that attempts to elicit explanations from informants runs the risk of being misled by 'official' accounts. Cornwell's (1984) research in East London illustrated how 'public' and 'private' accounts given by individuals of their beliefs and understandings give different insights into the ways in which their living and working environments shape their beliefs about health and illness.

The body of qualitative research on health difference is enormous (selections from the literature are reviewed, for example in: Helman 1984, Fitzpatrick *et al.* 1984, Scambler 1997, Hillier and Kelleher 1996). Many of these studies require to be contextualised in terms of the specific social group, time and place in which they are conducted, and thus they explore, either implicitly or explicitly, the contextual effects of place. However, more relevant to this discussion are studies, particularly those conducted by geographers, which have used intensive methods to explore specifically the role of place in the social construction of health and illness. (Illustrations of these studies are overviewed, for example by: Eyles and Donovan 1990, Jones and Moon 1993, Kearns and Joseph 1993, Curtis and Taket 1996). Fieldwork for these studies has employed a number of different techniques (*e.g.* intensive interviews, mental mapping techniques, life histories and observation). The subjects researched are also varied. By their nature these studies are not amenable to generalisation or comparison, but they do provide some insights which may be important to our understanding of the processes by which geography may influence health difference.

The diversity of extensive statistical strategies

Varying statistical approaches are used in the analysis of contextual effects. Alternative methods include tabulations (*e.g.* Fox and Goldblatt 1982, Blaxter 1990, Phillimore and Reading 1992) and separate regression analyses for different areas (*e.g.* Carstairs and Morris 1991, Eames *et al.* 1993). Further strategies are conventional regression analysis incorporating variables relating to the area of residence as well as individual characteristics (*e.g.* Sloggett and Joshi 1994) or examining geographical variation in the residuals from regression analysis of national samples (*e.g.* Bentham *et al.* 1995). Some authors (Duncan *et al.* 1993, Humphreys and Carr Hill 1991) suggest that the 'tabulation' and conventional regression methods of comparing social group differences for different areas are not very efficient strategies to test for contextual effects, and are also possibly biased in neglecting autocorrelation within districts. They recommend multi-level modelling, or some alternative, by which the hierarchical structure of the data can be represented. Research which uses multi-level modelling techniques to represent the simultaneous effects of both compositional and contextual influence more effectively includes: Humphreys and Carr-Hill (1991), Duncan *et al.* (1993), Gould and Jones (1994), Duncan and Jones (1995), Congdon (1994), Shouls *et al.* (1996), Haynes *et al.* (1997), Congdon *et al.* (1997).

Statistical evidence concerning contextual effects emerges from extensive analyses based on different research designs. Research using data on individuals, combined with information about their place of residence, provides evidence concerning contextual effects which seem to be statistically 'independent' of health difference at the individual level. Other studies use aggregated ecological data for smaller areas nested within larger regions to provide evidence concerning effects operating at different geographical scales.

A fundamental question addressed by most of this extensive research concerns whether statistically significant variation operates independently at different hierarchical levels. If so, then contextual effects may be considered relevant to our understanding of the health differences measured in these studies. If not, then one might conclude that health variation is best understood in terms of compositional effects only. The review below, therefore, begins with a discussion of the statistical evidence concerning independent contextual effects.

Some of the analyses go further to investigate whether certain attributes of places are associated with contextual effects. Three types of contextual (or environmental) variables seem to emerge from these studies of geographic variation in mortality and morbidity in Britain. These are associated with:

a. the socio-economic environment;
b. urbanization/rurality;
c. north/south position in the UK space.

We therefore go on to discuss the evidence for these dimensions of contextual effects and how they relate to the theoretical arguments considered above. We also attempt to make more explicit some of the links between this empirical evidence and the theories considered at the beginning of the chapter, drawing in some cases on the insights from more intensive research.

Evidence concerning statistically 'independent' contextual effects.
Some research has analysed data on individuals linked to information on the ecological context of their residential location. Examples using the tabulation method includes Fox and Goldblatt (1982), showing that males in the

same categories of class, housing tenure or employment had different mortality ratios according to the characteristics of their residential area (measured for electoral wards). Blaxter (1990) linked individual data on morbidity and fitness from the Health and Lifestyle Survey (HALS) to data on residential areas, showing that these health measures varied for people in similar social groups but living in different types of wards.

In contrast, Sloggett and Joshi (1994) introduced ecological variables (representing type of area of residence) into a regression analysis of individuals. They concluded that there is little residual variation in risk of death associated with area variables, once individual differences are accounted for. (However, some residual variation seemed to be linked to northern regional position, and this translates into increases in odds ratios for males which seem as important as those distinguishing social classes; Sloggett and Joshi 1994: Table 1.)

Humphreys and Carr-Hill (1991) and Duncan and Jones (1995) used multi-level modelling with the HALS data on individuals and their areas of residence. A large part of the health inequalities observed were found to be statistically explained by association with individual attributes, but some residual variation appeared to be associated with area level variables. Duncan and Jones emphasise that 'cross level intersections' demonstrate how individual variables have a changing effect according to context. Ecob (1996) shows that in survey data on a variety of health measures from Clydeside there was little evidence for area effects at the scale of postcode sectors. However Hart et al. (1997) demonstrated district level variation in coronary heart disease risk factors in data from the Scottish Heart Health Study. Duncan et al. (1993) also report that differences in individual health-related behaviour are associated with contextual effects at the level of regions, as well as attributes of the individuals in the sample. Gould and Jones (1994) and Shouls et al. (1996) have used multi-level modelling to examine data on long-term limiting illness collected in the 1991 Census. These researchers used the sample of anonymised records which provides census data for individuals, and can also be linked to information on the district where they lived. The models nested information on individuals (level one) within data on the district of residence (level two). Again, individual health difference was explained mainly by the level one variation (individual attributes) but a significant, albeit smaller, area effect remained at level two, suggesting that there may also be some association between health and geographical context.

It is often argued that ecological associations are best explored using data for small areas, which is relatively homogeneous in terms of both health and social structure, so associations between health and social conditions will be seen more clearly. Some of the authors referred to here have commented that they would have preferred to use contextual data at the very local scale (of electoral wards, for example) rather than regional or district information available to them. Others have been able to use smaller-scale ecological data. However, there are arguments in favour of investigating the effects of conditions over larger areas. Some environmental factors (such as climate, water and air quality, urbanisation, and other organisation of labour markets), operate over wider areas, and their effects may not be well identified at the small area level. Just as the individual's health may show variation associated with contextual effects, so small area effects may operate differently according to characteristics of the regions where they are located.

This becomes more apparent when considering the results of ecological research which relate to populations aggregated at more than one geographical scale. These studies seek to establish whether the regional setting influences the micro-scale ecological relationships between population health and socio-economic profile. Considering ward and area effects in the north of England, Phillimore and Reading (1992) examined ward level indicators of premature mortality and birthweight using a tabulation approach to demonstrate differences in ward level inequality between urban and rural areas. In another study of two industrial towns, Phillimore and Morris (1991) examined health of the populations of wards with similar levels of social deprivation and found that the wards in one town showed worse health than in the other. They concluded that this might be caused by contextual effects influencing population health at the scale of the whole town, rather than the very local scale of the ward.

Broader regional comparisons, using separate regression methods, include that by Carstairs and Morris (1991), who noted that the correlation coefficients for the association between deprivation score and mortality were higher for Scottish postcode areas than in the study of Northern England by Townsend and colleagues (1988b). Eames et al. (1993) carried out separate regression analyses of the association between ward level mortality and ward level deprivation in different Regional Health Authorities. They concluded that the associations at ward level depended on the region in which the wards were situated. Bentham et al. (1995) regressed data for local government districts on long term illness from the 1991 census against information on social deprivation and mapped the regional pattern of residuals in illness level which were not statistically 'explained' by the regression model.

Several studies have used multi-level modelling to demonstrate hierarchical structure in the statistical variation of small area indicators of health outcomes. These include Congdon (1994) who reported some hierarchical structuring by district in variation in health indicators for wards in East Anglia and in Greater London. At the national scale, Congdon et al. (1997) analysed differences in self-reported long term illness and in mortality using multi-level modelling at ward (level 1) and district (level 2) scales. Haynes et al. (1997) also used multi-level modelling to examine the (level 1) ward level relationship between social deprivation and health measured by self-reported illness and mortality and how this varied between travel to work areas (at level 2). Both studies found evidence for variation operating at both (level 1 and level 2), and both suggest that the 'level 2' effects were generally stronger for self-reported illness than for mortality.

On balance, the research reviewed above seems to suggest that, while individual or micro-level information explains a larger part of health variation, there is some statistical evidence for contextual effects in health variation in the British population, which can be expressed in terms of information on geographic setting. These contextual effects may operate at more than one geographic scale. They may be stronger for some measures of health than others, as there is some evidence that indicators of self-reported health (which may be more strongly influenced by differences in social construction of health) are more subject to these contextual effects than measures such as mortality (which are more 'objective'). We now turn to a consideration of the characteristics of places which seem to be statistically associated with these contextual effects.

Effects of the socio-economic environment.
Some studies of contextual effects have suggested that the health of individuals with similar social characteristics varies according to the socio-economic setting in which they live. The analysis of mortality data from the Longitudinal Study (*e.g.* Fox and Goldblatt 1982) and of data on reported health from the Health and Lifestyle Survey (HALS) (Blaxter 1990) showed that for individuals of similar social class, health measures varied in association with conditions in their residential area (defined using the ward cluster typologies of Webber 1977, Craig 1987). These studies both pointed to differences between individuals living in rural-or semi-rural areas, and individuals in declining urban/industrial areas (where health tended to be poorer). In apparent contrast with Fox *et al.* (1982), Sloggett and Joshi (1994), in their analysis of Longitudinal Study data, concluded that there were no independent effects of area deprivation on risk of death once individual deprivation was taken into account. This could be because their regression analysis simultaneously controlled for a number of different individual deprivation variables. On the other hand, in their multi-level analysis of the sample of anonymised individual records from the 1991 Census, Shouls *et al.* (1996) show that greater deprivation in the district population seemed to have a detrimental effect on individual reporting of long-term illness, and this was in addition to the effects of several individual deprivation measures which were included in the model.

The effects of socio-economic context also emerge from analyses showing that the small area ecological links between health and deprivation depend on the wider geographic context. Congdon *et al.* (1997) and Ben-Shlomo *et al.* (1996) demonstrated in different ways that wards in deprived districts showed greater prevalence of illness than wards with a similar social profile in more privileged districts. Ben-Shlomo *et al.* (1996) also suggest that the ward level association between mortality and deprivation is associated with both average level of deprivation and the variability of deprivation of the local authority area where the ward is located.

Conditions in the local labour market and the effects of industrial restructuring may have relevance for health variation. Phillimore and Morris (1991) invoke the differences in environmental impact of the industries in Middlesborough and Sunderland to help to explain differences in health experience in the two towns. Haynes *et al.* (1997) found that for wards in travel-to-work areas with high levels of unemployment, self-reported illness ratios were comparatively high, even allowing for ward deprivation. They suggest that the propensity to report long-term illness may be related to the perceived lack of employment opportunity. This would suggest that social constructions of health, linked to fitness for work, may interact with local labour market conditions to produce differences in the perception of illness (even though this is not reflected in mortality differences). Senior (1998) and Beatty and Fothergill (1996) suggest that the high levels of reported illness in Wales and in the North East of England are associated with indicators of decline in the coal mining industry (although Senior's results suggest that, in the case of Wales, a history of local coal mining does not fully explain the excess reporting of illness).

Thus there is some evidence that health disadvantage is exacerbated in socially and economically impoverished settings, particularly in declining industrial areas. As we have argued above, this might be theoretically explained in a number of ways. The theoretical framework offered by Macintyre *et al.* (1993), supported by theories concerning the ecological impact of socio-economic processes on the physical environment, the structures imposed by materialist landscapes in particular locales, and the impact of the habitus on patterns of consumption and lifestyle, provide a theoretical basis for supposing that individual health experience might be negatively affected by living in an area of high levels of socio-economic deprivation and industrial decline, as summarised in Table 3.

Urbanisation/rurality.
The second dimension which may have significance for contextual effects is associated with differences between more urban and more rural areas. The analyses of individual data in the UK Longitudinal Study reported by Britton *et al.* (1990) and Fox and Goldblatt (1982), suggest, for example, that, after controlling for social class or housing tenure, mortality ratios were higher for people who lived in an area classified as an 'urban council estate' as opposed to an area classified as 'rural'.

Some studies of ward level associations between health and deprivation, also show apparent differences between urban and rural areas, such that the association between indices of health and deprivation appears stronger in more urban areas than in more rural areas. This is reported by Townsend *et al.* (1988) for the North of England and Carstairs and Morris (1991) for

Table 3 *Theoretical perspectives on the health disadvantage of living in deprived areas*

Materialist landscapes, e.g.:
poor housing
lack of employment opportunities

Landscapes of consumption, e.g.:
poor health facilities
poor retail outlets for food
lack of play/leisure facilities

Ecological landscapes, e.g.:
pollution due to noxious industry
poor cleansing of public spaces
congestion/pollution/accidents due to through traffic

Scotland. Phillimore and Reading (1992) also found that inequalities in health between more and less deprived wards were more pronounced in urban areas than in rural areas. However, this might be due to the smaller population size of rural wards; the correlation coefficients between deprivation and health were found to become stronger for rural areas when wards were aggregated up into larger units. Congdon (1994) found that the small area association between deprivation and health was stronger in Greater London than in the more rural setting of East Anglia, though some of the strongest links between deprivation and health were found in metropolitan suburbs rather than in the inner city.

Thus it appears that health does not improve straightforwardly as rurality increases. Shouls *et al.* (1996), found the contextual effects due to rurality to be rather unclear in their analysis of individual reporting of illness in the 1991 census and they suggest that this may be because the statistical association between health and rurality may be non-linear. Some studies suggest that while populations of suburban and semi-rural areas have more favourable health status, than in inner cities, the populations of the most remote rural areas may suffer some health disadvantage (Bentham 1984).

While the impact of socio-economic context on health inequalities may be mediated by differences in levels of urbanisation/rurality, it is quite difficult to separate out effects of urbanisation or rurality from the more general contextual effects of socio-economic environment. Differences in the impact of socio-economic conditions in urban and rural areas probably partly reflect a tendency for social deprivation to be more extreme and more geographically concentrated in inner cities than in rural areas (Sim 1984). We have considered above theoretical accounts of mechanisms such as development of the 'service dependent ghetto' and 'urban desertification' which may help to explain how such concentrations of deprivation tend to develop in inner cities, and exacerbate health inequalities.

An alternative perspective on urban/rural inequalities in health explores whether the dimensions of social deprivation which are salient for health differences between wards may differ in urban and rural settings. For example, physical accessibility is sometimes argued to be a particularly significant dimension of deprivation in rural settings. Thus, for those lacking a car, problems of poorer access to infrastructure such as health-care facilities, places of work and shopping facilities might have a special significance in rural areas (Watt *et al.* 1994). A large geographical literature (from both extensive and intensive research) is devoted to whether physical accessibility affects use of health services, and the ways that physical accessibility relates to other dimensions of access. Social and economic dimensions of access are often more important, but in certain very isolated rural areas and for certain types of individual with very limited mobility physical accessibility may be a significant issue (Haynes and Bentham 1979, Curtis 1982, Joseph and Phillips 1984, Curtis and Taket 1996).

The significance of urbanisation may not lie merely in contrasts of material conditions between urban and rural areas, but also in the functioning of interconnected places in urban *systems*. We have already noted the relevance for epidemiology of geographical theories about urban hierarchies and communication networks. This is demonstrated by statistical evidence concerning the effects of urbanisation on health variations resulting from the diffusion of diseases (especially infectious diseases) in space and over time. Studies of the diffusion of HIV with the associated patterning of AIDS are often cited as recent examples (*e.g.* Smallman-Raynor *et al.* 1992, Gould 1993). One feature of the spatial diffusion of such diseases is a tendency to cascade down through the urban hierarchy, so that central areas of larger cities in the urban system, which are linked by rapid and well-used lines of communication are affected first, while smaller and more isolated settlements feel the effects of epidemics later. It is possible that changes in social organisation, public attitudes and health-related behaviour affecting risks of other, non-contagious diseases are also channelled in space by the structure of the urban system.

The difficulty of distinguishing a clear pattern of health difference between urban and rural areas does not necessarily imply that there are no differences in the processes affecting health in the two types of setting. Survey data reported by Cloke *et al.* (1997) show that rural dwellers are conscious of both benefits and disadvantages for wellbeing which are specific to rural settings. Thus, for example, lower levels of industrial and traffic pollution are balanced against other forms of pollution from agricultural activity. The tranquillity, social support and cohesion of rural social life needs to be set against the problems of lack of stimulation, tensions between long-term residents and newer and sometimes less permanent 'incomers', and social isolation and exclusion which can develop in small communities (Table 4).

Table 4 *Health experience of rural areas: theoretical frameworks*

Type of landscape	Health advantage	Health disadvantage
ecological landscapes	lower industrial pollution.	pollution by agricultural industry.
materialist landscapes	cheaper, less crowded accommodation.	lack of employment opportunities; limited housing stock; housing lacking amenities; lack of personal mobility.
landscapes of consumption	better access to green space; cheap 'at source' food outlets.	lack of public transport; lack of access to facilities.
therapeutic landscapes	the 'rural idyll': tranquillity; natural settings.	social isolation; lack of cultural stimulation.

North/south location.

There are regional north-south mortality and morbidity gradients in Britain, such that individuals from northern areas tend to have worse health than people with a similar social position living in the south. Fox and Goldblatt (1982), Britton (1990), Britton *et al.* (1990) and Blaxter (1990) all report that individual risk of mortality shows regional variation which is not entirely explained by differences in local area type discussed above. For example, males living in urban council estates have a worse mortality rate in northern and western regions than in southern and eastern regions. As noted above, Sloggett and Joshi's (1994) results seem to suggest differences in risk of death between north and south of the country, although the authors themselves do not stress this point. Congdon *et al.* (1997) show that for ward level differences in mortality and (more especially) for self-reported illness, there are significant differences associated with north/south position, after allowing for socio-economic characteristics of the wards and the districts where they were located. Bentham *et al.* (1995) showed that districts in Wales and in North East England had levels of reported morbidity well above those predicted by regression against district level socio-economic variables, suggesting that regional effects may be operating on the district level variation.

If socio-economic disparities between regions do not account fully for the North/South divide, then the complete explanation remains unclear. It might simply be due to shortcomings in the data (*e.g.* statistical studies have failed to capture sufficient socio-economic detail of local materialist landscapes). Otherwise, theories, which might explain the disparities, include the impact of ecological landscapes. Britton *et al.* (1990) examined the possible effects of physical environmental differences on mortality rate, but there was no conclusive evidence that these effects explained the regional differences. One might also hypothesise that broad cultural differences between north and south of the country, associated with varying landscapes of consumption might provide an explanation. However, there are significant potential pitfalls here, given the difficulty of studying such a complex phenomenon as 'culture' over such large geographic areas. For example, it is interesting to consider the North/South divide using Bourdieu's schema and to reflect on how working class lifestyles became presented as vulgar and unhealthy, as epitomised by Edwina Curry's perception of Northern 'pie and chips' culture. Such narratives may form powerful and distorting components of explanatory accounts for North/South health inequalities.

Conclusion: the significance for health policy

We have pointed to several theoretical perspectives on health difference which would suggest that health variation is caused both by the characteristics of individuals, and also by the setting in which they are situated. There is also empirical evidence, derived by using several different research strategies, to suggest that contextual effects operating at the level of places, seem to have some power to explain health inequalities, independently of the strong effects of individual attributes. In addition, some of this research has revealed contextual effects operating at different geographical levels (the immediate local area as well as the district or wider region).

Contextual effects are not, however, manifested consistently in all research results, and in some cases these effects are relatively weak (or even, apparently absent). Since health is affected by a range of individual behaviours, attributes and life experience, it is not surprising that much of the research reviewed above suggests that individual characteristics 'explain' more of the statistical variability in health between people than the characteristics of the areas where they live. Some of the inconsistency in research results seems likely to result from differences in theoretical or methodological approach, but it also seems likely that contextual effects operate differently for different indicators of health.

We conclude that geography does have a place in our understanding of inequalities in the health experiences of individuals and communities. Contextual effects associated with place and space, which may be quite complex, need to be considered together with other more individual theories about the processes and explanations relevant to health variation. If we are to construct effective policy responses to health inequalities, especially at the local level, then it is essential that these are informed by an understanding of the potential importance of place for health.

One of the obvious policy issues arising from this discussion concerns whether it is useful to target specific health policies towards particular areas. Some commentators who have not found contextual effects associated with places to be very significant for health variation, have argued against such a strategy. There are at least two strands to their argument. First, that policies targeted at areas rather than individuals are 'blunt instruments' which will not necessarily reach the individuals who are most in need of intervention to improve their health. This seems a very reasonable argument; there is strong evidence that individual characteristics are very important for health difference and that not all individuals in a geographically defined community will be equally able to benefit from an intervention which is targeted only at the collective and not toward the individual. We would also certainly agree that if inaccurate perceptions of contextual effects are applied to health policy this will be unhelpful in reducing health inequalities. Coombes (1993) has examined the ways that neighbourhoods were stereotyped as relatively 'healthy' or 'unhealthy' by public health experts. This had implications for the perceived level of health need in different neighbourhoods, and thus for allocation of resources. Daker-White (1995) also shows how ideas about community characteristics were inappropriately applied by some health service professionals in the field of provision of services for people with drugs dependency.

A second assertion sometimes made in relation to contextual effects is that there is no difference between places in the way that similarly deprived individuals experience health disadvantage. In the light of the above discussion this would seem more contentious. We would argue that there is theoretical and empirical evidence that health disadvantage may be experienced differently by socially disadvantaged individuals according to their geographic setting. This has several possible implications which deserve consideration in health policy. First, an intervention to influence some aspect of health for a particular type of individual may not be equally effective in every different setting. Second, the effects of regional geographic setting may be associated with even greater health inequality than one would expect from social and economic information on individuals in the population, or on small areas. This could be important if socio-economic data are used to estimate relative health needs in the population across the country. Thirdly, measures which are targeted only at individuals will probably not be adequate to tackle health inequalities because aspects of the collective social group and physical environment may also need to be changed in order to reduce health variations.

Acknowledgements

The authors would like to thank three anonymous referees for their helpful comments on an earlier draft, although the authors are solely responsible for the content of the chapter.

References

Bauman, Z. (1995) *Life in Fragments*. Cambridge: Polity Press.

Beatty, C. and Fothergill, S. (1996) Registered and hidden employment in areas of chronic industrial decline: the case of the UK coalfields. In Lawless, P., Martin, R. and Hardy, S. (eds) *Unemployment and Social Exclusion: Landscapes of Labour Inequality*. London: Jessica Kingsley.

Beck, U. (1992) *Risk Society: towards a New Modernity*. London: Sage.

Bell, D. and Valentine, G. (1997) *Consuming Geographies*. London: Routledge.

Ben-Shlomo, Y., White, I. and Marmot, M. (1996) Does the variation in the socio-economic characteristics of an area affect mortality? *British Medical Journal*. 312, 1013–14.

Bentham, C.G. (1984) Mortality rates in the more rural areas of England and Wales, *Area*, 16, 219–26.

Bentham, G., Eimermann, J.R., Lovett, A. and Brainard, J. (1995) Limiting long term illness and its associations with mortality and indicators of social deprivation, *Journal of Epidemiology and Community Health*, 49, suppl. 2, s57–64.

Benzeval, M., Judge, K. and Whitehead, M. (1995) *Tackling Health Inequalities: an Agenda for Action*. London: King's Fund.

Blane, D. (1987) The meaning of social class differences in health: people's experiences of risk factors, *Radical Community Medicine*, Spring, 31–7.

Blaxter, M. (1990) *Health and Lifestyles*. London: Tavistock/Routledge.

Bourdieu, P. (1984) *Disillusion: a Social Critique of the Judgement of Taste*. London: Routledge.

Bourdieu, P. (1990) *The Logic of Practice*. Cambridge: Polity.

Britton, M. (1990) Geographic variation in mortality since 1920 for selected causes. In Britton, M. (ed) *Mortality and Geography: a Review in the mid-1980s England and Wales*. London: HMSO.

Britton, M., Fox, A., Goldblatt, P., Jones, D. and Rosato, M. (1990) The influences of socio-economic and environmental factors on geographic variation in mortality. In Britton, M. (ed) *Mortality and Geography: a Review in the mid-1980s England and Wales*. London: HMSO, 57–78.

Brown, M. (1995) Ironies of distance: an ongoing critique of the geographies of AIDS, *Environment and Planning D: Society and Space*, 13, 159–83.

Carstairs, V. and Morris, V. (1991) *Deprivation and Health in Scotland*. Aberdeen: Aberdeen University Press.

Castel, R. (1991) From dangerousness to risk. In Burchell, G., Gordon, C. and Miller, P. (eds) *The Foucault Effect: Studies in Governmentality*. London: Harvester Wheatsheaf.

Chorley, R. and Haggett, P. (1974) *Network Analysis in Geography* (2nd Edition). London: Edward Arnold.

Cliff, A. and Haggett, P. (1988) *Atlas of Disease Distributions: Analytic Approaches to Epidemiological Data.* Oxford: Blackwell.

Cloke, P., Milbourne, P. and Thomas, C. (1997) Living lives in different ways? Deprivation, marginalization and changing lifestyles in rural England, *Transactions of the Institute of British Geographers*, 22, 2, 210–30.

Congdon, P. (1994) The impact of area context on long term illness and premature mortality: an illustration of multi-level analysis, *Regional Studies*, 29, 4, 327–44.

Congdon, P., Shouls, S. and Curtis, S. (1997) A multi-level perspective on small area health and mortality: a case study of England and Wales, *International Journal of Population Geography*, forthcoming.

Coombes, Y.J. (1993) A geography of the new public health, unpublished Ph.D thesis, Queen Mary and Westfield College, University of London.

Cornwell, J. (1984) *Hard Earned Lives: Accounts of Health and Illness from East London.* London: Tavistock.

Craig, J. (1987) An urban-rural categorisation for wards, and local authorities, *Population Trends*, 47, 6–11.

Curtis, S. (1982) Spatial analysis of surgery locations in general practice, *Social Science and Medicine*, 16, 303–13.

Curtis, S. and Taket, A. (1996) *Health and Societies Changing Perspectives.* London: Arnold.

Daker-White, G. (1995) Perceptions of illicit drug use and the accessibility of treatment services in an inner-London borough, unpublished Ph.D thesis, Queen Mary and Westfield College, University of London.

Dandeker, C. (1990) *Surveillance Power and Modernity.* Cambridge: Polity Press.

Dear, M. and Wolch, J. (1987) *Landscapes of Despair: From Deinstitutionalization to Homelessness.* Cambridge: Polity Press.

Dolk, H., Mertens, B., Kleinschmidt, I., Walls, P., Shaddick, G. and Elliott, P. (1995) A standardization approach to the control of socio-economic confounding in small area studies of environment and health, *Journal of Epidemiology and Community Health*, 49, suppl. 2, s9–14.

Duncan, C., Jones, K. and Moon, G. (1993) Do places matter? A multi-level analysis of regional variation in health related behaviour in Britain, *Social Science and Medicine*, 37, 725–33.

Duncan, C. and Jones, K. (1995) Individuals and their ecologies: analysing the geography of chronic illness within a multi-level modeling framework, *Journal of Health and Place*, 1, 27–40.

Dunn, J., Taylor, Elliott, S. and Walter, D. (1994) Psychosocial effects of PCB contamination and remediation: the case of Smithville, Ontario. *Social Science and Medicine*, 39, 8, 1097–104.

Eames, M., Ben-Shlomo, Y. and Marmot, M. (1993) Social deprivation and premature mortality: regional comparison across England, *British Medical Journal*, 307, 1097–102.

Ecob, R. (1996) A multi-level approach to examining the effects of area of residence on health and functioning, *Journal of Royal Statistical Society A*, 159, 1, 61–75.

Environment and Planning A (1991) 23, 2, 155–308. Special issue: new perspectives on the locality debate.

Eyles, J. and Donovan, J. (1990) *The Social Effects of Health Policy: Experiences of Health and Health Care in Contemporary Britain.* Aldershot: Avebury.

Fitzpatrick, R., Hinton, J., Newman, S., Scambler, G. and Thompson, J. (1984) *The Experience of Illness*. London: Tavistock.

Foucault, M. (1977) *Discipline and Punish, the Birth of the Prison*. London: Allen Lane.

Fox, A. and Goldblatt, P. (1982) *The Longitudinal Study: Socio-demographic Mortality Differentials*. OPCS Series L5.1. London: HMSO.

Gesler, W.M. (1992) Therapeutic landscapes: medical issues in light of the new cultural geography, *Social Science and Medicine*, 34, 7, 735–46.

Gesler, W.M., Bird, S.T. and Oljeski, S.A. (1997) Disease ecology and a reformist alternative, *Social Science and Medicine*, 44, 5, 657–71.

Giddens, A. (1984) *The Constitution of Society: Outline of a Theory of Structuration*. Cambridge: Polity Press.

Giddens, A. (1991) *The Consequences of Modernity*. Cambridge: Polity Press.

Golledge, R. (1993) Geography and the disabled, a survey with special reference to vision impaired and blind populations, *Transactions of the Institute of British Geographers*, 18, 1, 63–85.

Gould, M. and Jones, K. (1994) Analysing perceived limiting long term illness using the UK census microdata. Proceedings of 6th International Medical Geography Symposium, Vancouver, Canada, 12–16 July 1994.

Gould, P. (1993) *The Slow Plague*. Oxford: Blackwells.

Hagerstrand, T. (1982) Diorama, path and project, *Tidschrift vor Economische en Sociale Geografie*, 73, 323–39.

Haggett, P. (1994) Prediction and predictability in geographical systems. *Transactions of Institute of British Geographers*, 19, 1, 6–20.

Hart, C., Ecols, R. and Smith, G.D. (1997) People, places and coronary heart disease risk factors: a multilevel analysis of the Scottish Heart Health Study archive, *Social Science and Medicine*, 45, 6, 893–902.

Haynes, R. and Bentham, G. (1979) *Community Hospitals and Rural Accessibility*. Farnborough: Saxon House.

Haynes, R., Bentham G., Lovett, A. and Eimermann, J. (1997) Effect of labour market conditions on reporting of limiting long term illness and permanent sickness in England and Wales, *Journal of Epidemiology and Community Health*, 51, 3, 282–8.

Helman, C. (1984) *Culture, Health and Illness*. Bristol: Wright.

Higgs, P. (1998) Risk, governmentality and the reconcepualization of citizenship. In Scambler, G. and Higgs, P. (eds) *Modernity, Medicine and Health*. London: Routledge.

Hillier, S. and Kelleher, D. (1997) *Researching Cultural Differences in Health*. London: Routledge.

Humphreys, K. and Carr-Hill, R. (1991) Area variation in health outcomes: artefact or ecology, *International Journal of Epidemiology*, 20, 1, 251–8.

Imrie, R. (1996) *Disability and the City: International Perspectives*. London: Paul Chapman.

Jackson, P. (1991) Mapping meanings: a cultural critique of locality studies, *Environment and Planning A*, 23, 2, 215–28.

Jones, I.R. and Curtis, S.E. (1997) Health. In Pacione, M. (ed) *Britain's Cities: Geographies of Division in Urban Britain*. London: Routledge.

Jones, K. and Moon, G. (1987) *Health, Disease and Society*. London: Routledge.

Jones, K. and Moon, G. (1993) Medical geography: taking space seriously, *Progress in Human Geography*, 17, 4, 515–24.

Joseph, A. and Phillips, D. (1984) *Accessibility and Utilization: Geographical Perspectives on Healthcare Delivery*. New York: Harper and Row.

Kearns, R. (1991) The place of health in the health of the place: the case of the Hokianga special medical area, *Social Science and Medicine*, 33, 4, 519–30.

Kearns, R.A. and Joseph, A.E. (1993) Space in its place: developing the link in medical geography, *Social Science and Medicine*, 37, 6, 711–17.

Learmonth, A. (1988) *Disease Ecology*. Oxford: Blackwell.

Levy, S. (1997) Disability and housing: the geographies of wheelchair users in Dundee. Paper presented at Conference for Emerging Young Researchers in the Geography of Health, Queen Mary College University of London, 1–11.7, 97.

Loytonen, M. (1991) The spatial diffusion of human immunodeficiency virus type I in Finland, *Annals of the Association of American Geographers*, 81, 1, 127–51.

Macintyre, S., Maciver, S. and Soomans, A. (1993) Area, class and health: should we be focusing on places or people, *Journal of Social Policy*, 22, 2, 213–34.

Macintyre, S. and Soomans, A. (1995) Health and perceptions of the local environment in socially contrasting neighbourhoods in Glasgow, *Health and Place*, 1, 1, 15–26.

Meade, M., Florin, J. and Gesler, W. (1988) *Medical Geography*. New York: Guilford.

Phillimore, P. (1993) How do places shape health? Rethinking locality and lifestyle in North-East England. In Platt, S.D. Thomas, H., Scott, S. and Williams, G. (eds) *Locating Health: Sociological and Historical Explanations*. Aldershot: Avebury.

Phillimore, P. and Morris, D. (1991) Discrepant legacies: premature mortality in two industrial towns, *Social Science and Medicine*, 33, 2, 139–52.

Phillimore, P. and Reading, R. (1992) A rural advantage? Urban-rural health differences in Northern England, *Journal of Public Health Medicine*, 14, 290–9.

Pinch, S. (1997) *Worlds of Welfare: Understanding the Changing Geographies of Social Welfare Provision*. London: Routledge.

Pyle, G. (1969) The diffusion of cholera in the United States in the nineteenth century, *Geographical Analysis*, 1, 59–75.

Pyle, G. (1980) Geographical perspectives on influenza diffusion: the United States in the 1940s. In Mead, M. (ed) *Conceptual and Methodological Issues in Medical Geography*, Chapel Hill: University of Carolina.

Sack, R. (1986) *Human Territoriality: its Theory and History*, Cambridge: Cambridge University Press.

Scambler, G. (1997) *Sociology as Applied to Medicine* (4th Edition). London: W.B. Saunders.

Schwartz, S. (1994) The fallacy of the ecological fallacy: the potential misuse of a concept and the consequences, *American Journal of Public Health*, 84, 5, 819–24.

Senior, M. (1998) Area variations in self-perceived limiting long-term illness in Britain, 1991: is the Welsh experience exceptional? *Regional Studies*, 32, 3, forthcoming.

Shaper, A. (1984) Geographic variations in cardiovascular mortality in Great Britain, *British Medical Bulletin*, 40, 366–74.

Shouls, S., Congdon, P. and Curtis, S. (1996) Modelling inequality in reported long term illness in the UK: combining individual and area characteristics, *Journal of Epidemiology and Community Health*, 50, 3, 366–76.

Sibley, D. (1995) *Geographies of Exclusion*. London: Routledge.

Sim, D. (1984) Urban deprivation: not just the inner city, *Area*, 16, 299–300.

Sloggett, A. and Joshi, H. (1994) Higher mortality in deprived areas: community or personal disadvantage, *British Medical Journal*, 109, 1470–74.

Smallman-Raynor, M., Cliff, A. and Haggett, P. (1992) *London International Atlas of AIDS*. Oxford: Oxford University Press.

Smith, D. (1994) *Geography and Social Justice*. Oxford: Blackwell.

Smith, G. (1997) Reflections on a journey: geographical perspectives on disability. In Marks, L. and Jones, M. (eds) *Disability, Diversability and Legal Change*. Kluwer International, forthcoming.

Susser, S. (1994) The logic in ecological I: the logic of analysis, *American Journal of Public Health*, 84, 5, 825–9.

Thrift, N. (1992) *Spatial Formations*. London: Sage.

Townsend, P., Davidson, N. and Whitehead, M. (1988a) *Inequalities in Health*. London: Penguin.

Townsend, P., Phillimore, P. and Beattie, A. (1988b) *Health and Deprivation: Inequality in the North*. London: Croom Helm.

Wallace, R. (1990) Urban desertification, public health and public order: 'planned shrinkage', violent death, substance abuse and AIDS in the Bronx, *Social Science and Medicine*, 31, 801–13.

Wallace, R., Fullilove, M., Fullilove, R., Gould, P. and Wallace, D. (1994) Will AIDS be contained within US minority urban populations? *Social Science and Medicine*, 39, 8, 1051–62.

Watt, I.S., Franks, A.J. and Sheldon, T.A. (1994) Health and health care of rural populations in the UK: is it better or worse? *Journal of Epidemiology and Community Health*, 48, 16–21.

Webber, R. (1977) The classification of residential neighbourhoods: an introduction to the classification of wards and parishes, *PRAG Technical Report TP23*. London: Centre for Environmental Studies.

West, P. (1991) Rethinking the health selection explanation for health inequalities, *Social Science and Medicine*, 32, 4, 373–84.

Williams, S.J. (1995) Theorising class, health and lifestyles: can Bourdieu help us? *Sociology of Health and Illness*, 17, 5, 577–604.

Wright, E.O. (1995) The class analysis of poverty, *International Journal of Health Services*, 25, 1, 85–100.

Yi Fu Tuan (1974a) Space and place: humanistic perspective, *Prog Geography*, 6, 211–52.

Yi Fu Tuan (1974b) *Topophilia*. USA: Prentice Hall.

Young, I.M. (1990) *Justice and the Politics of Difference*. Princeton, NJ: Princeton University Press.

II: Social and spatial inequalities in health

5. Gender and disadvantage in health: men's health for a change

Elaine Cameron and Jon Bernardes

Introduction and background

Until recently, where health disadvantage has been linked to gender, the focus has typically been on women rather than on men (Arber 1990). This chapter addresses men's disadvantage in health, drawing on current research into men's experiences of prostate illhealth and its impact on their lives and their families (Bernardes *et al.* 1998).

Analyses of inequalities in health in relation to gender typically involve comparisons of groups of people (for example, Townsend and Davidson 1982). This may be simply groups of men and women, or men and women from different social class or ethnic groups. Gender, then, is often superimposed onto biological sex and tends to remain unproblematic. The emphasis here on disadvantage rather than inequalities, leads us to question gender, rather than take it as read, and to begin to unravel and understand some of the complex ways it links with health. Instead of comparing mortality or morbidity patterns, the more familiar territory of health inequalities and gender, this discussion shows how focusing on the workings of gender may contribute to a clearer understanding of those comparisons. Before discussing empirical evidence from the study, some key questions are raised, indicating the context within which this research and associated issues are located.

Why has men's health been neglected? Turning this question round to ask why women have had more of the attention leads to the more familiar reasons. Women are generally sicker than men (though Macintyre *et al.* 1996 question this), make more use of health care services and are regarded generally as the custodians of health for their partners and families as well as themselves (Miles 1991). Feminism, which has incorporated health into its exploration of women's wider disadvantage in society, has had important theoretical and political impact (Doyal 1995, Wilkinson and Kitzinger 1994). Its underlying framework for understanding disadvantage and gender centres on women and has until recently cast men as a rather homogenous group. It also has tended to assume perhaps over-simplistic sex/gender associations and an uncritical notion of the 'normal nuclear family'.

Asking why men's health has been neglected offers a different angle of approach. It was not until the early nineties that men's health became articulated as a specific area of policy concern (Department of Health 1992).

Due attention has been given by policy and services to some health conditions associated with men, notably heart disease and lung cancer, but little to 'hidden' morbidity such as mental health or prostate problems. Can theorising around gender offer any explanations concerning health agendas or are there more fruitful approaches; for example, those which consider power and the role of the medical profession? It is known that prostate problems are notoriously difficult to cure or treat effectively (Hamand 1991).

What is known about disadvantage in men's health? Lloyd (1996) summarises some of the more well documented aspects. For every age group, male mortality is higher than that of females, life expectancy is lower for men, men tend to use primary health services less than women, are more likely to delay help-seeking when ill and are more likely to adopt health damaging or 'risky' behaviours, for example smoking, drinking, violence, fast driving. But there is a need to unpick the complexities of gender and find better explanatory frameworks to spell out the links between epidemiology and behaviours and to consider agency-structure issues. This is quite a task.

Why is there a need to learn more about men's health? First, for sociologists, working to make sense of substantial social and economic changes in society, particularly the nature and extent of inequalities, issues around gender, family life and health are central. Researching men needs to relate to a shift in focus from that of 'the normal nuclear family' to a more radical perspective which accepts widespread diversity both in families and in the pathways whereby people experience and construct their lives (Bernardes 1997). Unravelling gender and masculinities as concepts then, is part and parcel of the business of sociology in documenting, understanding and accounting for its central concern with social change. Sociology has recently found health a fertile arena for airing new debates around mainstream shifts in theorising, for example sociology of the body (Scott and Morgan 1993) and 'risk' society (Beck 1992); the study of men's health similarly offers new challenges to existing theorising around gender as well as giving sociology new territory to document.

Second, men are in the news. Hard on the heels of the arrival of 'new man', has come recent public concern for men's health. A rise in media coverage, more debate about men's health, the portrayal of men's health as problematic and the specific advent of men's health magazines, can all be linked to the growth of men's movements and various men's health projects. Much of this public attention, however, centres on younger rather than older men, yet health is clearly something which concerns older men too. Arber and Ginn (1991), for example, note that when older men and women think about their future, health is a dominant concern.

Third, recent policy shifts have brought economic issues and restraints on resources into sharper focus. More knowledge is needed to understand and measure both effectiveness and efficiency of care services. Health and social care systems based on user-centred, needs-led service arrangements, mean that men and women need to be considered as people, not just as items of care of units of need. Increasing emphasis on health promotion and preventative care has implications for exploring the widest possible view of health, and gender has a key role in the complex construction and patterning of health. The last Conservative Government's record on addressing health inequalities has been notoriously poor (Townsend and Davidson 1982), but if equal opportunity issues in health are more likely to be raised following the change of Government in 1997, men's health ought to be one of these concerns. Patterns and trends in health continue to show widening inequalities as the papers in this issue demonstrate, but the picture and explanatory frameworks are by no means complete, as the 1997–2002 ESRC major research programme on variations in health suggests (ESRC 1997). Clearly, all the above issues rely on better knowledge and ways of understanding health in relation to gender.

The Prostate Health Research Project is concerned with men's health for a change. Its aim is not simply to document and understand a neglected area of men's health, but also to contribute to wider political debates around health through raising awareness and informing policy and practice. It is the first major social study of men with prostate problems, centres on the men themselves and their perspectives, and focuses on the way their ill-health affects themselves and their families. Funded by King's Fund, the study is being carried out collaboratively by two sociologists and the Prostate Help Association (PHA), thought to be the only voluntary support group for prostate sufferers and their families in Britain.

The research focuses on two chronic conditions, Benign Prostatic Hyperplasia (BPH) and prostatitis, and though reliable statistics are lacking, these conditions are currently thought to affect more than one in three men over 50 in the UK (Bradford 1995). BPH is the swelling of the prostate gland which makes urination less easy, leads to night time urination and, if untreated, retention and possible serious complications. Prostatitis is a blanket term for a variety of conditions which are assumed to be linked. The condition takes several forms, from a short-lived 'flu like infection with some passing of blood and mild pain to a chronic abacterial condition which is extremely painful in some cases (Hamand 1991).

The study feeds into many sociological areas, but is particularly appropriate as a platform for exploring issues about disadvantage and men's health, given the dominance of chronic health problems in the patterning of ill-health more generally, the typically hidden nature of prostate conditions, and the fact that in an ageing and ageist society, these particular health problems tend to affect older rather than younger men. Also as prostate health is sex-linked, there are interesting parallels to be drawn with equivalent female conditions.

The findings suggest that not only is there a substantial array of unmet needs among men with prostate problems, but also a greater than anticipated willingness among the men to tell their stories, and a definite pressure from them for public and professional awareness to be raised. When the PHA organiser appeared on the BBC radio Jimmy Young Show in 1993, talking briefly about this new support group, there were several thousand responses by letter and phone.

A brief overview of the key features of the research design will set the scene for a consideration of some of the detailed findings. A postal questionnaire survey of men listed as having contacted the PHA over the four years since it was established, was carried out during 1996–7, plus a small number of in-depth interviews. Together, these have produced a quantitative and qualitative data set which forms the basis for the analysis. Many respondents to the survey sent in additional qualitative information about their experiences and issues which concerned them; sometimes these were of avalanche proportions.

The 25 per cent response rate was satisfactory especially in view of the reduced number of 'live' cases from the main mailing list due to relatively rapid membership turnover. The final sample of 565 cases is thought to be the largest survey sample so far in the UK or USA of men with these conditions. The selective nature of the sample means that findings need to be assessed with due caution. The sample covers an age range of 20–92 years, the mean age is 66 with over half the subjects over 66 years; approximately three-quarters are from non-manual or professional groups, 98 per cent are white and almost 80 per cent live with partners. There are few reliable statistics for comparison, but it is likely that though the age range and marital status profile of sufferers may be roughly representative, class and ethnicity patterns are not. Further research, using different designs is needed to tap the likely substantial numbers of sufferers from working class and minority ethnic groups so that important comparisons can be made. (Further details of the project and methodology can be obtained from the authors.)

Of the respondents, 70 per cent had BPH, 25 per cent prostatitis and two per cent both conditions. Over 60 per cent had had their prostate problems for less than five years, with 18 per cent between six and nine years, though five had had symptoms for 30 years or longer. Almost all reported being in good health before the onset of their prostate problems.

Ninety five per cent reported increased frequency of daytime urination with almost all (98 per cent) an increased night time frequency. Eighty five per cent of the men needed to get up four times a night or less, and 15 per cent more often – one man got up 22 times a night on average. Almost seven out of ten men said they had problems starting urination and 93 per cent experienced urgency. Another symptom, more usually associated clinically with prostatitis, is pain. Thirty-five per cent said it was painful to urinate – an unexpectedly high figure given that only 27 per cent had prostatitis or both conditions. A substantial minority of BPH sufferers (eight per cent) reported painful urination. Just over half the men (56 per cent) said they had other kinds of pain connected with their prostate problem.

The figures say little about what prostate illhealth means to men. This comment by a retired financial advisor in his seventies, was typical of many who experienced severe or prolonged bouts of pain:

> Unless you have experienced prostatitis, it is impossible to fully explain the pain you suffer and how ill you feel: I explain it as feeling completely 100 per cent ill and feel that this is not an exaggeration.

Prostate illhealth can have a major effect on men's family relationships as in the case of a man who has had prostate problems since his student days:

> The impact on my family has been terrible. I constantly feel guilty that I do not spend as much time with my kids as I ought to, nor do I pay my wife the attention she deserves. During this last year I have been particularly withdrawn and anti-social. It's hard to be jolly when you have such intrusive pain . . . My career has suffered in that I have been absent from work more than is normal. In trying to put all my efforts into working effectively I find myself even less able to be an active participant at home.

Some men had changed jobs or retired early because of prostate problems. This comment from an education consultant who had had prostatis for ten years, shows how work can be affected: ' . . . I have just had to cancel a lecture tomorrow because of the problem – second in two weeks . . . '.

Over half of the sample reported changes in their social life and travelling, more than one in three felt their behaviour had changed due to prostate illhealth and also their day to day activities.

One younger prostatitis sufferer said: ' . . . prostatitis isn't just a disease, it is a life ruiner'.

Men's biological sex of course means that all men are at risk of developing these conditions, but in what ways does men's gender link with prostate illhealth? What disadvantages do men experience because of their gender? Are there any advantages of masculinity for health?

The research findings, giving quantitative data drawn from the questionnaires and qualitative data from both questionnaires and interviews, are set rather simply against some common assumptions about gender and health, to see how far the evidence fits the picture. A brief look at age is also included, as it will become clear that these variables are fundamentally interconnected. The analysis then considers how the growing literature on masculinities might offer some welcome clarification of the complexities surrounding gender and health and draws on shifts from a modernist to a postmodernist perspective on family living and from 'the normal nuclear family' towards family pathways.

Gender, men and their prostate health

Health is women's, not men's business and responsibility
In a range of ways, the findings support common gender role assumptions about concern and responsibility for people's health being generally and properly the domain of the woman. Some men acknowledged this as being both the norm and how they themselves behave in their families:

> Men don't talk about health when they're together [Mr 515].

> Men are reluctant to talk about health, I never did 'til I had problems [Mr 329].

> Men don't talk about their health as much as women – she [wife] can discuss hers with friends – it's good to discuss things [Mr 110].

One man, now retired, was proud of the way his wife took due charge of all his health appointments, kept track of his treatments and came in with him at every consultation:

> She's a brick . . . takes care of everything, comes with me every time. She knows more about these things . . . I'm not saying that because she's sat there! [Mr 174].

Some men were proactive about their health, yet still saw health as the proper concern of women; also, approximately one in five of the respondents had no partners.

Men know little about men's health
Men across the age range tend to have a lack of knowledge about the prostate, where it is and what can happen to it:

> Five years ago if you had mentioned the word prostate to me, I would have immediately thought of someone old. If you had mentioned the word prostatitis to me I wouldn't even have known what you were talking about [Mr 124, aged 20].

> Before I had my prostate problem, I didn't know about it, but I wouldn't have wanted to know . . . didn't realise it was the prostate . . . I didn't understand the mechanisms of the prostate then! [Mr 243, aged 60].

However, the few wives we spoke to also said they had known very little about these problems; evidence from correspondence to the PHA suggests that it is likely that neither sex knows enough about prostate health. In fact need for information of all kinds about the prostate is the single most important issue raised by sufferers.

Once aware of a problem though, many men became proactive in getting information. Some had amassed huge quantities of information from a range of sources including the PHA, libraries, books, articles, reviews. One man had tracked down research articles from the USA and drug trials. Also, use of the internet, perhaps accessed generally more by men than women, was mentioned in some cases, and the PHA reports a substantial growth in internet activity on its own web-site.

This typical comment comes from a prostatitis sufferer: 'I've joined the PHA and have acquired a box file full of related data from most relevant sources' [Mr 466].

Men tend to keep quiet about their health problems
It is interesting that while men generally tend not to talk about their health, regarding it as women's territory, a substantial minority of men with prostate problems (six per cent) had not even told their partners or close families about their problems.

One man in his mid-eighties, a retired local government officer, had not told his wife about his prostate problems, though they had known each other for 60 years. He said he didn't discuss his health and never had. He had not consulted his GP about his prostate problem, though he did talk about his asthma with him. He said he felt his older friends did have prostate problems but they never said. He was content to manage his prostate problems himself and believed firmly in 'mind over matter' and a positive view of health [Mr 110]. This case indicates that gender roles may interplay with age in terms of attitudes and behaviours around health, but shows also another edge to the idea that prostate sufferers 'suffer in silence'. A large majority of the men (90 per cent), however, had told their partners or close family members about their prostate problems.

One man who had had prostatitis for ten years commented:

I have never hidden the problem – even amongst friends and work colleagues. The frequency of urination is all to obvious and therefore I offered explanation [Mr 278].

Another [Mr 466] said: 'I am not one of the won't-talk-about-it-or-ask-questions men!'

Prostate problems, after the early stages, are not easily hidden from the view of close family members and work mates, so the condition itself may mean that men have to 'come out'. Interestingly, the men who shared their prostate problems with family and friends seemed to be aware that they were going against what is normally accepted as the man's role. The relationship between the public and the private seems to be challenged by men's prostate illhealth experiences. The following case is typical of those few who feel that they now have almost a responsibility to step beyond their traditional male role in order to serve fellow men's interests:

I tell everybody about the prostate, those with and without problems! Some people don't want to know . . . I'm open, not like some [Mr 399].

Another man said that it was the very nature of the problem, the symptoms and, most of all the kinds of physical examinations and intrusive interventions entailed, which had given him the impetus and confidence to change his previous way of behaving with his mates.

Health/health promotion is 'female' so being a man means being denied a self-monitoring role

For those men in the sample who had ignored their symptoms for many years, it is likely that masculinity was an important factor in failing to take notice of or take action about symptoms. Some were aware of this and acknowledged it. With some kinds of health problems, there is opportunity for women to take on this monitoring and prompting role for their menfolk, yet for women partners or other female close kin of prostate sufferers, the early symptoms are likely to remain largely out of sight.

However, once linked into the health care system and with a prostatitis or BPH diagnosis, some men in the study kept meticulous records of their symptoms, treatments, diet and bodily functions over long periods of time, and were clearly and actively in the monitoring business. Mr 243 has kept a record of every time he has urinated, and the difficulties involved, for five years together with details of all his liquid intake. Is this a gendered activity or way of responding to a health problem? Does traditional masculinity, with its emphasis on action and taking charge, advantage men in that they may 'track' their own health systematically once a problem is recognised?

Prostate problems represent a threat to masculinity/the 'self'

Men told us about the impact that prostate illhealth had on many areas of day to day living, including relationships, family life, work and leisure. Over half the sample reported changes in their social life, over a third, changes in levels of activity, and less than a quarter, changes in their job/work. Seven out of ten of those who answered reported changes in their sex life; symptoms and treatments can affect sexual functioning. The nature of these changes can be seen to tap into the heart of the arenas in which masculinity is conventionally acted out. Are prostate problems then a threat to the gendered identity and 'self', perhaps more than other disabling conditions?

The youngest man in the sample had had prostatitis for two years:

> I am only 20 years old and used to be out constantly, now all of a sudden
> I'm trapped because of this disease. My worst problem is sitting down
> and even lying down, if I put pressure on the prostate for some time I'm
> left in agony, my friends say to me 'we don't mind, come down the pub.' I
> would like to see them or anyone sit down on a bloody toilet seat in a pub
> or stand up all night, not only is it extremely painful, and I wouldn't have
> said anything like this three years ago because nothing or no-one both-

ered me. I could take anything really . . . I am at my sexual peak, but I am not allowed to indulge, I'm living life a monk, compared to how I used to be [Mr 124].

Another man in his seventies talked of how he believes a drug adversely affected his sex drive.

[My sex life] . . . now seems over and has made me feel inadequate with my wife – who is supportive and understanding. It has left me feeling nevertheless, less of a man and I know there is no going back [Mr 175].

Both younger and older men, then, can feel that their prostate problems do attack some central aspects of their sense of self, sexual issues rating highly for some. The wife of one sufferer wrote that her husband's prostate problem, in particular his embarrassment with urinary accidents, was more disabling to him personally than his artificial legs.

However, this is not the same for all. Some men seemed to use the experience as an opportunity to adapt and take on new attitudes, values, behaviours or ways of being, such as being more open about their body, emotions, sex functions and relationships. What is interesting is that such men didn't see themselves as 'less of a man'.

Men cope less well because they fear losing control

Chronic conditions are characterised by unpredictability and by a range of uncertainties (Bury 1991) which together may represent a threat to traditional masculinity, with its emphasis on control and taking charge. Women are often thought able to cope better with chronic illhealth, because acceptance and passivity align more with the traditional female gender role. Certainly, prostate diseases are beset by a multiplicity of uncertainties, perhaps more than most chronic conditions. These range from treatments having different effects on a man at different times, to expressed uncertainties by doctors about diagnoses and likely outcomes from interventions. The study shows variations among the men in coping with uncertainties.

Another traditional masculine trait is that of actively overcoming hurdles despite challenges, of 'coming through' whatever the knocks. These were apparent in some of the responses. For example:

. . . the best course appears to be just soldier on [Mr 126].

Life throws a lot at you and you can come through [Mr 243].

Perhaps these aspects of masculinity then are resources for men to draw on in times of great challenges to their health and lives.

Men tend to see the body as a machine

The literature on conceptions of health and the sociology of body supports the idea of the gendered body (Scott and Morgan 1993). Men's perspectives on the healthy body, the 'body as project' and behaviours involved in becoming 'healthy' can be seen to be different from women's; they may also, ironically, place men's health at risk (White *et al.* 1995). The evidence from the prostate study does suggest that men tend to deal with the mechanics of their bodies –inputs, outputs and effects – rather than emotions and feelings.

A teacher with BPH believed firmly that health was about cause and effect, and that it would soon be possible to use computers to determine exactly what dietary needs a body required to be perfectly healthy. He used the unlikely example of an acquaintance who ran a health shop who had cured a great dane dog's prostate problem simply with scientific dietary controls. Even the substantial proportion of sufferers who had used alternative therapies sometimes saw these interventions via a narrow cause and effect rather than a holistic viewfinder.

Many men also appeared to have an individualistic view of health. Men wanted to know about other men's prostate experiences, but at a distance and without personal contact. Attempts by the PHA to arrange group get-togethers have failed to find support. Women, on the other hand, were thought to belong to social networks where health issues were shared and these networks in turn help shape how they manage their illness (Miles 1991). Perhaps the written accounts, monitoring and record-keeping which many prostate sufferers produce, represent a gendered alternative to women's more oral ways of dealing with health concerns?

Again there are examples which show a different picture. A few men did seem to subscribe to a more holistic view of health, complete with due respect for emotion, more typical perhaps of a 'female' view of health. Yet they felt comfortable with this, largely seeing it as being a situation thrown up by their illhealth.

Men and services

Men tend to delay seeking help
Although there was variation among the men in the study, for many men the onset of symptoms did not lead immediately to help-seeking. For some it did not come until a health crisis occurred or a particular incident which acted as a trigger to consult. A 60-year-old man had had symptoms for seven years without consulting anyone until his BPH was diagnosed following emergency admission to hospital with retention of urine. He described the seven-year spell: 'I lived with it, adapted to the symptoms, didn't define myself as unwell, just accepted it'.

Interestingly, this same man also mentioned his impotence problems which he has had for some time, yet hasn't consulted his male GP about it:

It's not so easy to talk about . . . I think my GP would turn his head down in embarrassment [Mr 243].

Another man was finally prompted into consulting a doctor following a socially embarrassing moment when he needed to urinate unexpectedly:

[I was] in a friend's motor – a critical moment – I had to dive in opposite the bus depot [Mr 399].

Men make 'bad' patients

Masculinity may impede some treatments or interventions. One man gave up reflexology after one session, according to his wife solely because of pressure from his male friends. Some men showed they were not used to intrusive medical examinations and resisted investigations. A joke about the fictional television vet, James Herriott was one man's way of expressing his feelings on this.
Another said:

The whole episode of DRE [digital rectal examination], cytoscopy etc. was a *nightmare*. I have avoided going back for ten years!

Several respondents mentioned the sex of the doctors or health workers they saw. Some men felt that the sex of health staff was important – particularly regarding intimate or invasive procedures. As one man said, 'Men understand what you're going through' [Mr 243]. This raises the question of whether some men might benefit from same sex health care, as many women do.

Health policy and professionals

The so-called killer diseases for men are seen to have much greater attention and attract more resources than prostate illhealth: relatively less is known about these conditions compared to women's sex-linked illnesses. Prostate cancer, drawing relatively fewer resources than breast cancer, has a higher public profile than BPH or prostatitis, but this disease, too, is thought to be undergoing sidelining, with medical opinion recently rejecting calls for screening programmes (Linehan 1995). Is it that medical interest is reduced because it has as yet no effective treatment or cures for these conditions? Whatever the answers, men do seem aware of shortfalls in medical care, as some of their comments suggest:

The medics have no firm idea of causes [Mr 39].

Clearly the medical profession does not know enough about the prostate . . . [Mr 313].

My GP had little knowledge about prostate problems . . . he shows little interest in how my condition is progressing [Mr 236].

I felt totally let down by the medical profession . . . and feel that the medical profession don't consider it serious [Mr 76].

There was considerable evidence to support the view that doctors, particularly specialists, do not welcome the 'lay expertise' which many men had about their own condition, often recorded in great detail:

Some of us know our bodies better than any GP or medical test can [Mr 95, who has had BPH for 15 years].

The GP was helpful, but I feel I am more knowledgeable about the subject than he is [Mr 278, a man in his forties who has had prostatitis for ten years].

One man became so frustrated with the urologist taking so little notice of the written details of his urinary problems which he brought along to consultations, that he has considered hiring a video to record himself urinating, to show the doctor.

Traditional masculine assertiveness which may help men seek out the information they need, can be interpreted by doctors as inappropriate patient behaviour. One man spoke of how his persistence in asking for information about his prostate problem led to his being labelled 'aggressive' by the specialist. He felt this subsequently adversely affected the care he received.

Age

It is almost impossible to extricate gender and masculinities from considerations of age in this health study, as age has so many links into the image and reality of prostate problems. There are, for example, issues to do with generation, biographical experiences and cohort, all mediated via gender and vice versa, which show that age is as much in danger of being used as a blunt instrument by sociologists and policy makers as is gender. Men don't all live out their gender from the same structural positions in society; age and its many forms, is just one of the locators.

A few ideas can be teased out from the research to get a feel for this interplay. To begin with, prostate disease is not just seen as a disease of old age, but an old man's disease. There are therefore important repercussions for sufferers who fall outside the stereotype. Younger men can be disadvantaged:

This is definitely a concept of an 'old man's disease' and associated stigma. I developed prostatitis in my 30s [a man in his forties].

Also, younger men are unlikely to expect or be wary of early signs of symptoms. A man who has had BPH for nine years reflects on this: 'Younger men think it's a joke and do nothing to safeguard their futures' [Mr 301].

Disrupted biographies and the destabilising which prostate illhealth often brings can have major knock-on effects for younger men. Long-term repercussions may follow, for example, concerning relationships and economic status. One man had suffered from BPH for 20 years. He worked as an independent insurance and financial adviser. He felt that his need to go to the toilet often, made his clients feel suspicious of him, which definitely affected his career adversely.

In contrast, older men may tend to see symptoms as part of the 'normal' ageing process, rather than an illness, which may contribute to late referral. Older age may compound disadvantages of masculinity. Are masculinities among older men less flexibly negotiated or with more rigid distinctions between the private and public?

Is ageism evident in diagnosis? Diagnosis of the two diseases included in our study seem to be heavily age dependent. First, there is a very clear age difference between BPH (average 69 years, range 37–92 years) and prostatitis (average 57 years, range 20–80 years). This, of course, may simply reflect the fact that, as the vast majority of medical textbooks and self-help manuals suggest, BPH is a progressive disease with an onset in older age. Our data, however, suggest that something else may be at work here. Taking a sample of cases with very similar symptoms, preliminary analysis suggests that for men below 60 to 65 years the diagnosis was likely to be prostatitis; above those ages, BPH. This in itself is interesting, but diagnostic labels may also lead on to different treatment regimes.

Other key factors which locate men and their gendered experiences are ethnicity and class. While this research does not explore prostate health and ethnicity and class, it does point to some further puzzles. Where are the likely large numbers of men from ethnic minority, and from working class, groups currently getting their information and support, if any? Are prostate sufferers from these groups somehow doubly disadvantaged?

Discussion and conclusions

The study suggests men's gender can and does disadvantage them via both structure and agency with regard to prostate health. Structural disadvantage for prostate sufferers can be seen within health policy, the health care system and the medical profession, and disadvantage via agency through traditional masculinity and male gender roles. While men's gendered behaviour and attitudes may not place them 'at risk' of contracting prostate problems (as they might with many conditions such as broken limbs from driving too fast or heart disease from dietary habits), it certainly may affect what happens when they have them.

As often, it is more complex than that. For example, the data show that men's traditional gendered roles do not always signify disadvantage but often advantage; masculinity can be a resource in dealing with a serious health problem. The challenge then is to find ways to tune in more sensitively to the multiplicity of ways gender and health link together and to revisit the concept and use of 'gender'. As Segal (1993) says, gender role theory based around Parsons' ideas is no longer useful (Parsons and Bales 1956).

The growing literature on masculinity may prove valuable here and has potential for development and application within the sociology of health and illness more widely. Three ideas are particularly helpful.

1. Multiple and multidimensional masculinities (Connell 1987),
2. Hegemonic masculinity (Connell 1987),
3. Negotiated gender (Cornwall and Lindisfarne 1994).

Masculinities rather than masculinity is a useful concept because it allows for a wide range of possible ways men can live out their maleness. Multi-dimensional masculinities allow for variability within individual and group experiences both at one time and longitudinally. It also affords biographical pathways and family diversity central roles, and chimes with postmodernity.

Hegemonic masculinity, representing the ideological construction of masculinity serving the interests of dominant male groups, offers a way into accounting for structural frameworks and issues of power relations between different groups of men. Gordon gives the characteristics of the much quoted American dominant male sex role by Brannon (Gordon 1995). These are the need to be different from women (no sissy stuff), to be superior to others (the big wheel), to be independent and self-reliant (the sturdy oak) and to be more powerful than others, through violence if necessary (give 'em hell). The gender order and hegemonic version of masculinity frames relations of inequality, showing that men dominate both women and other groups of men.

Health of course is an important component of social inequality, and hegemonic masculinity can be seen as dangerous to men's health. 'Health seems to be one of the most clear-cut areas in which the damaging impacts of traditional masculinity are evident' (Sabo and Gordon 1995: 17). As men strive for this dominant version of masculinity, it places their health at risk. Canetto's work on suicide suggests men are more likely to die in suicide attempts than women because men are better achievers (Canetto 1995). Men whose position in the social order shifts because of, for example, job changes due to prostate illness, can become relegated to marginalised masculinity in the gender order. Hegemonic masculinity can be seen as a key risk factor associated with men's illness – a risk factor in disease aetiology, but also a definite barrier to developing a consciousness about health and illness, though as we have seen, some qualities may be a resource for health. Sabo quotes Soltenberg in suggesting that more men ought to refuse to be men (Sabo and Gordon 1995). Perhaps our study shows that in various ways some men actually do this.

The idea of *negotiated gender* is useful because of its emphasis on processes whereby gender is constantly being redefined and renegotiated in interaction. It fits well with the idea of men negotiating their own life-courses, paying regard to other family members and wider elements of social structure in redefining their masculinity. Charmaz suggests that in chronic illness, threats to identity typically confront the individual again and again, as chronic illness is characterised by long duration and uncertainties (Charmaz 1995). Traditional masculine identity becomes a 'two-edged sword' for men with chronic illhealth; it can lead to men achieving a valued life after illhealth and also to men being diminished by it, as our findings show. Chronic illness can be one process whereby some men are reduced to 'marginalised masculinity' in the gender order (Connell 1987). Masculine identities reflect lifelong participation in the gender order and when men's lives become destabilised, men are more likely to begin to consider their own masculinity. Bury's notion of 'biographical disruption' as a feature of chronic illness is also relevant here (Bury 1982).

Negotiated gender makes sense of our findings. Prostate illhealth tends to be fundamentally destabilising, but our findings show that situations vary and the 'self' is not necessarily threatened by damage to what might at first be thought of as central features of masculinity e.g. sexual functioning. Gordon's work on testicular cancer also supports this. Most men with this disease respond positively once they physically recover and feel no less masculine, achieving redefinition of masculinity via both traditional and non-traditional models of masculine characteristics. Gordon emphasises the negotiated element by arguing that men do have some control over this process of self definition (Gordon 1995). In our research, then, some of the men with prostate problems were perhaps not simply refusing to be men, but rather negotiating new and sometimes 'better' ways to be masculine.

Blakemore and Boneham (1994) in their discussion of ethnicity and identity suggest that at different times and settings people may consider various factors as central to their identity – ethnicity may be dominant at some times or in some settings but not in others. Gender or masculinity may not always be central in men's perceptions of their identity or in their interaction. So it is vital to be cautious about assuming too much about the impact of gender in all settings and for all men at all times. The literature on masculinities is useful only in so far as gender has relevance for the area under investigation. This is important because unquestioned assumptions or overgeneralisations can lead to false research trails and insensitive service responses.

For example, separate services for older people from minority ethnic groups may be developed based on services' perception that ethnicity is the dominant feature in these people's lives, when the older people themselves place commonalities with others, such as via age or gender, as more central in relation to some of their needs for services (Cameron *et al.* 1996).

The literature on masculinities therefore provides a framework for understanding power relations and inequalities. It also opens up analysis of the different ways gender and health are linked and how masculinities can signify both advantage and disadvantage. It helps us move past the straitjacket of an over-simplistic view of gender, where sex and gender are simple equivalents, and where gender is just something to be 'added and stirred' into a variables mix (Annandale and Hunt 1990).

Other useful frameworks involve postmodern perspectives on families and biographical pathways. The term postmodern family life was developed by Stacey 'to signal the contested, ambivalent, and undecided character of contemporary gender and kinship arrangements' (Stacey 1990: 17). Morgan has recently concluded that the focus on the issue of family practices gives some sense of the 'flow and fluidity [which] is probably part of a postmodernist understanding' (Morgan 1996: 200). Taken together, these seem to capture the image of family living that we wish to explore here along with theoretical strategies developed to study such family lives. Bury's (1982) ideas of lifecourses and biographies can be usefully extended via the notion of pathways to incorporate social structures. This combines both individual lifecourses and family pathways (Bernardes, 1997). An individual occupies and moves through different structures relating to, for example, being a baby, a child, a teenager, a single adult, a spouse, a parent, as well as structures linked to health or disease. At all times the individual negotiates a pathway through these structures; the lifecourse is multidimensional, being seen in terms of, say, health, education, career, hobbies or sport. Families, therefore can be viewed as processes as well as a multiplicity of structures. People may face similar experiences, such as chronic illness, but come to these events via different routes and respond quite differently. Nunnally suggests that 'most families encounter external or internal stresses at different points in the life span of each member. These stresses vary from one family to another depending on many factors in the environment and the family' (Nunnally *et al.* 1988: 13). Facing and coping with similar events or situations does not mean that these are experienced in the same way, so this approach sheds fresh light on what is both unique and common to men's experiences concerning health.

In conclusion, the study of prostate health provides new evidence and ideas about a neglected area in men's health. It also generates ideas about men's health more generally to help sharpen analysis of wider health inequalities. It raises questions about the concept of 'gender' as a social dimension and its use as an analytical tool. Research into men's health can be hindered by assumptions that all males are equivalent in the gender order or in the social construction of their gender. Disaggregating gender from sex therefore, is a good starting point. It keeps gender on its toes.

Current theorising around masculinities has a great deal to contribute, both in developing conceptual frameworks and methodologies. In particular, the ideas of hegemonic masculinity, the gender order, multiple and multi-dimensional masculinities and negotiated gender can help tie both structure and agency into the frame. They also allow other variables such as class, ethnicity, generation and age to have a more incisive entry point into analyses of men's health. Another benefit of masculinity theories is that by placing masculinities alongside or instead of gender, it necessitates bringing femininities into the picture too. Family diversity and biographical pathways provide parallel frameworks which afford gender new and flexible working space. Theories around masculinities seem particularly relevant for understanding chronic illness.

Bringing masculinity into men's health also spills into relevant debates around the gendered body. Saltonstall's discussion on the healthy body and gender shows how gender is implicated in everyday experiences of health (Saltonstall 1993). Highlighting the different approaches of men and women towards body maintenance may have practical spin-offs for health promotion. Like most research which touches on health inequalities, the prostate research is concerned throughout with identifying ways to reduce disadvantage in men's health.

Which way forward from here?

In terms of seeking evidence and explanation about men's health, more knowledge is needed about how various masculinities are constructed, how difference in socio-economic locations of male groups is linked to this, and how power and hegemonic masculinity liaise with men's health. Another area to pursue is the way men's and women's health are linked to other inequalities. Analytical work on the links between these and health needs to encompass not just descriptive epidemiology, but exploration of the diversity of disadvantage among men in different class, age and ethnic groups. Important also is how this relates to the experiences of wives and families.

Setting up a dialogue with feminists and theorists working on femininities is important, as is to avoid establishing narrow 'men's studies' with associated elephant traps such as feminists have struggled to escape from. Sabo warns of 'becoming a fresh set of choir boys (or girls) singing new arrangements of timeworn patriarchal scores' (Sabo and Gordon 1995: 17).

Does sociological investigation of men, disadvantage and health present any particular challenges for methodology? The prostate research suggests that an approach which incorporates interpretive perspectives, actively involves men themselves and self-help groups in the research process, and which relates directly to policy and practice in health, is a good start in generating useful data and stretching existing conceptual apparatus.

Feminists have challenged sexism in research methodology in so far as it disadvantages or excludes women (Roberts 1990). Does sexism in methodology and epistemology also disadvantage some groups of men? Should we then be looking for methodologies which actively ensure all men are represented in knowledge and the business of generating it? Answers are starting to appear. Coltrane (1994) suggests strategies which incorporate both structural and agency dimensions. Morgan (1992) offers a very thorough examination of theoretical, methodological and practical issues involved in researching men, showing how this involves a revisiting of what is understood by 'feminist' methodologies. These represent important reading for anyone involved with men's health.

However, going back to the earlier point which Blakemore and Boneham (1994) raise about identity, there needs to be some caution. Although gender is a major basis for identity, it is not the only one and methodologies must not grasp hold of masculinities to the point of achieving a stranglehold. Researching men is also about researching people. Men may be older or younger, middle class or working class, white or black. Sensitive methodologies perhaps will be those which remain awake to the range of methodological alternatives always waiting in the wings, and those which keep a constant reflective eye on the interrelationship between theory, method and data.

What ways forward are there now for men with prostate problems? The men, themselves had various suggestions. There were views concerning macro-level changes – prioritisation of prostate health in policy, health care and research and provision of more information. One man said that men don't know what's normal, so how could they possibly recognise early symptoms? Others' suggestions were about 'changing' men, but saw many difficulties. Men readily rationalise away early symptoms, for example giving nervousness as an excuse for difficulty starting to urinate in public lavatories. Older men may be quick to consider 'dribbling' of urine as just caused by the ageing process. A wife of a prostate sufferer felt that change can only come about generationally, by starting to give better information to younger men and boys and letting it 'work its way up'.

It seems unlikely, as Sabo and Gordon (1995) argue, that there can be significant individual change without structural changes. Political pressures are needed to help change policy and practice, to redress male over male, as well as male over female, hierarchies, to challenge hegemonic masculinity and find ways to legitimate diverse masculinities. But there may also be ways to identify, legitimate and build on the positive resources which different men, and different masculinities, bring to health.

The feminist movement has in many ways led the way in engaging with health disadvantage and gender, and men's health is now poised to build on what has been learned, make use of new frameworks and take some strides of its own. A comment by a man in the study picks up the two key dimensions of structure and agency which are at the heart of the puzzle that is men's health: ' . . . the world is run by men but they don't listen to health messages'.

Acknowledgements

Thanks are due to the men who took part in this research and to King's Fund, London for funding and supporting the project.

References

Annandale, E. and Hunt, K. (1990) Masculinity, femininity and sex: an exploration of their relative contribution to explaining gender differences in health, *Sociology of Health and Illness*, 12, 1, 24–46.

Arber, S. (1990) Opening the black box: inequalities in women's health. In Abbott, P. and Payne, G. (eds) *New Directions in the Sociology of Health*. Basingstoke: Falmer Press.

Arber, S. and Ginn, J. (1991) *Gender and Later Life*. London: Sage.

Beck, U. (1992) *Risk Society: towards a New Modernity*. London: Sage.

Bernardes, J. (1997) *Family Studies: an Introduction*. London: Routledge.

Bernardes, J., Cameron, E. and Dunn, P. (1998) *Prostate Health: Common Conditions other than Cancer. A Summary Report on the Impact of Prostatitis and Benign Prostatic Hyperplasia on Men's Lives and those of their Families*. Wolverhampton: University of Wolverhampton.

Blakemore, K. and Boneham, M. (1994) *Age, Race and Ethnicity: a Comparative Approach*. Buckingham: Open University Press.

Bradford, N. (1995) *Men's Health Matters*. London: Vermillion.

Bury, M. (1982) Chronic illness as biographical disruption, *Sociology of Health and Illness*, 4, 2, 167–82.

Bury, M. (1991) The sociology of chronic illness: a review of research and prospects, *Sociology of Health and Illness*, 13, 4, 455–68.

Cameron, E., Badger, F. and Evers, H. (1996) Ethnicity and care management. In Phillips, J. and Penhale, B. (eds) *Reviewing Care Management for Older People*. London: Jessica Kingsley in association with The British Association of Gerontology.

Canetto, S.S. (1995) Men who survive a suicidal act. In Sabo, D. and Gordon, F. (eds) *Men's Health and Illness: Gender, Power and the Body*. London: Sage.

Charmaz, K. (1995) Identity dilemmas of chronically ill men. In Sabo, D. and Gordon, F. (eds) *Men;s Health and Illness: Gender, Power and the Body*. London: Sage.

Coltrane, S. (1994) Theorizing masculinities in contemporary social science. In Brod, H. and Kaufman, M. (eds) *Theorizing Masculinities*. London: Sage.

Connell, R.W. (1987) *Gender and Power: Society, the Person and Sexual Politics*. Cambridge: Polity Press.

Cornwall, A. and Lindisfarne, N. (eds) (1994) *Dislocating Masculinity: Comparative Ethnographies*. London: Routledge.

Department of Health (1992) *The Annual Report of the Chief Medical Officer.* London: Department of Health.

Economic and Social Research Council (1997) *Variations in Health Programme.* Lancaster. Website: http://www.lancs.ac.uk/users/apsocsci/hvp.htm

Doyal, L. (1995) *What Makes Women Sick: Gender and the Political Economy of Health.* Basingstoke: Macmillan.

Gordon, D.F. (1995) Testicular cancer and masculinity. In Sabo, D. and Gordon, F. (eds) *Men's Health and Illness: Gender, Power and the Body.* London: Sage.

Hamand, J. (1991) *Prostate Problems – the Complete Guide to their Treatment.* London: Thorsons.

Linehan, T. (1995) Preventing prostate cancer: to screen or not to screen *Healthlines,* October, 17–19.

Lloyd, T. (1996) *Men's Health Review.* London: Men's Health Forum, Royal College of Nursing.

Macintyre, S., Hunt, K. and Sweeting, H. (1996) Gender differences in health: are things really as simple as they seem? *Social Science and Medicine,* 42, 617–24.

Miles, A. (1991) *Women, Health and Medicine.* Buckingham: Open University Press.

Morgan, D. (1992) *Discovering Masculinities.* London: Routledge.

Morgan, D.H.J. (1996) *Family Connections: an Introduction to Family Studies.* Cambridge: Polity Press.

Nunnally, E.W., Chilman, C.S. and Cox, F.M. (eds) (1988) *Troubled Relationships.* Newbury Park: Sage.

Parsons, T. and Bales, R. (1956) *Family Socialization and Interaction Process.* London: Routledge and Kegan Paul.

Roberts, H. (ed) (1990) *Doing Feminist Research.* London: Routledge.

Sabo, D. and Gordon, F. (eds) (1995) *Men's Health and Illness: Gender, Power and the Body.* London: Sage.

Saltonstall, R. (1993) Healthy bodies, social bodies: men's and women's concepts and practices of health in everyday life, *Social Science and Medicine,* 36, 1, 7–14.

Scott, S. and Morgan, D. (1993) *Body Matters: Essays on the Sociology of the Body.* London: Falmer Press.

Segal, L. (1993) Changing men: masculinities in context, *Theory and Society,* 22, 5, 625–41.

Stacey, J. (1990) *Brave New Families: Stories of Domestic Upheaval in Late Twentieth Century America.* New York: Basic.

Townsend, P. and Davidson, N. (1982, Penguin edition 1990) *Inequalities in Health: the Black Report.* Harmondsworth: Penguin Books.

White, P.G., Young, K. and McTeer, W.G. (1995) Sport, masculinity and the injured body. In Sabo, D. and Gordon, F. (eds) *Men's Health and Illness: Gender, Power and the Body.* London: Sage.

Wilkinson, S. and Kitzinger, C. (eds) (1994) *Women and Health: Feminist Perspectives.* London: Taylor and Francis.

6. Changing the map: health in Britain 1951–91

_Mary Shaw, Danny Dorling and
Nic Brimblecombe_

Introduction

While it is undoubtedly true that we are all going to die, some of us will die
sooner rather than later – our life chances are intimately connected to our
social and economic circumstances, which are inextricably linked to influences of behaviour and intergenerational advantages and disadvantages. As
well as _social_ inequality in health, there is also an interlinked _geographical_
dimension to health: people living in different places have differing life
chances, irrespective of their social status. In this chapter we briefly review
the literature on the geographical distribution of health in Britain as gauged
by mortality data. This body of literature suggests that not only is there
inequality in health between regions and areas in Britain but that the extent
of this inequality is increasing. Possible explanations for the geographical
patterns observed are briefly discussed. A unique analysis of national
mortality data for local areas is then presented. Attention focuses upon the
methodological issue of changing geographical boundaries, and how this
process of area redefinition may have obscured the observation of underlying patterns of inequality. Constant geographical boundaries are constructed to allow for the comparison of standardised mortality ratios
(SMRs) over the period 1951–1991. The results indicate that changes in the
definition of boundaries have led to the underestimation of geographical
inequalities in health (at least in terms of mortality) in contemporary
Britain.

Geographical patterns in health

Mortality has traditionally been, and continues to be, the most commonly
used indicator of the geographic distribution of health. In this country, the
topic has been investigated since the publication of vital statistics, including
information on area of residence, were first collected in England and Wales
in 1837 (Britton, 1990). Patterns can be observed on a number of geographical levels: between countries, between regions and also between districts and
wards. There are quite remarkable differences between the mortality and life
expectancy of groups of different countries – the World Bank reports that

life expectancy in Sub-Saharan Africa stands at 52 years, whereas in 'established market economies' it reaches 76 years (World Bank 1993). Large differences are also apparent between the countries of the European Community (Kaminski *et al.* 1986). Generally, mortality is lower in richer countries (Curtis and Taket 1996). However, as Wilkinson (1992) asserts, it appears that the health of a nation is determined not only by its level of economic development but also by the distribution of health services and the distribution of wealth – the more equal the society economically, the better the overall health of that society.

Many researchers have reported regional inequalities in mortality within the UK. Patterns have been documented for over a century in Britain, and it has been consistently found that mortality rates are higher in the north and in Scotland and lower in the south. Similar evidence of a north/south divide is presented by Britton (1990) who, looking at data up to 1983, argued that there was a continuation, and if anything a worsening of the regional gradient in mortality, from high in the north and west to low in the south and east for both men and women. This is the case for almost all the main causes of death. Regarding particular causes of mortality, Strachan *et al.* (1995) report regional variations in cardiovascular disease and stroke with a southeast to northwest gradient in mortality, the northwest having the higher mortality. Similarly, Howe (1986) found regional differences in heart disease and lung cancer for males; for females the number of deaths overall from these conditions was less, however, the pattern of regional differences was similar to that for males. As observed in the Black Report Britain can be divided into two zones of relatively high and low mortality (DHSS 1980). Howe (1986) proposes an imaginary line reaching from the Bristol Channel to the estuary of the Humber separating those experiencing favourable and unfavourable life chances, whereas Britton (1990) suggests a divide from the Severn to the Wash separating areas of low and high mortality.

However, this pattern is not all-encompassing. Illsley and Le Grand (1993) used the large standard regions to look at specific age groups and found that it was only in adults aged 45–64 that the inter-regional variation in mortality conformed to the familiar north/south gradient; differences were greater for men than for women. Others have also found that the regional gradient in mortality does not hold for all age groups. For example, Britton (1990) found that the only exception to the continuing inequalities in health was for post-natal mortality (28 days to one year). Gordon and Sutherland (1987) state that there has also been a disappearance of the north/south differentials in neonatal mortality (less than 28 days), although this is disputed by Britton (1990).

Comparisons of rural and urban places also have a long history – urban/rural differences in mortality have been manifest since the production of vital statistics by area in Britain. William Farr (1885) found that average life expectancy at birth in the 1840s in rural areas was in the upper 40s, but in urban areas, such as Liverpool and Manchester, it was 20 years below this. More recently, rural/urban differences in Britain have been reported by Bentham (1984), Britton (1990) and Watt *et al.* (1994) who found that mortality rates are lower in rural areas and higher in conurbations and larger towns. However, there is some variation to this pattern. Phillimore and Reading (1992) found that inequalities in mortality between more and less deprived wards were more extreme in urban areas than in rural areas. Looking at specific causes of death, Saunderson and Langford (1996) investigated the geographical variation of suicide rates in England and Wales and found that both males and females experience a high rate in densely populated urban areas, but that males also experience high rates in agricultural (rural) regions. Whilst the recent pattern in Britain has generally been that mortality rates are higher in urban than rural areas, there have been exceptions to this in the past, most notably in the Pennines in the 1930s and the Great Irish Famine of the 1840s. Likewise in other countries, there are examples of rural death rates exceeding those of urban areas.

A number of studies have reported variations in mortality on a more local level, looking at counties, wards and neighbourhoods. For example, Britton (1990) found differences between counties within the UK, with north and west and also metropolitan areas having higher mortality. Townsend *et al.* (1988) present data on differences by ward. Differences were such that the worst ward had (proportionately) almost five times as many deaths as the best ward. Interestingly, Congdon (1995) found that ward level differences in health were stronger in metropolitan suburbs and inner city areas than in rural areas and Eames *et al.* (1993) found that the association between deprivation at the ward level and mortality depended upon the Regional Health Authority in which the ward was situated. Townsend *et al.* (1984) and Townsend *et al.* (1988) also found that local neighbourhood was more strongly associated with health than was region. Skrimshire (1978) suggested that a working class person was at greater disadvantage if living in a predominantly working class area than in a mixed area, indicating that the localities themselves had an effect upon a person's health. However, Ben-Shlomo *et al.* (1996) in a study of mortality and deprivation by ward, found that variations in mortality were least in the most affluent and most deprived areas.

Intra-urban differences in health have also received some attention. For example, Howe (1986) reports a clear core-periphery pattern for SMRs in London. For heart attacks in males, for example, SMRs range from 51 in Sutton in Inner London to 122 in Dagenham in Outer London. Howe (1986) notes that the mortality ratio for Glasgow as a whole is one-third above the UK average, but that in some parts of Glasgow SMRs are well below this level, whereas in other areas SMRs are in excess of 170. Areas with the highest mortality tend also to be the most deprived areas. A number of studies have compared areas on the basis of their socio-economic characteristics. McCarron *et al.* (1994) found substantial differences in mortality between the most and least deprived areas of Glasgow. In a study of infant mortality within the city of Southampton, with areas divided according to socio-economic characteristics, Robinson and Pinch (1987) found that there were four times as many child deaths in the worst areas compared with the best areas – there was a clear division of mortality and social deprivation in the city. Such comparisons of places according to socio-economic characteristics and in particular the degree of deprivation are common. Differences between rich and poor areas (as defined by a material deprivation index based on factors such as car ownership and housing tenure) have also been found by Townsend *et al.* (1988). They found that, in the main, deprivation in an area was linked to high mortality rates, although some equally deprived areas had differing rates.

Looking at the concept of 'place' on a more micro level, there are also differences in health according to housing tenure; indeed, Jones and Goldblatt (1996) claim that tenure is a better predictor of mortality than area. Fox and Goldblatt (1982) report that owner occupiers have lower mortality than those in rented accommodation; Britton (1990) found higher mortality in council estates, in particular low-status urban or inner city estates, with mortality rates 20 per cent over the national average for council house renters compared with near average mortality rates for owner-occupiers in the same areas. Tenure, in conjunction with car access, is increasingly used as a measure of social position in preference to the traditional marker of occupation. Goldblatt (1990) found a connection between mortality and both tenure and car ownership. Tenure, of rather the lack of tenure, is also important in that homelessness has been found to be linked with a number of health problems – the life expectancy of the street homeless has been estimated to be 42 years (Grenier 1996), lower than in Sub-Saharan Africa. It should also be noted that while there has been a dramatic rise in the number of owner occupiers in Britain in the last two decades, there has also been a striking increase in the number of homeless people (Dorling 1995).

To summarise the findings of this literature, although patterns are not entirely the same for different causes of death, for males and females and for different age groups, these studies of the geographical patterns of mortality in Britain clearly indicate that there is a strong north/south and urban/rural divide in health in Britain. These patterns in mortality are also generally reflected in patterns in morbidity (Blaxter 1990, Haynes 1991, Gould and Jones 1996). Moreover, several studies indicate that in recent years the difference is becoming greater – that there is polarisation of mortality between areas. Britton (1990) notes that over the period 1979–1983 the familiar northwest/southeast gradient in mortality was becoming more pronounced, and other authors have also reported this pattern of polarisation (Phillimore *et al.* 1994, Staines and Cartright 1994, Congdon 1995). Bryce *et al.* (1994) report that although mortality as a result of coronary heart disease is falling overall, geographical inequalities are increasing, at least for older people. In reporting widening mortality differentials within the city of Glasgow between 1980–2 and 1990–2, McCarron *et al.* (1994) quantify the extent of polarisation – for men, mortality increased in the most deprived areas by nine per cent whereas in the least deprived areas it *decreased* by 18 per cent. In this chapter we update these studies by considering geographical changes in mortality rates at the local area level for the whole of Britain over the past forty years.

Explanations of geographical patterns in health

Various explanations have been proposed for the geographical patterning of mortality in Britain. A significant debate surrounds the issue of whether these differences are because of people or places, or in other words, the relative contribution of compositional and contextual factors (MacIntyre *et al.* 1993). A number of studies have considered this question. Sloggett and Joshi (1994) used data from the ONS Longitudinal Study to look at whether high mortality in deprived wards was caused by the aggregate effect of personal factors or a community level factor. In terms of years of life lost they found that (what they chose to term) individual factors (such as car access and housing tenure) were stronger predictors than ward of residence. They report:

> For men, the increased risks of death associated with living in such [deprived] areas were entirely explained by the levels of personal disadvantage experienced by the individual. The deprivation effect was therefore entirely due to the concentration of disadvantaged men in the area. (1994: 1471)

Thus they found no residual area effect at ward level. However, they did find higher excess mortality in the North as compared with the South, even after controlling for individual factors, a finding which they chose not to highlight. A number of other studies also report a residual area effect. The Alameda county study in the US reported a residual area effect (Haan *et al.* 1987), as well as various British studies (Charlton *et al.* 1983, Carstairs and Morris 1991, Humphreys and Carr-Hill 1991, Duncan and Jones 1995, Shouls *et al.* 1996). Langford and Bentham (1996) used the technique of multi-level modelling and found that

> . . . even after adjusting for such factors [level of deprivation and area type] there is a distinct regional contrast with areas to the North and the West of an approximate line between the Severn and the Wash showing high levels of all-cause mortality. (1996: 907)

These findings thus lend support to the contextual argument – that health is not only a product of individual characteristics but also determined by the context in which a person lives. Phillimore and Morris (1991) suggest that we need a deeper socio-cultural understanding of what constitutes a 'place' in order to take this further. From their study of two towns with similar levels of social deprivation but varying premature mortality rates, Middlesbrough and Sunderland, they conclude that we need to look beyond general explanations of health inequalities and more closely examine the social and economic histories of particular localities, such as the pattern of deprivation over a number of decades and the provision of social housing. Phillimore (1993) suggests that the characteristics of a place may be as important as the characteristics of people when trying to understand health. He specifically mentions such factors as the industrial environment, internal inequality and lifestyles in a broad sense, including fears, values and beliefs. MacIntyre *et al.* (1993) likewise suggest that it is not just the *level* of deprivation that is important to a place, but the *experience* of that deprivation. However, few have looked at the features of particular places – the social, cultural or economic environment – that affect health by area (MacIntyre *et al.* 1993).

Another debate surrounds the role of migration as a possible explanatory factor of spatial differences in mortality although there are only a few studies which address this issue. It is proposed that geographical differences in health could be produced as a consequence of healthy or unhealthy people being more or less likely to migrate. Britton (1990) reports Longitudinal Study data over the period 1971–1981, finding that migrants who had moved within a county had excess mortality (5–10 per cent) but migrants who moved a longer distance had 10 per cent less mortality, so, in general, the greater the distance moved the lower the mortality. Britton notes that socio-demographic characteristics affect the propensity to move, those with more economic and educational resources tending to move further. Strachan *et al.* (1995) have also used the Longitudinal Study to look at the possibility that regional differences in mortality from ischaemic heart disease and stroke could be the result of migration. They conclude that region of origin and region of adult life were equally related to mortality. Bentham (1984) has also looked at migration as a possible explanation of rural/urban patterns in mortality. He found that there was not a simple gradient of mortality according to whether areas were rural or urban, but that the urban and the most rural places had higher mortality rates than semi-rural areas. This could be explained by certain types of people migrating from rural areas – the young, healthy and better qualified. Thus when considering the relationship of migration to mortality we need to consider not only the individual characteristics of migrants, but also where they move from and where they move to.

Finally, as in the debate regarding inequalities in health in general, there has been some discussion of the artefact explanation – that observed differences are due to measurement. A number of methodological issues have been discussed and investigated in the literature on health inequalities, such as numerator/denominator bias and the ecological fallacy, the use of mortality as an indicator of health, and so on (see for example, Davey Smith *et al.* 1994). The geographical debate has its own measurement issues, such as the need for longitudinal data in order to look at the causes and effects of migration in relation to health. For instance, there is virtually no information on the characteristics of people who have emigrated from Britain.

There is also the issue of changing area boundaries; just as disease classifications change over time, so do geographical boundaries. Administrative boundaries are altered continuously, but the most serious changes were in 1965 to London and in 1974 to the rest of Britain. Within the geographical literature the problem of changing boundaries is addressed many times. (For a summary of the difficulties faced when analysing data by area see Openshaw 1992.) In essence, the problem is that different results are obtained when different boundaries are used to calculate statistics. For instance, if we were to compare changing mortality rates between England and Scotland with Wales, we would assume Britain was becoming more equal, whereas between England and Wales as compared with Scotland, mortality rates are diverging. It is also possible to obtain very different results through only minor changes. The basic solution adopted by most studies is to choose a single geographical definition of areas and freeze that over time. This can only be done if data are available for units small enough to be able to reconstitute the old areas from the new small areas. Fortunately, this is possible in studies of mortality in Britain because since 1981 in England and Wales (and 1974 in Scotland) all mortality records have been stored on computer, with the postcode of the last residence of the deceased attached. Thus mortality rates can be calculated for very small areas, once data from the population censuses are added, and these rates can be combined to produce statistics for administrative areas that no longer exist, but for which statistics were calculated in the past. The main disadvantage of this method is that the areas for which statistics are calculated are no longer in administrative use. However, without taking this approach, no robust comparisons over time can be made.

Data and methods

For this study, changing levels of mortality were calculated for a consistent set of local areas in England, Wales and Scotland for the period from 1950 onwards using official records. The areas used are County Boroughs, and urban and rural remainders of counties existing in 1951. A Geographical Information System was used to monitor boundary changes. The 1971 Census provides a link between 1971 and 1974 administrative geographies for every 1971 enumeration district. This was the main source of information used, along with the manual digitising of other boundaries. Further details are given in a short report published by the Joseph Rowntree Foundation (Dorling 1997) which also gives more details of the statistics quoted here. These are usually either mortality rates expressed as a percentage, or rates standardised to allow for the age-sex structure of the population.

Results

Table 1 below lists those areas where standardised mortality ratios were above average in 1981 and are still rising, showing how many fewer people would have died in those areas in the latest period (1990–92) if the national mortality rates had applied. These are some of the areas being left behind by the general improvement in mortality. Only areas where the ratio has been rising steadily in recent years have been included. The ratios for the early 1950s are included so that a comparison can be made with the past. Exactly the same geographical areas are being considered in each case. The ratios in this study have been constructed on a consistent basis using twelve age and sex groups to classify the population. This has been done because these are the only groups for which sufficient information was available from past publications. If more detailed population breakdowns are used, the results in terms of inequality, become more dramatic. The same is true if smaller geographical areas are used.

The three areas with the highest mortality rates in the 1990s, Oldham, Salford and Greenock, had mortality ratios only a fifth higher than the national average in the early fifties. Table 1 shows that their rates are now rising towards being a third higher than the national rate. The table shows that almost a thousand deaths a year would be avoided, were the mortality rates not excessive, in just these three places. Here excess deaths are calculated as deaths above the average rate, not deaths above the best rate, which would produce far higher numbers and a much more dramatic summary. At the other extreme, the ratio in Plymouth was fairly average at the start of the 1980s but is rising, although it is still less than it was in the early 1950s. Nevertheless, 237 deaths would not have occurred in 1990–92 had the mortality rates in this town been the same as the average rates for England and Wales as a whole.

The figure at the end of the table shows the total number of excess deaths in these areas, deaths which wouldn't have occurred in the last three-year period (1990–92) had the mortality rates not been higher than average. The 22,400 deaths represent 16 per cent of all mortality in these areas. Nationally there were 77,000 such excess deaths representing about four per cent of all mortality.

The total proportion of excess deaths in the country can be calculated for each period for which data are available on a consistent basis using identical

Table 1 *Places where Standardised Mortality Ratios are high and rising in Britain 1981–1992*

Area	Standardised Mortality Ratio				Excess deaths
	1950–53	1981–85	1986–89	1990–92	1990–92
Oldham	120	121	124	131	1102
Salford	121	125	126	131	1161
Greenock	120	123	127	130	696
Manchester	118	117	119	121	3390
Birkenhead	112	112	116	121	1001
Clydebank	112	116	119	120	312
Newcastle upon Tyne	112	112	115	119	1461
Bolton	117	112	113	118	926
Nairn County	102	109	113	117	76
Liverpool	118	115	116	117	3033
Falkirk	108	106	116	117	241
Sunderland	112	107	111	117	693
Hackney	99	109	110	116	581
Smethwick	98	103	110	115	249
rural Stirling County	108	109	113	115	755
Southwark	116	103	110	114	250
Edinburgh	109	108	112	114	2192
Huddersfield	109	110	112	114	646
Bermondsey	104	106	109	114	212
Lambeth	102	110	112	113	632
Zetland County	110	105	107	112	88
Perth Burgh	102	108	111	112	168
rural Durham	108	109	110	111	1475
Great Yarmouth	102	107	110	111	235
Islington	104	105	106	108	350
rural Perth County	98	102	104	106	240
Plymouth	105	102	103	104	237
Total					22400

areas and population groups for each period. This is done in Table 2 for each of the six periods considered, for the whole population and for the two sub-groups in which most premature deaths occur: men and women aged 45–64. The table shows that the overall proportion of excess deaths has remained fairly stable over time at between 4.1 per cent and 4.3 per cent of all deaths. However, for both men and women aged between 45 and 64, the

Table 2 *Excess mortality in Britain by local areas (figures are per hundred deaths)*

Period	All groups	Men 45–64	(change)	Women 45–64	(change)
1950–1953	4.3	7.5		5.6	
1959–1963	4.1	6.9	(−0.6)	5.4	(−0.2)
1969–1973	4.2	7.1	(+0.2)	6.8	(+1.4)
1981–1985	4.2	8.8	(+1.7)	7.8	(+1.0)
1986–1989	4.3	9.8	(+1.0)	8.4	(+0.6)
1990–1992	4.1	9.6	(−0.2)	8.9	(+0.5)

proportion of excess deaths has risen steadily, particularly in the 1980s, after having fallen in the 1960s. A growing proportion of premature deaths in Britain can be attributed to some aspect of rising spatial inequalities. Now almost 10 per cent of deaths to men of these ages occur in areas as an excess over the national mortality rates. The 'all groups' figure conceals this concentration in mortality because of the large and rising proportion of deaths occurring over the age of 65.

Within Britain, premature mortality is becoming more concentrated in certain areas as it also becomes more rare at young ages across Britain nationally. The overall picture is not a simple one: more people are living in areas of average overall mortality, but more are also living in areas of relatively high mortality; the 1980s have seen a deterioration in equality for many age and sex groups although for some (such as women aged 45–65) geographical inequality began to increase earlier.

The Department of Social Security in the publication on households below average income (1996) divides the population into 10 equal sized groups based on income. The same methodology is used here but the population is divided by SMR rather than income. These decile groups can then be compared, and the relative changes in their mortality charted over time. Because the subject of this paper is area inequalities, the population of Britain is divided into 10 groups of areas at each period. Areas are selected according to the standardised mortality rate for people below the age of 65. They do not have to be made up of contiguous areas, nor do they need to be the same areas over time. What is important is that each of the 10 decile areas contains a tenth of the population at the time it was created. Table 3 shows the absolute mortality rate in each of 10 geographically defined equal population sized areas of the country over the study period, not adjusted for their age and sex distribution. Even without allowing for population structure, it is evident that by the end of the period the mortality rate of those aged under 65 living in the worse decile of areas, at 3.25 per thousand, is more than two-thirds higher than that in the best (it was 56 per cent higher in the 1950s and fell to 43 per cent higher in the early 1960s). This rate is still

Table 3 *Absolute mortality rate per 1000 of the population at risk aged under 65 by decile area*

Population decile	1950–53	1959–63	1969–73	1981–85	1986–89	1990–92
1	5.72	5.20	5.01	4.10	3.61	3.25
2	5.22	4.86	4.46	3.58	3.20	2.89
3	5.13	4.52	4.30	3.48	3.05	2.68
4	4.71	4.49	4.06	3.31	2.88	2.56
5	4.64	4.25	3.96	3.12	2.73	2.45
6	4.46	4.08	3.72	2.93	2.62	2.27
7	4.17	3.73	3.58	2.79	2.45	2.27
8	4.01	3.82	3.41	2.68	2.44	2.19
9	3.86	3.70	3.31	2.60	2.29	2.05
10	3.68	3.64	3.07	2.38	2.15	1.94

worse than that experienced by people living in the best areas 20 years earlier (3.07 per thousand). There has thus been no convergence in mortality rates between these equal sized groups of the population.

When the mortality rates are corrected to allow for the differences in the population structure of each group, the divergence in mortality rates by area becomes even more evident, as Table 4 shows. The 10 per cent of people living in the highest mortality areas of the country have the worst ever recorded relative mortality rates in the most recent period, with an SMR of 142.3. Since 1981 the standardised mortality ratio of this group has

Table 4 *Age Sex Standardised Mortality ratio for deaths at ages under 65 by decile area*

Population decile	1950–53	1959–63	1969–73	1981–85	1986–89	1990–92
1	131.0	135.5	131.2	135.0	139.2	142.3
2	118.1	123.0	115.6	118.6	120.9	121.4
3	112.1	116.5	112.0	114.2	113.9	111.3
4	107.0	110.7	108.1	109.8	106.9	104.9
5	102.5	104.5	103.0	102.1	102.2	99.0
6	98.6	97.4	96.9	95.7	95.6	93.5
7	93.1	90.9	91.8	91.6	91.9	90.9
8	88.7	87.6	88.9	89.3	89.1	86.5
9	85.7	83.1	87.0	84.3	83.0	80.4
10	81.8	77.1	83.0	79.2	78.1	76.2

risen by 7.4 percentage points and that of the second decile of the population has risen by 2.7 per cent. All other decile groups have seen their relative mortality rates fall over this period. When standardised for age and sex distributions, people living in the worst tenth of areas of Britain are 42 per cent more likely to die before age 65 than the average person. In the 1950s they were 31 per cent more likely to die than average, while people in the best areas were 18 per cent better off in terms of their relative life chances. Mortality rates are now 24 per cent below average for people living in the best decile area. The gap is clearly growing.

Conclusion

This study supports the findings of the studies cited above. By using a consistent and detailed national geography we have found that in recent years mortality rates by area have been polarising in Britain and, further, that this pattern of excess mortality is very similar for men and women. Indeed, the extent of inequality in mortality in Britain is so strong that, if the Registrar General of 1951 were to repeat the study of mortality carried out then, he would no doubt be shocked by the extent, persistence and widening of the basic divided in British society. Moreover, using a set of consistent geographical boundaries this pattern of polarisation is not a statistical artefact, and because the areas are smaller than regions and counties the polarisation found is more extreme.

Why construct consistent boundaries? If we make efforts to ensure 'good data', we not only minimise the possibility of artefactual explanations, but we are then in a position to move on to discuss possible explanatory factors, in this case, to what extent geographical patterns in mortality are due to the characteristics of people, places or migration. Further studies are needed to assess the relative contribution of these various factors. Such studies should address the extent to which this observed polarisation in mortality is due to changes in the socioeconomic circumstances of individuals, to contextual factors which have altered places, or to differential migration. There is also the important question as to why these changes have occurred.

Geographical inequalities in health are not simply a passive reflection of social inequalities, although social inequalities lie behind a large part of the map of health in Britain. For instance, particular health damaging effects, such as traffic accidents, have a very marked geography (being more prevalent among rural populations). Most important, recent *changes* to the geography of health in Britain – falling mortality rates in remote rural areas and rising mortality rates in London boroughs, for instance (Dorling 1997) – do not mirror changes in the social class composition of these areas as it is conventionally measured. Social classes have actually become slightly more evenly mixed over space in 1990s Britain (Dorling and Woodward 1996). There are many reasons why this mismatch of geographical and social changes might be so, which the authors of this paper are currently investigating.

The evidence we have presented of increasing polarisation shows that, at least until 1992, the government was not on target to reach its commitment to reduce geographical inequalities in health by the year 2000 (Target 1 of the WHO targets for countries in the European Region). Yet as Davey Smith (1993) points out, the fact that mortality rates vary temporally and geographically means that reduction *is* possible. Knowing that something needs to be done and that something can be done about geographical inequalities in health provides us with a solid basis for considering the best ways of reducing such inequalities. Although many interventions are possible the most direct approach is to improve the health service. An increase of NHS funds to areas with high mortality, although preferably not at the expense of other areas, may well be one effective policy. However, this is only likely to be part of the solution. Increases in resources and services do not necessarily result in an increase in use of those services. Differences in health by tenure also suggest the need for the specific targeting of resources and community-based health services, and also indicate the need for other measures such as an improvement in housing and in neighbourhood facilities and services. These are only some of the measures that might be considered. There are likely to be others, in particular interventions based on the finding that deprivation is strongly linked to early mortality. As we move from analysis of data and consideration of validity issues to an exploration of the reasons for the patterns found, we can increasingly suggest ways of reducing those inequalities as well as describing them.

Acknowledgements

This research was conducted under ESRC grant number L128251009.

References

Ben-Shlomo, Y., White, I. and Marmot, M. (1996) Does the variation in the socioeconomic characteristics of an area affect mortality? *British Medical Journal*, 312, 13–14.

Bentham, (1984) Mortality rates in the rural areas of England and Wales. *Area*, 16, 219–26.

Blaxter, M. (1990) *Health and Lifestyles*. London: Routledge.

Britton, M. (ed) (1990) *Mortality and Geography: a Review in the mid-1980s, England and Wales*. OPCS, Series DS No. 9, London: HMSO.

Bryce, C., Curtis, S., and Mohan, J. (1994) Coronary heart disease: trends in spatial inequalities and implications for health care planning in England, *Social Science and Medicine*, 38, 5, 677–90.

Carstairs, V. and Morris, R. (1991) *Deprivation and Health in Scotland.* Aberdeen: Aberdeen University Press.

Charlton, J.R.H., Hartley, R.M., Silver, R. and Holland, W.W. (1983) Geographical variations in mortality from conditions amenable to medical intervention, *The Lancet*, March 26, 691–6.

Congdon, P. (1995) The impact of area context on long term illness and premature mortality: regional comparisons across England, *Regional Studies*, 29, 327–44.

Curtis, S. and Taket, A. (1996) *Health and Societies: Changing Perspectives.* London: Arnold.

Davey Smith, G. (1993) Socioeconomic differentials in wealth and health: widening inequalities in health – the legacy of the Thatcher years, *British Medical Journal*, 307, 1085–6.

Davey Smith, G., Blane, D. and Bartley, M. (1994) Explanations for socio-economic differentials in mortality: evidence from Britain and elsewhere, *European Journal of Public Health*, 4, 131–44.

Department of Health and Social Security (1980) *Inequalities in Health: Report of a Research Working Group.* London: DHSS.

Department of Social Security (1996) *Households Below Average Income: Methodological Review.* Report of a working party, Analytical Services Division.

Dorling, D. (1995) *A New Social Atlas of Britain.* Chichester: Wiley.

Dorling, D. (1997) *Changing Life Chances in Britain 1950–1990.* York: Joseph Rowntree Foundation.

Dorling, D. and Woodward, R. (1996) *Social Polarisation 1971–1991: a Micro-geographical Analysis of Britain.* Monograph in the *Progress in Planning* Series, 45, 2, 1–67.

Duncan, C. and Jones, K. (1995) Individuals and their ecologies: analysing the geography of chronic illness within a multilevel modelling framework, *Journal of Health and Place*, 1, 27–40.

Eames, M., Ben-Shlomo, Y. and Marmot, M.G. (1993) Social deprivation and premature mortality: regional comparisons across England, *British Medical Journal*, 307, 1097–102.

Farr, W. (1885) *Vital Statistics.* London:

Fox, A.J. and Goldblatt, P.O. (1982) *Longitudinal Study: Socio-demographic Mortality Differentials.* OPCS Series LS No. 1, London: HMSO.

Goldblatt, P. (1990) Mortality and alternative social classifications. In Goldblatt, P. (ed) *Longitudinal Study: Mortality and Social Organisation 1971–1981*, 164–92, OPCS Series LS No. 6, London: HMSO.

Gordon, R. and Sutherland, R. (1987) Equality in death: disappearance of differences in post-neonatal mortality between northern and southern regions in England and Wales, *British Medical Journal*, 295, 528–9.

Gould, M. and Jones, K. (1996) Analysing perceived limiting long-term illness using UK census microdata, *Social Science and Medicine*, 42, 6, 857–69.

Grenier, P. (1996) *Still Dying for a Home.* London: Crisis.

Haan, M., Kaplan, G. and Camacho, T. (1987) Poverty and health: prospective evidence from the Alameda County Study, *American Journal of Epidemiology*, 125, 6, 989–98.

Haynes, R. (1991) Inequalities in health and health service use: evidence from the General Household Survey, *Social Science and Medicine*, 33, 4, 361–8.

Howe, G.M. (1986) Does it matter where I live? *Transactions of the Institute of British Geographers*, 11, 387–414.

Humphreys, K. and Carr-Hill, R. (1991) Area variations in health outcomes: artefact or ecology? *International Journal of Epidemiology*, 20, 1, 251–8.

Illsley, R. and Le Grand, J. (1993) Regional inequalities in mortality, *Journal of Epidemiology and Community Health*, 47, 444–9.

Jones, D.R. and Goldblatt, P.O. (1996) Social and environmental epidemiology in the inner city: some leads from the OPCS longitudinal study, *The Statistician*, 39, 247–75.

Kaminski, M., Bouvier-Colle, M.-H. and Blondel, B. (1986) *Mortalite des Jeunes dans les Pays de la Communaute Europeeane (de la Naissance a 24 Ans)*. Paris: Doin.

Langford, I.H. and Bentham, G. (1996) Regional variations in mortality rates in England and Wales: an analysis using multi-level modelling, *Social Science and Medicine*, 42, 6, 897–908.

McCarron, P., Davey Smith, G. and Womersley, J. (1994) Deprivation and mortality in Glasgow: changes from 1980 to 1992, *British Medical Journal*, 309, 1481–2.

MacIntyre, S., MacIver, S. and Soomans, A. (1993) Area, class and health: should we be focusing on places or people? *Journal of Social Policy*, 22, 2, 213–34.

Openshaw, S. (1992) Developing appropriate spatial analytical methods for GIS. In Maguire, D.J., Goodchild, M.R. and Rhind, D.E. (eds) *Geographical Information Systems: Principles and Applications*. Harlow: Longman Scientific and Technical.

Phillimore, P. (1993) How do places shape health? Rethinking locality and lifestyle in North-East England. In Platt, S., Thomas, H., Scott, S. and Williams, G. *Locating Health: Sociological and Historical Explanations*. Aldershot: Avebury.

Phillimore, P.K. and Morris, D. (1991) Discrepant legacies: premature mortality in two industrial towns, *Social Science and Medicine*, 33, 2, 139–52.

Phillimore, P. and Reading, R. (1991) A rural advantage? Urban-rural health differences in northern England, *Journal of Public Health Medicine*, 14, 3, 290–9.

Phillimore, P., Beattie, A. and Townsend, P. (1994) Widening inequality in health in Northern England, 1981/91, *British Medical Journal*, 308, 1125–8.

Robinson, D. and Pinch, S. (1987) A geographical analysis of the relationship between early childhood death and socio-economic environment in an English city, *Social Science and Medicine*, 25, 1, 9–18.

Saunderson, T.R. and Langford, I.H. (1996) A study of the geographical distribution of suicide rates in England and Wales 1989–92 using empirical Bayes estimates, *Social Science and Medicine*, 43, 4, 489–502.

Shouls, S., Congdon, P. and Curtis, S. (1996) Modelling inequality in reported long term illness in the UK: combining individual and area characteristics, *Journal of Epidemiology and Community Health*, 50, 366–76.

Skrimshire, A. (1978) *Area Disadvantage, Social Class and the Health Service*. Oxford: University of Oxford, Department of Social and Administrative Studies.

Sloggett, A. and Joshi, H. (1994) Higher mortality in deprived areas: community or personal disadvantage? *British Medical Journal*, 309, 1470–4.

Staines, A. and Cartright, R. (1994) Deprivation and mortality in Yorkshire: changes from 1981–91, *Journal of Epidemiology and Community Health*, 49 (Suppl.) S79.

Strachan, D.P., Leon, D.A. and Dodgeon, B. (1995) Mortality from cardiovascular disease among interregional migrants in England and Wales, *British Medical Journal*, 310, 423–7.

Townsend, P., Simpson, D. and Tibbs, N. (1984) *Inequalities of Health in the City of Bristol*. Bristol: Department of Social Administration, University of Bristol.

Townsend, P., Phillimore, P. and Beattie, A. (1988) *Health and Deprivation: Inequality and the North*. London: Croom Helm.

Watt, I.S., Franks, A.J. and Sheldon, T.A. (1994) Health and health care of rural populations in the UK: is it better or worse? *Journal of Epidemiology and Community Health*, 48, 16–21.

Wilkinson, R. (1992) Income distribution and life expectancy, *British Medical Journal*, 304, 165–8.

World Bank (1993) *World Development Report 1993: Investing in Health*. Oxford: Oxford University Press.

7. Genetic, cultural or socio-economic vulnerability? Explaining ethnic inequalities in health

James Y. Nazroo

Introduction

Over the last three decades there has been considerable interest in both class inequalities in health and the health of ethnic minority populations. A relatively early, but key, publication in both of these fields has influenced the direction they took – the Black Report (Townsend and Davidson 1982) on class inequalities in health and Marmot *et al.*'s (1984) study of immigrant mortality. Importantly, these two pieces of work came to quite different conclusions. The Black Report placed emphasis on material explanations for class inequalities in health, which, given the class locations of ethnic minority people at that time (Brown 1984), would suggest that such issues might also be relevant to ethnic inequalities in health. However, the data published on immigrant mortality rates, a few years after the Black Report, indicated that class and, consequently, material explanations were unrelated to mortality rates for most migrant groups, and made no contribution to the higher mortality rates found among those who had migrated to Britain (Marmot *et al.* 1984). Indeed, for one group, those born in the 'Caribbean Commonwealth', the relationship between class and overall mortality rates was the opposite of that for the general population. Marmot *et al.* concluded:

> (a) that differences in social class distribution are not the explanation of the overall different mortality of migrants; and (b) the relation of social class (as usually defined) to mortality is different among immigrant groups from the England and Wales pattern. (1984: 21)

The two fields have subsequently taken quite different directions. Those interested in class inequalities have, on the whole, concentrated on providing additional evidence for a material explanation and on unpacking the mechanisms that might link material disadvantage with a greater risk of poor health (*e.g.* Macintyre 1997, Vågerö and Illsley 1995, Davey Smith *et al.* 1994, Lundeberg 1991). While, with a few notable exceptions (Ahmad *et al.* 1989, Fenton *et al.* 1995, Smaje 1995, Harding and Maxwell 1997), class has largely disappeared from investigations into the relationship between ethnicity and health, particularly in the UK. For example, in an overview of existing data produced for the NHS Executive and NHS Ethnic Health

Unit, there is no mention of class, even though there is some discussion of other demographic features of the ethnic minority population of Britain (Balarajan and Soni Raleigh 1995).

In contrast to Marmot *et al.*'s (1984) data, work in the US (Rogers 1992, Sterling *et al.* 1993, Davey Smith *et al.* 1996, 1997a) and recent work in the UK has suggested both that material factors are relevant to the health of ethnic minority people and that they make the key contribution to differences in health between different ethnic groups (Nazroo 1997a). The work undertaken in the UK was based on a nationally representative survey of ethnic minority and white people living in England and Wales (the *Fourth National Survey of Ethnic Minorities*) that was identified through a process of focused enumeration (Brown and Ritchie 1981, Smith and Prior 1997). One or two adults in the identified households underwent a structured face-to-face interview conducted by an ethnically matched interviewer in the language of the respondents' choice. In addition to physical (Nazroo 1997a) and mental health (Nazroo 1997b), the questionnaire covered a comprehensive range of information on both ethnicity and other aspects of the lives of ethnic minority people, including demographic and socio-economic factors (see Modood *et al.* 1997 for a full report on these data). Its novel findings were, at least in part, a reflection of its methodological strengths and the depth of the data collected.

In some ways, findings suggesting a material base for ethnic inequalities in health run counter to the wider sociological literature on ethnicity and 'race'. Although, within this work there appears to be complete agreement that 'race' is a concept without scientific validity (see, for example, the collected works of Barot 1996) – an artificial construct, used to justify the hierarchical ordering of groups of people and the exploitation of 'inferior races' – in contrast, most writers give credence to a notion of ethnicity, which reflects self-identification with cultural traditions that both provide strength and meaning, and boundaries (perhaps fluid) between groups. So, although socio-economic disadvantage might contribute to health differences, it is suggested that there remains an essential component to ethnicity that could make a major contribution to differences in health, that when explaining the relationship between ethnicity and health, ethnicity cannot be 'simply emptied into class disadvantage' (Smaje, 1996).

This chapter sets out to explore in more detail these various approaches to understanding the relationship between ethnicity and health and some of the implications of these for policy. Data from the *Fourth National Survey* will be used to illustrate the points made.

Un-theorised ethnicity – epidemiological approaches

Researchers and commentators in the field of ethnicity and health seem divided over whether this work should be empirically or theoretically driven. Not surprisingly, those with a more epidemiological bent tend to argue for the former. If differences in rates of disease are present between groups that have been identified on the basis of an emergent 'ethnic' classification, these differences will provide a useful starting point for the identification and exploration of aetiological factors associated with those groups at higher risk. For example, Senior and Bhopal state:

> Epidemiology is the study of the distribution and determinants of disease. The main method of study, particularly for investigating the causes of disease, is to compare populations with different risks of disease.
> Ethnicity is a variable that is used increasingly to define populations for epidemiological studies. (1994: 327)

A good example of this approach can be found in the work of McKeigue and colleagues (e.g. McKeigue et al. 1988, 1989 and 1991). This focuses on a particular disease (Coronary Heart Disease – CHD), rather than health per se, and uses the variation in the pattern of this disease across ethnic groups to provide clues for an understanding of its aetiology.

If the empirically driven approach of this work is accepted, criticism inevitably falls to the accuracy with which key variables are measured. Most epidemiological research on health and ethnicity has taken a crude approach to the allocation of individuals into ethnic groups. As might be expected, because country of birth is recorded on death certificates and in the census, much of the published data in this area have allocated ethnicity according to country of birth, a strategy that is clearly limited. In addition, many studies use 'ethnic' groupings with quite inappropriate boundaries, such as Black or South Asian. The data are then interpreted as though the individuals within them are ethnically (i.e. genetically and culturally) homogeneous, even though such categories are heterogeneous, containing ethnic groups with different cultures, religions, migration histories, and geographical and socio-economic locations (see Bagley's (1995) comments on a similar situation in the US).

Such criticisms lead to a focus on the technical problems with assigning individuals to ethnic categories during the research process, and a concern with such things as: collecting sufficiently detailed information to differentiate between distinct groups; recording ethnic background in a consistent way; and dealing with issues such as mixed parentage (see Chaturvedi and McKeigue's (1994) comments on the British data, and McKenney and Bennett's (1994) comments on the data provided by the US Bureau of the Census). Solutions proposed involve more sensitive strategies for collecting information on ethnicity, for example by allowing individuals to define their ethnic group in their own terms. It is argued that this reduces the use of groups which are artefactual and without 'real' meaning (Aspinall 1995) and avoids the construction of ethnic boundaries on the basis of the racist assumptions of researchers (Sheldon and Parker 1992). (Although in most research using this model respondents are offered only a limited number of categories to choose from.)

In apparent support of this position, recent work based on the *Fourth National Survey* (Nazroo, 1997a) has shown that a more detailed approach to the assignment of individuals into ethnic groups reveals important additional differences between them. In that survey, individual respondents could be allocated into particular ethnic groups on the basis of a number of criteria. Figure 1 uses a categorisation based on the respondents' replies to a question on the country of their family origin. It shows the relative risk compared with whites for reporting fair or poor general health for various ethnic minority groups. (Relative risk is the chance of the member of a group having a particular attribute compared with a member of a reference group – in this case whites. In Figure 1, and subsequent figures, the relative risk for each minority group is represented as the range within which there is a 95 per cent statistical probability of the true value lying, with the mid point of the range also indicated. If the range does not cross the solid line at the value of '1', the value for the comparison white group, differences are, of course, statistically significant.) If the first three groups are examined, the data show that the use of an overall ethnic minority group obscures important differences between Caribbeans and South Asians. And, if the final four groups are compared, the data show that the use of an overall South Asian group obscures important differences between Indians on the one hand and Pakistanis and Bangladeshis on the other.

Of course, the refining of our ethnic classification need not stop here. For example, those ethnic minority people with Indian family origins are ethnically very diverse. They can be broadly divided into at least three cultural/geographical groups: Hindus from the Gujarati region of India; Sikhs from the Punjabi region of India; and Muslims from a number of areas. Figure 2 shows how the rate of reported fair or poor health compared with whites varied across these three groups, identified on the basis of their religion, and a fourth, Christian Indians. It suggests that the health experience of Indians also varies along religious/cultural lines, with Muslims appearing to have worse health than the other groups (although the differences shown are not statistically significant).

Similar refinements can be made for the other ethnic groups included in Figure 1, for example Caribbeans can be divided into African and Indian Caribbeans, and whites can be divided in many ways. The implication of these figures is that further refining the assessment of ethnicity used in epidemiological research will improve its power. More accurate assignments of ethnicity reveal additional differences and should allow a more careful generation of aetiological hypotheses and a more finely tuned programme for intervention.

It is here that the lack of theoretical work done by such researchers becomes important. Despite this lack, it is a mistake to assume that the

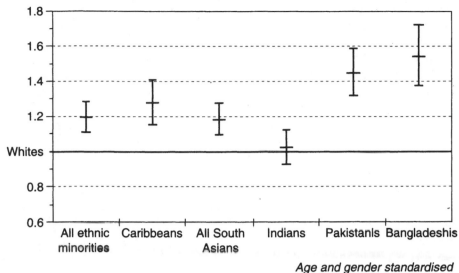

Figure 1: *Relative risk of reporting fair or poor health compared with whites*

process of identifying 'ethnic' groups is theoretically neutral (hence my use of the term 'un-theorised' rather than atheoretical). Take the example of Marmot *et al.*'s (1984) immigrant mortality study, which in some ways could be seen as opportunistic, being based on the combination of country of birth data that is recorded on death certificates and at the 1981 Census. When discussing the rationale for their analysis, Marmot *et al.* have in mind a clear notion of the significance of their 'country of birth' variable:

> Comparisons of disease rates between immigrants and non-immigrants in the 'old' country, between immigrants and residents of the 'new' country, and between different immigrant groups in the new country have helped elucidate the relative importance of genetic and environmental factors in many diseases. (1984: 4)

And, in his discussion of equivalent data relating to the period covered by the 1991 Census, Balarajan suggests that differences could be due to 'biological, cultural, religious, socio-economic or other environmental factors' (1995: 119).

However, in this work these explanatory factors are rarely assessed with any accuracy and the search for clues regarding aetiology is typically done with a focus on the *assumed* genetic or cultural characteristics of individuals within the ethnic group at greater risk. Consequently, explanations tend to fall to unmeasured genetic and cultural factors based on stereotypes, because such meanings are easily imposed on ethnic categorisations (see Bhopal (1997) for a critique of this 'Black Box' approach to epidemiology).

Theory is brought in surreptitiously – ethnicity, however measured, equals genetic or cultural heritage. This then leads to a form of victim blaming, where the *inherent* characteristics of the ethnic (minority) group are seen to be at fault and in need to rectifying (Sheldon and Parker 1992). It is the ways in which ethnic and racial groups are constructed during this process, and the kinds of attributes focused on, that raise a concern with racialisation.

An example of this can be found in the well publicised greater risk of 'South Asians' for CHD. A *British Medical Journal* editorial (Gupta *et al.* 1995) used research findings to attribute this problem to a combination of genetic (*i.e.* 'race') and cultural (*i.e.* ethnicity) factors that are apparently associated with being 'South Asian'. Concerning genetic factors, the suggestion was that 'South Asians' have a shared evolutionary history that involved adaptation 'to survive under conditions of periodic famine and low energy intake'. This resulted in the development of 'insulin resistance syndrome', which apparently underlies 'South Asians'' greater risk of CHD. From this perspective 'South Asians' can be viewed as a genetically distinct group with a unique evolutionary history – a 'race'. In terms of cultural factors, the use of ghee in cooking, a lack of physical exercise and a reluctance to use health services were all mentioned – even though ghee is not used by all of the ethnic groups that comprise 'South Asians', and evidence suggests that 'South Asians' do understand the importance of exercise (Beishon and Nazroo 1997) and do use medical services (Nazroo 1997a, Rudat 1994). It is important to note how the policy recommendations flowing from such an approach underline the extent to which the issue has become racialised. The authors of the editorial recommend that 'community leaders' and 'survivors' of heart attacks should spread the message among their communities and that 'South Asians' should be encouraged to undertake healthier lifestyles (Gupta *et al.* 1995). The problem is, apparently, viewed as something inherent to being 'South Asian', nothing to do with the context of the lives of 'South Asians' and as only solvable if 'South Asians' are encouraged to modify their behaviours to address their genetic and cultural weaknesses.

Given this risk of racialisation, it is not helpful to refine an ethnic classification scheme in a way that allows further assumptions to be made about the importance of culture and genetics when neither are measured, and environment continues to be ignored. For example, analysis of the *Fourth National Survey* showed that, while a South Asian group had a greater risk of indicators of CHD, once the group was broken down into constituent parts, this only applied to Pakistanis and Bangladeshis – Indians had the same rate as whites (Nazroo 1997a). In addition, within the Indian group Muslims had a high rate of indicators of CHD, while Hindus and Sikhs had low rates (producing very similar findings to those shown for reported general health in Figures 1 and 2). While this approach was useful in uncovering the extent to which convenient assumptions of similarity within

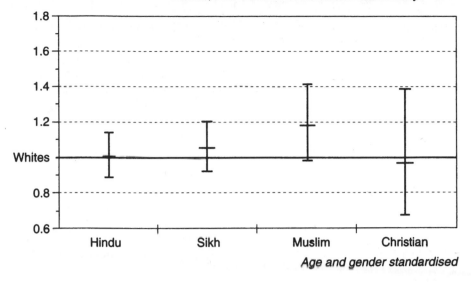

Figure 2: *Relative risk of reporting fair or poor health compared with whites –
Indians only*

obviously heterogeneous groups were false, it could be suggested that these
findings mean we can use the term 'Muslim heart disease', or 'Pakistani and
Bangladeshi heart disease', rather than 'South Asian heart disease', to
describe the situation. And explanations can be sought in assumptions
about Muslim, Pakistani and Bangladeshi cultural practices or their shared
evolutionary history. This potential results from the use of un-theorised and
apparently emergent ethnic classifications that allow ethnicity to be treated
as a *natural and fixed* division between social groups, and the *description* of
ethnic variations in health to become their *explanation* (Sheldon and Parker,
1992). Explanations are, consequently, based on cultural stereotypes or suppositions about genetic differences, rather than attempting directly to assess
the nature and importance of such factors, the contexts in which they operate and their association with health outcomes.

So, in addition to refining our measurement of ethnicity, in order to
progress we need to examine the degree to which the indicator used (country
of birth, country of family origin, self-assigned ethnic groups, etc.) reflects
an underlying construct (Williams *et al.* 1994, Bagley 1995, McKenzie and
Crowcroft 1996) – are we measuring genetics, biology, culture, lifestyle, the
consequences of racialisation, socio-economic position etc., and are the indicators used appropriate to whichever of these we are concerned with?

Ethnicity as structure – socio–economic status

As implied in the introduction, one of the key contexts relevant to the relationship between ethnicity and health should be socio-economic position. Indeed, findings from the *Fourth National Survey*, shown in Table 1, suggest important differences between different ethnic groups in socio-economic positions. Overall, there were few differences between the white and Indian groups, but Caribbeans, Pakistanis and Bangladeshis were, to varying degrees, worse off than the other two groups. Interestingly, these differences mirror those for health shown in Figure 1.

However, following Marmot *et al.*'s (1984) analysis, rather than puzzling over why such an important explanation for inequalities in health among the general population did not apply to ethnic minorities, researchers have ignored class and simply accepted that different sets of explanations for poor health apply to the ethnic minority and majority populations. In fact, there are a number of reasons why class effects might be suppressed in immigrant mortality data. Most important is that Marmot *et al.* (1984) had to use occupation as recorded on death certificates to define social class. The inflating of occupational status (where, according to Townsend and Davidson (1982), occupation is recorded on death certificates as the 'skilled' job held for most of the individual's life rather than the 'unskilled' job held for the last few years of life, will be particularly significant for immigrant mortality data if migration to Britain were associated with downward social mobility for members of ethnic minority groups, a process that both Smith (1977) and Heath and Ridge (1983) have documented. So, the occupation recorded on the death certificates of migrants may well be an inaccurate reflection of their experience in Britain prior to death. In addition, given the socio-economic profile of ethnic minority groups in Britain, this inflation of occupational status would only need to happen in relatively few cases for the figures representing the small population in higher classes to be distorted

Table 1   *Ethnic differences in socio-economic position*

	White %	Caribbean	Indian	Pakistani	Bangladeshi
Registrar General's Class					
I/II	35	22	32	20	11
IIIn	15	18	20	15	18
IIIm	31	30	22	32	32
IV/V	20	30	26	33	40
Unemployed	11	24	15	38	42

upwards. For example, Table 3.7 in Marmot *et al.* (1984) reports only 212 deaths occurring in the class I group to those born in the Indian sub-continent in 1970–72, and only 37 for those born in the Caribbean.

In fact, data from the *Fourth National Survey* suggest that class effects are similar for ethnic minority and white people. Figure 3 shows the relationship between class and reporting fair or poor health for different ethnic groups. (Here a distinction has been drawn between households that are manual and those that are non-manual, according to the Registrar General's criteria, and a third group of respondents from households containing no full-time worker has also been identified. Those aged 65 or older have not been included in any of the socio-economic analyses.) There was a clear and strong relationship between class and health for all the ethnic groups covered.

Others have presented similar findings, both in smaller scale regional studies (*e.g.* Fenton *et al.* 1995) and in the most recent analysis of immigrant mortality data (Harding and Maxwell 1997). The implication of this is clear, the second conclusion drawn by Marmot *et al.* (1984), that social class has a different relationship to health for ethnic minority compared to majority people, is not supported. However, a closer examination of the Figure suggests that their first conclusion, that differences in social class distribution do not explain ethnic differences in health, is supported. For example, within each class group Pakistanis and Bangladeshis (who Figure 1 suggests have the poorest health) were more likely than equivalent whites to report fair or poor health, and the same is true for non-manual and manual Caribbeans (who overall also had poorer health than whites). Similarly, the most recent analysis of immigrant mortality data found that adjustments for occupational class made little change to the differences between groups, despite finding a class gradient within country of birth groups, leading the authors to conclude that: 'social class is not an adequate explanation for the patterns of excess mortality observed [among migrant groups]' (Harding and Maxwell 1997: 120). The implication of both sets of data is that there remains some unidentified component of ethnicity that increases (some) ethnic minority groups' risk of poor health. It is tempting to reduce this unexplained variance to assumed cultural or genetic factors.

However, this interpretation is misleading. There has been an increasing recognition of the limitations of traditional class groupings, which are far from internally homogeneous. A number of studies have drawn attention to variations in income levels and death rates among occupations that comprise particular occupational classes (*e.g.* Davey Smith *et al.* 1990). And within an occupational group, ethnic minorities may be more likely to be found in lower or less prestigious occupational grades, to have poorer job security, to endure more stressful working conditions and to be more likely to work unsocial hours. Evidence from the *Fourth National Survey* illustrates this point clearly. Table 5.2 in Nazroo (1997a) showed that ethnic

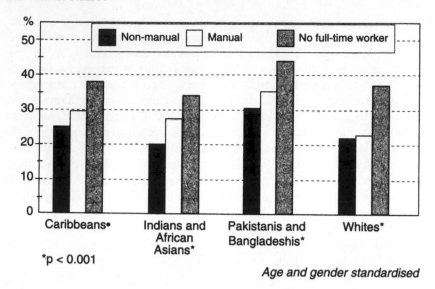

*p < 0.001

Age and gender standardised

Figure 3: *Reported fair or poor health by ethnic group and class*

minority people had a lower income than white people in the same class, that unemployed ethnic minority people had been unemployed for longer than equivalent white people, and that some ethnic minority groups had poorer quality housing than whites regardless of tenure. Similar findings have been reported in the US (Lillie-Blanton and Laveist 1996, Williams *et al.* 1994). The conclusion to be drawn is that, while standard indicators of socio-economic status have some use for making comparisons *within* ethnic groups, they are of little use for 'controlling out' the impact of socio-economic differences when attempting to reveal a pure 'ethnic/race' effect.

Figure 4 provides additional support for this conclusion. It shows changes in the relative risk of reporting fair or poor health for Pakistanis and Bangladeshis (the groups with the poorest health) compared with whites once the data had been standardised for a variety of socio-economic factors. Comparing the first bar with the second and third shows that standardising for class and tenure makes no difference. However, taking account of an indicator of 'standard of living' (a more direct reflection of the material circumstances of respondents – see Nazroo (1997a) for full details, leads to a large reduction in the relative risk (compare the first and last bars). Given that this indicator is also not perfect for taking account of ethnic differences in socio-economic status (see Table 5.4 in Nazroo 1997), such a finding suggests that socio-economic differences, in fact, make a large and key contribution to ethnic inequalities in health.

Another problem with using data that have been standardised for socio-economic status is worth highlighting. Such an approach to analysis and interpretation regards socio-economic status as a confounding factor (McKenzie and Crowcroft 1996) that needs to be controlled out to reveal the 'true' relationship between ethnicity and health. This results in the importance of socio-economic factors becoming obscured and their explanatory role lost. So, as described above, the presentation of 'standardised' data leaves both the author and reader to assume that all that is left is an 'ethnic/race' effect, be that cultural or genetic. Again, this gives the impression that different types of explanation operate for ethnic minority groups compared with the general population. While, for the latter, factors relating to socio-economic status are shown to be crucial, for the former, they are not visible, so differences are assumed to be related to some aspect of ethnicity or 'race', even though, as shown here, socio-economic factors are important determinants of health for all groups. This allows a theory regarding the essential component of ethnicity to be smuggled in to explain a redundancy in a model that claims to, but cannot, fully account for socio-economic factors.

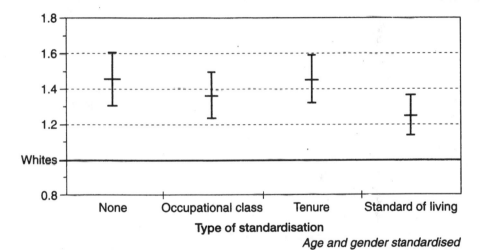

Figure 4: *Relative risk of fair or poor health standardised for socio-economic factors – Pakistanis and Bangladeshis compared with whites*

Here it is also important to remember that, as well as being imperfect, socio-economic indicators do not account for other forms of disadvantage that might play some role in ethnic variations in health. That is, the structural context of ethnicity needs to cover a number of additional issues, including:

1. A lifetime perspective – differences are likely to be a consequence of a lifetime accumulation of disadvantage (Davey Smith *et al.* 1997b), which may be particularly important for migrants who will have been through a

number of lifecourse transitions, and whose childhood might have involved significant deprivation.

2. Living in a racist society – in addition to being directly discriminated against, ethnic minority people know that they are disadvantaged and excluded compared with others, and hence have a clear perception of their relative disadvantage, which, as Wilkinson (1996) has argued, may well have a significant impact on health.

3. Ecological effects – ethnic minority people are concentrated in particular geographical locations that are quite different from those populated by the white majority (Owen 1994) and there is a growing body of work suggesting that the environmental circumstances may have a direct impact on health over and above individual circumstances (Townsend *et al.* 1988, Macintyre *et al.* 1993).

One possible interpretation of the *Fourth National Survey* findings on socio-economic effects is that ethnic inequalities in health can be reduced to socio-economic disadvantage. A position that has been supported by a number of commentators in the field and that raises questions about the legitimacy of using ethnicity as an explanatory variable (Navarro 1990, Sheldon and Parker 1992). This potentially reduces ethnicity to class, and shifts the focus to a concern with how racism leads to the disadvantaged socio-economic positions of 'ethnic minority' groups (see Miles's (1989) comments on this in relation to 'race'), a position that needs additional empirical support. Indeed, as I pointed out in the introduction, others have suggested that regardless of any socio-economic contribution, ethnic inequalities in health cannot be reduced to class, because ethnicity involves far more than this. And, of course, a similar debate is present in the wider literature on ethnicity. Consequently, it is worth considering how ethnicity might be brought back into the picture.

Ethnicity as identity

Smaje (1996) has commented that ethnicity needs to be considered both as identity and as structure. Insofar as ethnic minority status can be equated with various forms of disadvantage, ethnicity is perhaps best viewed as an 'external definition' imposed on ethnic minority people by the majority (Jenkins 1996). In this sense 'ethnicity' is used to signify the 'other', allowing the construction and maintenance of boundaries of exclusion and hierarchical relationships. Although most commentators on such a process of signification have emphasised the role of physical characteristics and the ideological notion of 'race', they recognise that this process also involves cultural characteristics (*e.g.* Miles 1989: 40, Mason 1996: 201). So, although the biological and cultural can be analytically separated, the ideological representations of 'race' and 'ethnicity' overlap, both representing notions of the inherent, inevitable and inferior biological and cultural characteristics of signified groups (Miles 1996). Indeed such a relationship between these two concepts is clearly present in the health field, as the example on CHD previously cited illustrates (Gupta *et al.* 1995). In terms of understanding ethnic inequalities in health, this leads to a focus on the process and origins of 'ethnic' signification (perhaps located in the wider demands of capitalism (Miles 1989)), how this leads to the disadvantaged position of ethnic minority groups, and the links between that (material) disadvantage and poor health.

In terms of ethnic identity, however, others have argued that underlying the 'racist categorisation' imposed on ethnic minority groups lie 'real collectivities, common and distinctive forms of thinking and behaviour, of language, custom, religion and so on; not just modes of oppression but modes of being' (Modood 1996: 95). This is the 'internal definition' where individuals and groups establish their own identity (Jenkins 1996). To emphasise this point, some have attempted to draw a distinction between the notions of 'race' and 'ethnicity'. While the former is a boundary of exclusion imposed on a minority group, the latter is a boundary of inclusion, providing a sense of identity and access to social resources. So relations between ethnic groups 'are not necessarily hierarchical, exploitative and conflictual' (Jenkins 1996: 71). In addition, Modood argues, in the context of his analysis and interpretation of data from the *Fourth National Survey*, that ethnic identity provides a political resource:

> Ethnic identity, like gender and sexuality, has become politicised and for some people has become a primary focus of their politics. There is an ethnic assertiveness, arising out of the feelings of not being respected or lacking access to public space, consisting of counterposing 'positive' images against traditional or dominant stereotypes. It is a politics of projecting identities in order to challenge existing power relations; of seeking not just toleration for ethnic difference but also public acknowledgement, resources and representation. (1997: 290)

In this sense a politicised and mobilised ethnic identity can be construed as a new social movement (Scott 1990) occurring in a vacuum provided by the disappearance of a class-based politics (Gilroy 1987).

It is important to recognise that this notion of ethnicity is also some considerable distance from the immutable and reified elements of 'race'. Ethnic identity cannot be considered as fixed, because culture is not an autonomous and static feature in an individual's life. Cultural traditions are historically located, they occur within particular contexts and change over time, place and person. In addition, ethnicity is only one element of identity, whose significance depends on the context within which the individual finds him/herself. For example, gender and class are also important and in certain situations may be more important. The implication is that there are a range of identities that come into play in different contexts and that identity should be regarded as neither secure nor coherent (Hall 1992).

This conception of ethnic identity promises exciting new avenues to follow in the exploration of the relationship between ethnicity and health. Ethnic identity as a source of pride and political power provides an interesting contrast to ethnicity as a sense of discrimination and relative disadvantage, a contrast which could be of great relevance to Wilkinson's (1996) arguments on the relationship between relative deprivation and health. Indeed, there is evidence to suggest that the concentration of ethnic minority groups in particular locations is protective of health (Smaje 1995), perhaps because this allows the development of a community with a strong ethnic identity that enhances social support and reduces the sense of alienation. Such a conception of ethnic identity also allows a contextualised culture to be brought into view. Identification with cultural traditions that may be both harmful and, now we can separate ethnicity from the outsiders' negative definition, beneficial to health, are of obvious importance to health promotion.

However, the fluid and contextual nature of ethnic identity, and the potential competition between multiple identities, makes this field of enquiry highly complex. For example, Ahmad's (1995) suggestion that we should research the relationship between ethnicity and health with the contextual nature of ethnicity explicitly in mind presents serious methodological problems. This is illustrated by Hahn and Stroup's (1994) suggestions that 'standard scientific criteria' may not apply to the measurement of ethnicity, and fluid ethnic boundaries mean 'fuzzy logic' might apply. Such work is also in its infancy, with virtually no empirical work being undertaken.

The level of complexity can be illustrated by data from the *Fourth National Survey*. Figure 5 shows how rates of smoking – presumably a culturally related practice – vary according to a number of criteria. For simplicity's sake only those with South Asian family origins are included.

The first section of the figure shows that smoking was related to a broadly defined ethnic background. This impression of cultural variation is confirmed if the data are analysed by religion rather than country of family origin (see Nazroo (1997a) Figure 4.14, which shows that among Indians, Sikhs have very low rates of smoking while Muslims have high rates). The next section of the figure suggests that this element of culture is not stable. Those who migrated to Britain aged 11 or older (described as migrants in the figure) reported lower rates of smoking, suggesting that this behaviour is related to differences in the cultural context of migrants' and non-migrants' childhoods. This emphasises the need to contextualise ethnic identity to capture its fluid nature; a need that is further emphasised by both the third and final sections of the figure. The third section shows that gender is also strongly related to smoking, so both ethnic and gender identities need to be considered together. The final section shows that class is also important.

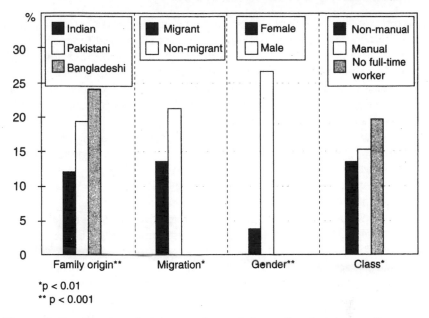

Figure 5: *Smoking by ethnicity, gender and class – South Asians only*

Continuing in the vein of the rest of the paragraph, it would make sense to suggest that this has something to do with a class identity, but class is also an indicator of material circumstances and these may play a more important role. This possibility forces us to reflect back on the interpretation of the other sections of the figure, because they also represent more than just a self-adopted and asserted culture or identity. They correlate with both socio-economic position and external imposed identities. Here the need for data that go far beyond what we currently have available, as Ahmad (1995) has recommended, becomes very apparent.

Conclusion

Following Smaje (1996), I have suggested that to understand the relationship between ethnicity and health we need to theorise ethnicity adequately. This involves recognising ethnicity as both structure and identity; hence the unresolved answer to this paper's title – although current evidence provides more support for a structural-material explanation (Nazroo 1997a). Insofar as ethnic differences in health can be seen as a consequence of class inequalities, the discussion so far indicates that work on the relationship between ethnicity and health has the potential to be at the leading edge of inequalities in health research.

In terms of the cluster of competing and complimentary explanations for inequalities in health, ethnic background is strongly related to most of them. There is variation in the class position of different ethnic minority and majority groups, and this is reflected in differing levels and types of material disadvantage. Ethnic minority groups are discriminated against, and recognise themselves as disadvantaged. This disadvantage not only occurs in the form of a failure to achieve the full potential of economic success, but also in everyday exclusion from elements of white, mainstream, society. Consequently, there is the potential to explore the psychological, as well as material, consequences of disadvantage. Ethnic minority people are concentrated in particular geographical locations and these locations have specific attributes that should allow us to explore both the extent and the nature of an ecological contribution to inequalities in health. Migrant ethnic minority people have been through a number of life-course transitions, some of which would be related to changes in material resources, others to changes in social networks and position in the social hierarchy. Exploring ethnicity also has the potential to allow an examination of the relationship between lifestyle and health and how this might contribute to inequalities. In particular it should allow a dynamic exploration of culture and the relationship between culture, context and class. There are important differences in the social position and expectations of women in different ethnic groups, allowing us to explore issues relating to gender inequalities. And, of course, there are purported differences in the genetic make-up of different ethnic groups.

In terms of methodological issues, exploring ethnic inequalities in health could help resolve a number of problems. Such work relies on indicators of health that are valid across different ethnic groups. Exposing the extent to which the validity of health assessments might vary across ethnic groups raises questions that are applicable to other forms of comparison, such as class and gender. The difficulties of finding indicators of socio-economic status that operate consistently across ethnic groups provides an impetus to be clear about what we mean by the concepts of 'class' and 'material disadvantage' in this research, and how these might apply to other forms of social division, such as gender. And operationalising a concept of ethnicity should make us focus on what we mean by ethnicity and which dimensions of ethnicity might be relevant to inequalities in health.

However, it is worth stepping back for a moment (at least) to reconsider our motives for undertaking work on inequalities in health. In terms of ethnic inequalities in health, I have suggested that motives for the work are related to competing desires to expose the extent and consequences of wider social inequalities, and to uncover aetiological processes, and I have argued that the latter approach has great potential for racialising inequalities in health (Nazroo 1997c). Although at first sight it seems that inequalities in health research are very much concerned with the former, a reconsideration of the preceding sections of this conclusion might suggest otherwise. The tight focus on the pathways that lead from disadvantage to poor health should contribute greatly to our understanding of aetiology. Particularly if we meet the requirement that material causes of inequalities in health must be biologically plausible. And there is no reason why such pathways should be identical for different health outcomes. This focus produces an exclusive concern with inequalities in health as an adverse outcome, and how the complex pathways leading to this outcome can be understood and broken. The root cause, wider social inequalities, becomes obscured from view. The policy implications of this are clear, the more difficult and dramatic interventions to address social inequalities can continue to be avoided and health promotion can focus on improving our understanding of pathways and designing interventions along them. Inequalities in health become a problem requiring technical interventions tailored to individual diseases and individual circumstances, they become a problem for individuals rather than a reflection of social malaise. Williams *et al.*'s comments in this regard are worth citing:

> There is a temptation to focus on identified risk factors as the focal point for intervention efforts. In contrast, we indicate that the macrosocial factors and racism are the basic causes of racial differences in health. The risk factors and resources are the surface causes, the current intervening mechanism. These may change, but as long as the basic causes remain operative, the modification of surface causes alone will only lead to the emergence of new intervening mechanisms to maintain the same outcome. (1994: 36)

We need to remember that we are concerned with (ethnic) inequalities in health because they are a component and a consequence of an inequitable capitalist society, and it is this that needs to be directly addressed.

Acknowledgements

I am grateful to Karen Iley, Chris Smaje, Satnam Virdee and anonymous referees for comments on an earlier version of this chapter. My current work is supported by a grant from the (UK) Economic and Social Research Council under the Health Variations Programme (L128251019).

References

Ahmad, W. (1995) Review article: Race and health, *Sociology of Health and Illness*, 17, 3, 418–29.
Ahmad, W.I.U., Kernohan, E.E.M. and Baker, M.R. (1989) Influence of ethnicity and unemployment on the perceived health of a sample of general practice attenders, *Community Medicine*, 11, 2, 148–56.

Aspinall, P. (1995) Department of Health's requirement for mandatory collection of data on ethnic group inpatients, *British Medical Journal*, 311, 1006–9.

Bagley, C. (1995) A plea for ignoring race and including insured status in American research reports on social science and medicine, *Social Science and Medicine*, 40, 8, 1017–19.

Balarajan, R. (1995) Ethnicity and variations in the nation's health, *Health Trends*, 27, 4, 114–19.

Balarajan, R. and Soni Raleigh, V. (1995) *Ethnicity and Health in England*. London: HMSO.

Barot, R. (ed) (1996) *The Racism Problematic: Contemporary Sociological Debates on Race and Ethnicity*. Lewiston: The Edwin Mellen Press.

Beishon, S. and Nazroo, J.Y. (1997) *Coronary Heart Disease: Contrasting the Health Beliefs and Behaviours of South Asian Communities in the UK*. London: Health Education Authority.

Bhopal, R.S. (1997) Is research into ethnicity and health racist, unsound, or important science? *British Medical Journal*, 314, 1751–6.

Brown, C. (1984) *Black and White Britain: the Third PSI Survey*. London: Heinemann.

Brown, C. and Ritchie, J. (1981) *Focussed Enumeration: the Development of a Method for Sampling Ethnic Minority Groups*. London: Policy Studies Institute/ SCPR.

Chaturvedi, N. and McKeigue, P. (1994) Methods for epidemiological surveys of ethnic minority groups, *Journal of Epidemiology and Community Health*, 48, 107–11.

Davey Smith, G., Shipley, M.J. and Rose, G. (1990) Magnitude and causes of socioeconomic differentials in mortality: further evidence from the Whitehall study, *Journal of Epidemiology and Community Health*, 44, 265.

Davey Smith, G., Blane, D. and Bartley, M. (1994) Explanations for socio-economic differentials in mortality: evidence from Britain and elsewhere, *European Journal of Public Health*, 4, 131–44.

Davey Smith, G., Wentworth, D., Neaton, J., Stamler, R. and Stamler, J. (1996) Socioeconomic differentials in mortality risk among men screened for the Multiple Risk Factor Intervention Trial: II. Black Men, *American Journal of Public Health*, 86, 4, 497–504.

Davey Smith, G., Neaton, J., Wentworth, D., Stamler, R. and Stamler, J. (1997a) Cause-specific and all-cause mortality differentials between black and white men in the United States: men screened for the Multiple Risk Factor Intervention Trial (MRFIT), *Lancet*, 351, March 28, 934–9.

Davey Smith G., Hart, C., Blane, D., Gillis, C. and Hawthorne, V. (1997b) Lifetime socioeconomic position and mortality: prospective observational study, *British Medical Journal*, 314, 547–52.

Fenton, S., Hughes, A. and Hine, C. (1995) Self-assessed health, economic status and origin, *New Community*, 21, 1, 55–68.

Gilroy, P. (1987) *'There Ain't No Black in the Union Jack': the Cultural Politics of Race and Nation*. London: Hutchinson.

Gupta, S., de Belder, A. and O'Hughes, L. (1995) Avoiding premature coronary deaths in Asians in Britain: spend now on prevention or pay later for treatment, *British Medical Journal*, 311, 1035–6.

Hahn, R.A. and Stroup, D.F. (1994) Race and ethnicity in public health surveillance: criteria for the scientific use of social categories, *Public Health Reports*, 109, 1, 7–15.

Hall, S. (1992) The question of cultural identity. In Hall, S., Held, D. and McGrew, T. (eds) *Modernity and its Futures*. Cambridge: Polity Press.

Harding, S. and Maxwell, R. (1977) Differences in mortality of migrants. In Drever, F. and Whitehead, M. (eds) *Health Inequalities: Decennial Supplement No. 15*. London: The Stationery Office.

Heath, A. and Ridge, J. (1983) Social mobility of ethnic minorities, *Journal of Biosocial Science*, supplement, 8, 169–84.

Jenkins, R. (1996) 'Us' and 'Them': ethnicity, racism and ideology. In Barot, R. (ed) *The Racism Problematic: Contemporary Sociological Debates on Race and Ethnicity*. Lewiston: The Edwin Mellen Press.

Lillie-Blanton, M. and Laveist, T. (1996) Race/ethnicity, the social environment, and health, *Social Science and Medicine*, 43, 1, 83–91.

Lundeberg, O. (1991) Causal explanations for class inequality in health – an empirical analysis, *Social Science and Medicine*, 32, 4, 385–93.

Macintyre, S. (1997) The Black Report and beyond: what are the issues? *Social Science and Medicine*, 44, 6, 723–45.

Macintyre, S., Maciver, S. and Soomans, A. (1993) Area, class and health: should we be focusing on places or people? *Journal of Social Policy*, 22, 2, 213–34.

Marmot, M.G., Adelstein, A.M., Bulusu, L. and OPCS (1984) *Immigrant Mortality in England and Wales 1970–78: Causes of Death by Country of Birth*. London: HMSO.

Mason, D. (1996) Some reflections on the sociology of race and racism. In Barot, R. (ed) *The Racism Problematic: Contemporary Sociological Debates on Race and Ethnicity*. Lewiston: The Edwin Mellen Press.

McKeigue, P., Marmot, M., Syndercombe Court, Y., Cottier, D., Rahman, S. and Riermersma, R. (1988) Diabetes, hyperinsulinaemia, and coronary risk factors in Bangladeshis in East London, *British Heart Journal*, 60, 390–6.

McKeigue, P., Miller, G. and Marmot, M. (1989) Coronary heart disease in South Asians overseas: a review, *Journal of Clinical Epidemiology*, 42, 7, 597–609.

McKeigue, P., Shah, B. and Marmot, M. (1991) Relation of central obesity and insulin resistance with high diabetes prevalence and cardiovascular risk in South Asians, *Lancet*, 337, 382–6.

McKenney, N.R. and Bennett, C.E. (1994) Issues regarding data on race and ethnicity: the Census Bureau experience, *Public Health Reports*, 109, 1, 16–25.

McKenzie, K. and Crowcroft, N.S. (1996) Describing race, ethnicity, and culture in medical research, *British Medical Journal*, 312, 1054.

Miles, R. (1989) *Racism*. London: Routledge.

Miles, R. (1996) Racism and nationalism in the United Kingdom: a view from the periphery. In Barot, R. (ed) *The Racism Problematic: Contemporary Sociological Debates on Race and Ethnicity*. Lewiston: The Edwin Mellen Press.

Modood, T. (1996) If races don't exist, then what does? Racial categorisation and ethnic realities. In Barot, R. (ed) *The Racism Problematic: Contemporary Sociological Debates on Race and Ethnicity*. Lewiston: The Edwin Mellen Press.

Modood, T. (1997) Culture and identity. In Modood, T., Berthoud, R., Lakey, J., Nazroo, J., Smith, P., Virdee, S. and Beishon, S. *Ethnic Minorities in Britain: Diversity and Disadvantage*. London: Policy Studies Institute.

Modood, T., Berthoud, R., Lakey, J., Nazroo, J., Smith, P., Virdee, S. and Beishon, S. (1997) *Ethnic Minorities in Britain: Diversity and Disadvantage*. London: Policy Studies Institute.

Navarro, V. (1990) Race or class versus race and class: mortality differentials in the United States, *The Lancet*, Nov 17, 1238–40.

Nazroo, J.Y. (1997a) *The Health of Britain's Ethnic Minorities: Findings from a National Survey*. London: Policy Studies Institute.

Nazroo, J.Y. (1997b) *Mental Health and Ethnicity: Findings from a National Community Survey*. London: Policy Studies Institute.

Nazroo, N. (1997c) Why do research on ethnicity and health? *Share*, 18, 5–8.

Owen, D. (1994) Spatial variations in ethnic minority groups populations in Great Britain, *Population Trends*, 78, 23–33.

Rogers, R.G. (1992) Living and dying in the USA: socio-demographic determinants of death among blacks and whites, *Demography*, 29, 287–303.

Rudat, K. (1994) *Black and Minority Ethnic Groups in England: Health and Lifestyles*. London: Health Education Authority.

Scott, A. (1990) *Ideology and the New Social Movements*. London: Unwin Hyman.

Senior, P.A. and Bhopal, R. (1994) Ethnicity as a variable in epidemiological research, *British Medical Journal*, 309, 327–30.

Sheldon, T.A. and Parker, H. (1992) Race and ethnicity in health research, *Journal of Public Health Medicine*, 14, 2, 104–10.

Smaje, C. (1995) Ethnic residential concentration and health: evidence for a positive effect? *Policy and Politics*, 23, 3, 251–69.

Smaje, C. (1996) The ethnic patterning of health: new directions for theory and research, *Sociology of Health and Illness*, 18, 2, 139–71.

Smith, D. (1977) *Racial Disadvantage in Britain*. Harmondsworth: Penguin.

Smith, P. and Prior, G. (1997) *The Fourth National Survey of Ethnic Minorities: Technical Report*. London: Social and Community Planning Research.

Sterling, T., Rosenbaum, W. and Weinkam, J. (1993) Income, race and mortality, *Journal of National Medical Association*, 85, 12, 906–11.

Townsend, P. and Davidson, N. (1982) *Inequalities in Health (the Black Report)*. Middlesex: Penguin.

Townsend, P., Phillimore, P. and Beattie, A. (1988) *Health and Deprivation: Inequality and the North*. London: Routledge.

Vågerö, D. and Illsley, R. (1995) Explaining health inequalities: beyond Black and Barker, *European Sociological Review*, 11, 3, 219–39.

Wilkinson, R.G. (1996) *Unhealthy Societies: the Afflictions of Inequality*. London: Routledge.

Williams, D.R., Lavizzo-Mourey, R. and Warren, R.C. (1994) The concept of race and health status in America, *Public Health Reports*, 109, 1, 26–41.

8. Mortgage debt, insecure home ownership and health: an exploratory analysis

Sarah Nettleton and Roger Burrows

Introduction

Wilkinson (1996) has recently argued that it is not only the *physical effects* of material deprivation which affect health, but also the *psycho-social processes* associated with the experience of such deprivation. He supports this argument by drawing on a wide range of empirical data deriving from the work of anthropologists, sociologists and physiologists. He points, for example, to evidence (Bartley 1994, Ferrie *et al.* 1995, Wilson and Walker 1993) which suggests that whilst the impact of loss of income and increased poverty associated with unemployment can impact upon health, what is also of significance is the *insecurity* which is experienced by people who lose their jobs (Wilkinson 1996: 78). In passing he also speculates that insecurity in relation to housing is likely to have similar consequences.

> Housing insecurity, whether caused by council plans or difficulty in keeping up the rent or the mortgage payments, has much in common with fears of unemployment. The high rate of housing repossessions reflects only the tip of an iceberg of housing insecurity . . . The numbers of people who lose their homes are in turn only the tip of the vast numbers who live with worrying debts. So far the effects of debt on health have not been adequately researched. (1996: 178–9)

This chapter is a direct response to this call for more research into housing insecurity and health in that it examines the consequences for the health of home owners of the onset of mortgage indebtedness. Hitherto the literature on housing and health has tended to focus on the impact of the physical aspects of housing on health (Best 1995, Hopton and Hunt 1996, Ineichen 1993, Smith 1989). The impact of the affordability of housing on health has been relatively unexplored and this is particularly so in relation to home ownership.

Throughout the last two decades there has been an increase of 17 per cent in the numbers of people in Britain owning their own homes. Home ownership has been 'sold' by politicians, and argued for by some sociologists (Saunders 1990), as a means of ensuring a more secure future and as a means of accessing a better quality of life. However, for large numbers of people this has not turned out to be the case and, in fact, for many people attempting to keep up with mortgage payments has become a source of great anxiety and has induced real fears of losing one's home (Ford *et al.* 1995, Davis and Dhooge 1993). For large numbers of households this fear has become a reality. In Britain between 1990 and 1996 almost 388,000 households with a mortgage, containing over one million individuals, had their homes possessed (Wilcox 1996: 139). Although the rate as which possessions are occurring has stabilised of late, an additional 820 households still lost their homes in this way every week (Ford 1997). Mortgage arrears also remain at historically high levels. Although levels peaked in 1991 at the end of 1995 there were still some 85,000 households with mortgage arrears of more than 12 months, almost 127,000 with arrears of between six and 12 months and almost 178,000 with arrears of between three and six months (Wilcox 1996: 139). These figures give some indication of the extent to which for many people in Britain home ownership has become *unsustainable*. This chapter sets out to explore what impact, if any, this increased level of insecurity amongst home owners has had upon their health status and their use of primary health care services.

The chapter is based on the results of a secondary analysis of the *British Household Panel Survey* (BHPS).[1] Using these data we attempt to explore whether or not the experience of the onset of mortgage indebtedness has an independent impact on the mental health of individuals and on their use of general practitioners (GPs). To make sense of our findings we then draw upon work on the sociology of insecurity. We begin, however, by setting the context for this analysis by describing the recent history of housing policy in relation to home ownership in the United Kingdom.

The growth of home ownership

A key thrust of the housing policies of successive British Governments since the second world war has been the expansion of home ownership. A minority of households were home owners at that time, now however they form 67 per cent of all households. The policy of increasing home ownership was significantly accelerated by the Conservative Governments in office between 1979 and 1997. In fact, 3.8 million more households now own their own home compared with 1979, an increase of some 38 per cent. The expansion of home ownership in recent decades formed part of the Tory Government's ideological commitment to private rather than public provision of welfare. Three policy initiatives in particular, combined with the formation of more households who wanted to buy their own homes, contributed to the accelerated growth of owner occupation(Hogarth *et al.* 1996). First, the selling of council houses[2] to tenants at discounted prices under the 'Right to Buy' (RTB) scheme which formed part of the 1980 Housing Act. Between 1981 and 1995 1.57 million council houses were sold (Wilcox 1996: 106). Second, restrictions were placed on local authorities who were unable to use their capital receipts to build new houses. This, combined with the RTB, resulted in a substantial reduction in and residualisation of, local authority housing available for rent. This also 'forced' some households towards home owner-ship which might otherwise have been housed in the social rented sector (Burrows 1999). Third, the Financial Service Act in 1985 and the Building Societies Act in 1986 deregulated the credit market. New players came onto the lending scene, expanded the market and offered mortgages to groups of people who had hitherto been regarded as 'riskier' customers.

These initiatives together unleashed the 1980s housing boom which came to an abrupt end as the decade closed. It is widely agreed that four processes combined to produce a substantial growth in the unprecedented levels of mortgage arrears and possessions. First, as a result of the financial deregula-tion noted above, a highly competitive market and rising property prices, high loan to value mortgages became widely available. Second, mortgage rates rapidly increased from 9.5 per cent in 1988 to peak at 15.4 per cent in February 1990 before slowly decreasing throughout the 1990s and then increasing again in 1997. Third, a deep economic recession led to job losses, under-employment and small business failure amongst substantial numbers of mortgagors. Fourth, the housing market itself entered a deep and persis-tent recession. Consequently many highly geared borrowers first faced rising mortgage costs and then often lost income from employment. However, many were denied the possibility of selling their way out of problems due to the housing recession (Forrest and Murie 1994). Consequently the number of households with mortgage arrears increased, as did the number of mort-gage possessions (Ford *et al.* 1995).

Although the housing recession has now ended, research evidence sug-gests that unsustainable home ownership will continue well into the next millennium (Ford and Wilcox 1998). This is because unsustainable home ownership is but one element in a set of circumstances which are associated with what some commentators refer to as the 'new insecurity' of social and economic life (Hutton 1995, Pahl 1995, Wilkinson 1996). Unless social and public policy is dramatically altered the historically high levels of mortgage indebtedness and possession currently being witnessed will remain during features of social life in England. This is caused by a set of fundamental structural changes which are currently transforming economic life.

Economic restructuring and unsustainable home ownership

These structural changes are numerous, but five in particular are interacting in order to produce increasing levels of insecurity amongst home owners (Ford and Wilcox 1998). First, in a low inflation economy, the long term (usually 25 years) nature of the credit contract means that the entry ratio of mortgage costs to earnings is prolonged. Second, the costs of credit are variable and unpredictable with interest rates varying between 7.5 per cent and 15 per cent during the last decade. Third, continuous and secure employment contracts are being displaced by more insecure and short-term employment contracts whilst the social security 'safety net' has been eroded (Oldman and Kemp 1996, Ford and Kempson 1997). Fourth, the expansion in owner occupation has brought into the sector households at greater risk from unemployment than had typically been the case previously. In particular the increase in the number of manual workers in the owner occupied sector has increased the risk to the sector as a whole. Fifth, rising house prices and relatively high interest rates have often meant that entry into sustainable home ownership now necessitates dual earner households. These two final features demonstrate the critical nature of the changing labour market for sustainable home ownership and it is likely that this constitutes the main reason why the 'problem' of unsustainable home ownership is going to remain significant during the coming decades.

Social security policies have compounded the situation by reducing eligibility and entitlements to benefits. For example, 'new' borrowers (from October 1995), in receipt of income support (IS) have to wait nine months before receiving help with mortgage interest (MI). 'Existing' borrowers eligible for IS also now have to wait longer (two months with nothing, then 50 per cent for four months) but not as long as new borrowers. Borrowers are encouraged instead to make their own arrangements by taking out private mortgage protection plans. These have been found to be inadequate because, not only are they relatively expensive but the policies have been found to have tight eligibility and claiming criteria. Ford *et al.* (1995) found that of those in arrears only about one quarter could have been helped by private insurance. One of the main reasons for this is that mortgage arrears are not always the consequences of a total lack of income, but a result of reduced income (for example, a new job at lower wages, loss of income earned etc.) yet there is currently neither an adequate public or a private safety net to deal with this situation (Ford and Kempson 1997). Whilst those people who are living in rented accommodation may be entitled to housing benefit, those who are buying their own homes are not.

The restructuring or 'flexibilisation' of work is resulting in continuous and secure employment contracts being displaced by more insecure and short-term employment contracts and/or increasing rates of self-employment. Mortgages, however, are premised on the assumption of stable employment over a long period of time. There is an increasingly clear disjuncture emerging between the supposed need for flexible labour markets and the ability of people to sustain mortgage costs over long periods (Burrows and Ford 1997, Ford and Wilcox 1998). It would seem reasonable to speculate, therefore, that for as long as this disjuncture exists home ownership will remain problematic and/or unsustainable for a significant proportion of home owners. Housing policy over the last two decades or so rests on the notion that individuals, or households, are able and should be encouraged to take responsibility for their own accommodation needs. However, individuals have to try and make rational choices within deregulated market contexts which in turn are vulnerable to the vagaries of the wider economy (Nettleton and Burrows 1998).

The antecedents of mortgage arrears

It is extremely difficult to decipher the precise reasons why people fall into mortgage arrears, not least because the reasons are extremely varied and also because it often appears to be a culmination of a number of factors. Doling *et al.* (1988) have usefully identified three related sets of factors which influence the chances that a household will fall into mortgage arrears. First, structural factors, such as income/loan ratios, interest rates, government subsidies, social security support levels and loan/value ratios. Second, household income and expenditure factors, such as unemployment, short-time working, marital breakdown, sickness, unanticipated repairs, and other household expenditure including other loan repayments. Third, personal factors such as money management skills, commitment to the house and personal priorities. A survey of 362 borrowers (Ford *et al.* 1995) who had fallen into arrears found that the most common reasons, in order of prevalence were: redundancy; a drop in earnings; small business failure; and relationship breakdown. It is therefore difficult and inappropriate to try and identify single factors which 'cause' people to have problems with paying their mortgage. Factors are likely to be multiple and compounding. Indeed, conceptually and pragmatically this is a salient feature of mortgage indebtedness; it is not an isolated life event but an experience which both results from and impacts upon other biographical changes.

The social distribution of mortgage indebtedness

Mortgage debt, like ill health, does not occur randomly – it is strongly socially patterned. Households with certain social characteristics are significantly more likely to experience unsustainable home ownership than are others. An analysis of data derived from the *Survey of English Housing* shows some clear patterns of relative disadvantage (Burrows 1998, Burrows and Ford 1997). First, households headed by younger people are at greatest risk. Second, households with dependent children, especially lone parents, are at greater risk than are couples with no children. Third, single males are at greater risk than are single females. Fourth, the divorced and separated are at greater risk than those who are not. Fifth, the currently economically inactive are at greater risk than are the employed. Sixth, there is a clear social class gradient, with those in the lower social classes being at greatest risk. Seventh, amongst employees those in the private sector are at greater risk than are those in the public sector. However, the self-employed (especially sole traders) are at greater risk than employees. Finally, households headed by individuals who identify themselves as being from 'minority ethnic groups' are at greater risk than are households headed by individuals who identify themselves as 'white'. Thus, although home owners tend, on average, to be more advantaged than are households living in either the social housing or private rented sectors, within the tenure there are clear patterns of relative disadvantage (Smith 1990).

Data also suggest that mortgage indebtedness does not just occur as a 'one off' event – it often involves a sustained struggle to keep one's 'head above water'. Recent survey work shows the extent to which mortgagors face financial difficulties with their mortgages but manage to pay, as well as the variety of missed payment patterns that contribute to the arrears figures. They also provide information on the incidence as well as the stock of arrears at any one time. Using the four year period between 1991 and 1994 Ford *et al.* (1995) have shown that roughly one in five home buyers at been 'at risk' (either in terms of financial difficulties or missed payments) during the period considered: three per cent had no current arrears but had previous arrears; three per cent were having difficulties paying and had arrears previously; one per cent were in arrears again, having cleared previous arrears; one per cent had been in arrears for the whole of the period under consideration; three per cent had fallen into arrears for the first time in the last three years; and nine per cent had no arrears over the period but had current payment difficulties.

Our concern in the rest of this chapter is to explore what impact this experience of mortgage indebtedness has on the mental health of individuals and their use of GPs. Our empirical focus is on the impact of the experience of the onset of mortgage arrears rather than on the more devastating consequences of the actual loss of a home through mortgage possession (Nettleton 1998) – something which only a minority of households who enter a period of mortgage arrears will have the misfortune to experience.

Methods

To investigate the pattern of association between the onset of mortgage indebtedness and mental health a sample of individuals was drawn from the British Household Panel Survey (BHPS). The BHPS is a complex data set, unique in the history of British social science, which enables a large nationally representative sample of households, and the individuals within them, to be tracked over time (Buck *et al.* 1994). Five waves of the data were available for analysis at the time of the study. The first wave of the BHPS was carried out in 1991/92 and the fifth, in 1995/96. The BHPS is designed as an annual survey of each adult (16+) member of a nationally representative sample of more than 5,000 households, making a total of about 10,000 individual interviews. The same individuals are re-interviewed in successive waves and if they split off from original households (as in the case of children leaving home, partners separating or groups of otherwise unrelated individuals reconfiguring their households) all adult members of their new households are also interviewed. Children in households are interviewed once they reach the age of 16. Thus, the sample remains broadly representative of the British population as it changes through the 1990s. Within each wave a whole series of factual and attitudinal questions are asked of individuals on topics such as housing, residential mobility, employment and unemployment, health, income, debt, consumption, education, leisure, politics, values and so on.

The BHPS is suited to analyses investigating the relationship between housing and health because it is one of the few sources of data which brings together variables covering these two domains. In addition its panel design has certain advantages over cross sectional designs in which we always have to infer the impact of change in some independent variable 'x' on changes in some dependent variable 'y' based solely on inter-unit variations at one point in time.

In what follows we examine the impact of the onset of mortgage problems on changes in mental health (as measured by a common subjective wellbeing scale, the GHQ12) and changes in the number of GP visits across waves 1 and 2 and again across waves 4 and 5. Although we are able to demonstrate an enduring relationship between the onset of mortgage problems and changes in subjective wellbeing across all of the waves of the data we present the results from just these two 'transition' periods here. The first represents the period in which the housing recession was at its deepest (Forrest and Murie 1994) – and also where the association was at its strongest – and the second represents the 'beginning of the end' of the same housing recession – and also where the association was at its weakest over the five waves.

For both 'transitions' (1991 to 1992 and 1994 to 1995) we constructed a (suitably weighted) sample of *individuals* made up of all heads of household and, if applicable, their partners (married or cohabiting) living in households with a mortgage, who reported in the first year of each 'transition' that they had no problems paying their mortgage. In the first 'transition' between 1991 and 1992 amongst our sample of over 3,700 individuals over 15 per cent either fell into arrears or were having problems paying their mortgage. This proportion fell year on year falling to under 10 per cent of our sample of 3,500 in the second 'transition' period considered here between 1994 and 1995.

Results

As we have already discussed, the onset of mortgage problems can be the product of a complex set of factors many of which may themselves be related to a change in health status and/or subjective wellbeing. Our task is to begin to disentangle the independent impact, if any, that the onset of mortgage problems has on subjective wellbeing.

Changes in subjective wellbeing

Two measures of change in subjective wellbeing were constructed for each individual in the sample by comparing GHQ12 scores (calculated to range from 0 (excellent) to 36 (very poor) in the second year of the 'transition' compared with GHQ12 scores in the first year. The first measure is simply the GHQ12 change score over the two years. So if an individual scored 10 in the first year and 20 in the second their change over the two years would be 10. Thus this variable score can logically take on any whole number value between −36 and +36, with negative values indicating an improvement in subjective wellbeing, and positive values indicating a worsening in subjective wellbeing. The second measure reduces these GHQ12 change scores to a simple dichotomy between those with an improved or static GHQ12 score on the one hand and those with a worsening GHQ12 score on the other.

If we examine the simple bivariate relationship between the onset of mortgage problems and changes in subjective wellbeing a clear and significant pattern of association is apparent ($p < 0.001$) using either measure and across both 'transitions'. However, our interest is in whether this relationship is maintained when we control for other factors which on *a priori* grounds we might suspect to impact upon a worsening of subjective wellbeing. In order to explore this a series of other variables were examined alongside mortgage indebtedness using *multiple regression* where the dependent variable was the GHQ12 change score, and *logistic regression* where the dependent variable was the dichotomy: income and income changes; physical health problems and changes in physical health problems; employment and changes in employment; and age.

Income and changes in income: A measure was constructed in order to examine *changes in household income*. The incomes for the households in which the individuals in the sample resided were calculated for 1991 and 1992 and again for 1994 and 1995. These figures were then weighted to take account of differences in household structures (a process known as 'equivalising') and then deflated. Estimates were then made of changes in household income over the two 'transition' periods.

Physical health problems and changes in physical health problems: A measure was constructed which attempted to operationalise any *changes in physical health status.* For each individual the number of physical health problems reported in the first year (out of a possible total of nine) of the 'transition' were compared to the number reported in the second so as to estimate if the number of health problems reported had increased or decreased. Logically, then, this change variable could run from –9 to +9 with a positive number representing an increase in the number of problems and a negative number representing a decrease in the number of problems.

Employment and changes in employment: A measure was obtained which attempted to operationalise *changes in employment status amongst household members* of which the individual was a part. This was based on a simple count of the number of adult household members currently in full-time or part-time employment. A household level measure of employment status was preferred over one measured at the level of the individual. This was because for those individuals who were economically active the two measures were (not surprisingly) highly co-linear, but for economically inactive individuals the household level measure was more strongly associated with changes in subjective wellbeing than were changes in the individual employment status of other household members.

Other factors: In addition to the above variables a number of others were also considered in various models – a measure of *residential mobility* between each of the two waves; a measure to show if a *new child* had been born in the household; and a measure to ascertain if individuals had *ended a relationship* (either through death, divorce or separation) during the 'transition' period; and so on. None of these variables showed any significant association with changes in subjective wellbeing and so are not reported here.

Table 1 shows the results of running multiple regression and logistic regression analyses using our two measures of worsening GHQ12 scores in 1992 compared to 1991. For each procedure two different models are shown – the 'simultaneous' model shows parameter estimates when all of the variables are entered into the model, whilst the 'best fitting' model shows the parameter estimates obtained via stepwise selection of the most significant variables. Following the suggestion by Arber (1991) models have been calculated for males and females separately. Table 2 reproduces the analysis for 1995 compared with 1994.

The 'best fitting' multiple regression results for the first 'transition' period shown in Table 1 indicate that for men, after controlling for other significant variables in the model, the onset of mortgage problems leads to a 1.64 increase in the GHQ12 change score (sig. at $p < 0.001$), and for women the increase is even higher at 2.51 (sig. at $p < 0.001$). In addition, for both men and women, after controlling for other factors, there exists an inverse relationship between the initial GHQ12 score in 1991 and the change in the

Table 1 *Worsening GHQ12 scores in 1992 compared to 1991: multiple regression and logistic regression results*

| Characteristics | Multiple regression | | | | Logistic regression | | | |
| | Simultaneous | | Best fitting | | Simultaneous | | Best fitting | |
	Male	*Female*	*Male*	*Female*	*Male*	*Female*	*Male*	*Female*
GHQ12 score in 1991	-0.48***	-0.54***	-0.49***	-0.54***	0.84***	0.82***	0.85***	0.82***
Mortgage problems								
No problems	–	–	–	–	1.00	1.00	1.00	1.00
Problems/arrears	1.61***	2.43***	1.64***	2.51***	1.70*	3.23***	1.81**	3.24***
Equivalised household income in 1991	0.00	0.00	–	–	1.00	1.00	–	–
Change in equivalised household income in 1992 compared to 1991	0.00	0.00	–	–	1.00	1.00	–	–
Number of health problems in 1991	0.61***	0.50***	0.58***	0.48***	1.11	1.21**	–	1.18*
Change in number of health problems in 1992 compared to 1991	0.65***	0.75***	0.62***	0.74***	1.07	1.32***	–	1.30**
Number of household members in employment in 1991	0.24	-0.01	–	–	1.00	1.00	–	–
Number of household members in employment decreased in 1992 compared to 1991?								
No	–	–	–	–	1.00	1.00	1.00	1.00
Yes	0.90**	1.21***	1.06	1.24**	1.48*	1.40	1.50***	1.41
Age	-0.01	-0.01	–	–	1.00	1.00	–	–
Constant/base odds	4.60	6.19***	4.75***	5.79***	5.18***	5.00***	4.24***	6.15***
Percentage of variation explained by model	19.4%	22.1%	19.4%	22.3%	7.3%	10.7%	7.1%	10.2%

* sig at $p<0.05$ **sig at $p<0.01$ *** sig at $p<0.001$

score – the higher the initial score the less likely it is to have increased. There is however no apparent relationship between either initial household incomes or changes in these incomes – probably because any effect here is picked up in the employment changes variable discussed below. There is, however, a significant association between both the number of health problems and a change in the number of health problems and changes in the GHQ12 score between the two years. Both the initial number of health problems and the change in the number of health problems lead to statistically significant increases in the change in GHQ12 measure (both sig. at $p < 0.001$). For both men and women each health problem in 1991 leads to a three-quarter unit change in GHQ12 change score, and each additional health problem in 1992 leads to another one-half unit change in the GHQ12 change score. Finally, although the initial number of household members in employment is not significantly associated with changes in subjective wellbeing any decrease in the number of members employed leads to a 1.2 unit increase in the GHQ12 change score ($p < 0.001$). In both cases the 'best fitting' models are able to explain about 22 per cent of the variation in the GHQ12 scores over the two years.

Broadly similar conclusions about these patterns of association between the onset of mortgage problems and a worsening in subjective wellbeing are reached using the cruder dichotomous version of the change in GHQ12 variable as the dependent variable. For men the 'best fitting' logistic regression equation includes the GHQ12 score in 1991, the onset of mortgage problems variable, and changes in the number of household members in employment but not any changes in the number of health problems. For women all of these variables can be included in the model. The conclusion of this logistic regression analysis for both men and women is that compared with those without mortgage problems those mortgagors with problems are more likely (sig. at $p < 0.001$) to have experienced a worsening in subjective wellbeing even after adjusting the odds for the influence of the other variables in the models. For men the odds are increased by a factor of 1.81 and for women the odds are increased by a factor of 3.24.

Table 2 shows that in the second transition period the relationship is not so strong. In the multiple regression analysis the impact of the onset of mortgage problems for men drops out of the final equation and is only just significant for women. However, in the logistic regression analysis the association is maintained. For men in households experiencing mortgage problems the odds of a worsening in subjective wellbeing is only increased by a factor of 1.5 (sig. at $p < 0.05$) whilst for women it is increased by a factor of 1.95 (sig. at $p < 0.01$) after controlling for the other variables in the model.

Visits to general practitioners
In Tables 3 and 4 we attempt to relate increase in the number of GP visits to the onset of mortgage problems. They show the results of a logistic

Table 2 *Worsening GHQ12 scores in 1995 compared to 1994: multiple regression and logistic regression results*

Characteristics	Multiple regression				Logistic regression			
	Simultaneous		Best fitting		Simultaneous		Best fitting	
	Male	*Female*	*Male*	*Female*	*Male*	*Female*	*Male*	*Female*
GHQ12 score in 1991	−0.57***	−0.58***	−0.57***	−0.58***	0.81***	0.84***	0.81***	0.84***
Mortgage problems								
No problems	–		–		1.00	1.00	1.00	1.00
Problems/arrears	0.53	1.17*	–	1.16*	1.51	1.97**	1.51**	1.95**
Equivalised household income in 1991	0.00	0.00	–	–	1.00	1.00	–	–
Change in equivalised household income in 1992 compared to 1991	0.00	0.00	–	–	1.00	1.00	–	–
Number of health problems in 1991	0.87***	0.69***	0.89***	0.69***	1.49***	1.30***	1.44***	1.30***
Change in number of health problems in 1992 compared to 1991	0.94***	0.98***	0.95***	0.98***	1.49***	1.44***	1.49***	1.44***
Number of household members in employment in 1991	0.00	−0.05	–	–	1.09	1.00	1.14*	–
Number of household members in employment decreased in 1992 compared to 1991?								
No	–		–		1.00	1.00	–	1.00
Yes	0.60	0.81*	0.61*	0.70*	1.18	1.32	–	1.31*
Age	0.00	0.00	–	–	0.99	0.99*	–	0.99*
Constant/base odds	5.09***	6.42***	5.43***	6.37***	5.84***	6.72***	4.57***	7.03***
Percentage of variation explained by model	30.1%	27.7%	30.1%	27.8%	12.7%	11.3%	12.5%	11.28%

* sig at $p<0.05$ **sig at $p<0.01$ *** sig at $p<0.001$

Table 3 *Increased number of GP visits in 1992 compared to 1991 logistic regression results*

| | Logistic regression | | | |
| | Simultaneous | | Best fitting | |
Characteristics	Male	Female	Male	Female
Number of GP visits in 1991	0.32**	0.44***	0.32***	0.44***
Mortgage problems				
No problems	1.00	1.00	1.00	–
Problems/arrears	1.95**	1.12	2.11**	–
Equivalised household income in 1991	1.00	1.00	–	–
Change in equivalised household income in 1992 compared to 1991	1.00	1.00	–	–
Number of health problems in 1991	1.60***	1.89***	1.59***	1.37***
Change in number of health problems in 1992 compared to 1991	2.44***	1.40***	2.45***	1.88***
Number of household members in employment in 1991	0.98	1.02	–	–
Number of household members in employment decreased in 1992 compared to 1991?				
No	1.00	1.00	–	–
Yes	1.18	0.87	–	–
Age	1.01	0.99	1.02*	–
Constant/base odds	1.08	2.04***	0.81	1.87***
Percentage of variation explained by model	13.45%	10.48%	13.2%	10.31%

regression analysis which models the odds that the onset of mortgage problems will lead to an increase in the number of visits made to a GP, controlling for other factors which are also likely to be associated with such an increase. Table 3 shows that in the first 'transition' period a significant increase in GP visits related to the onset of mortgage problems was evident for men (sig. at $p < 0.001$) but not for women. Table 4 shows that in the second 'transition' period although those with mortgage problems were more likely to have increased the number of visits they made to their GP the increases were not statistically significant.

Table 4 *Increased number of GP visits in 19952 compared to 1994 logistic regression results*

| | Logistic regression | | | |
| | Simultaneous | | Best fitting | |
Characteristics	Male	Female	Male	Female
Number of GP visits in 1991	0.35***	0.43***	0.35***	0.43***
Mortgage problems				
No problems	1.00	1.00	–	–
Problems/arrears	1.35	1.21	–	–
Equivalised household income in 1991	1.00	1.00	–	–
Change in equivalised household income in 1992 compared to 1991	1.00	1.00	–	–
Number of health problems in 1991	1.90***	1.56***	1.90***	1.57***
Change in number of health problems in 1992 compared to 1991	1.46***	1.62***	1.46***	1.64***
Number of household members in employment in 1991	1.00	0.97	–	–
Number of household members in employment decreased in 1992 compared to 1991?				
No	1.00	1.00	–	–
Yes	0.95	1.20	–	–
Age	0.99	0.98*	–	0.98*
Constant/base odds	1.40	4.24***	1.38*	4.10***
Percentage of variation explained by model	11.0%	11.8%	10.9%	11.6%

Discussion

From the analyses presented above we have shown how the experience of the onset of mortgage indebtedness is associated with changes in the subjective wellbeing of men and women, and that it increases the likelihood that men in particular will visit their GPs. Such findings would appear to support the thesis, posited at the beginning of this chapter, that housing insecurity can impact upon health. However, the nature of the associations presented above are complex and may merit further analysis. Whilst there is no clear cut *causal* relationship, the findings are consistent with the idea of association, and the relationship between difficulties with mortgage payments and poor mental health does appear to hold even when other variables (such as household income, employment status and physical health) are held constant.

Another finding worthy of further exploration is that the strength of the association between the onset of mortgage problems and a worsening in mental health is greater in the first transition period than it is in the second. Indeed, the strength of the association declines as the number of people experiencing mortgage problems declines. The first transition period (1991–92) represents the peak in the numbers of mortgage possessions[3] and the numbers of people who were experiencing difficulties with their payments. This implies that in times when more people are experiencing difficulties, the health effects may be greater. It may be that when there are high levels of arrears those who would not normally be at high risk of debt (see the discussion on the social distribution of indebtedness above) are more exposed to it. The problem may touch a wider diversity of people and may include those who are less likely to have experience of debt and financial hardship. Studies on the impact of financial debt more generally have found that those people who have little experience of this type of 'life event' find it more difficult to cope with (Kempson 1996: 10–16). One might speculate further that at times of greater economic insecurity the qualitative experience of mortgage indebtedness may be different during times of greater economic security. Whilst there may be greater numbers of people in arrears, it is not a life event which is experienced collectively, its antecedents and consequences are likely to be intensely personal.

The complexity of the associations presented in our findings make it difficult to judge the extent to which poor health is *caused* by the onset of mortgage indebtedness or whether those with worsening health are more likely to find themselves in difficulty. Whilst the data are suggestive of the former, it is likely that there is an element of both causal *and* selection processes at work here. Indeed, as we have noted above, mortgage indebtedness is rarely an isolated life event, but an experience which results from and impacts upon other biographical changes. In trying to make further sense of our findings the following discussion draws upon recent conceptual analyses and qualitative studies which might assist in the future exploration of this topic.

Mortgage indebtedness as a 'biographical disruption'
As we have indicated above, the reasons for mortgage indebtedness are varied and so too will be the *experience* of such indebtedness. It is likely that it is caused by a constellation of factors rather than simple cause and effect. The experience of arrears will therefore be related to other biographical changes. Although we have demonstrated that poor mental health may be associated with mortgage indebtedness, it is likely that changes in health and caring for others in ill health may also sometimes be an antecedent or compounding factor which led to job loss or a reduction of earnings. For

example, Ford *et al.* (1995: 29) cite the case of a woman in mortgage arrears who explained:

> My husband's overtime money disappeared, then he had a back injury which put him on the sick register. He was on full pay for four months, now he is on half pay. Also I've lost my wages because of the birth of my son

A man from the same study described how caring commitments and reduction of earnings contributed to his arrears.

> My wages dropped when the firm was taken over. They stopped the commission and Karen had to give up part-time work to look after her mum. Our income went down by £150 per week. (Ford *et al.* 1995: 29)

Thus, a feature of mortgage indebtedness appears to be that it is but one dimension of a series of biographical changes. Like illness it may be conceptualised as a 'biographical disruption' (Bury 1982) which may have profound consequences for a person's sense of self and social identity, and coping with it involves a series of complex strategies. Any attempt to explore the link between difficulties with mortgage payments and poor mental health therefore requires an analysis of the meanings and interpretations of such life situations from the point of view of members of the household where such problems have occurred. The results of the secondary analysis presented in this paper therefore should be treated as exploratory work which simply sets the context for a more intensive and primarily qualitative study of the social impact of housing insecurity.[4]

Mortgage indebtedness and ontological insecurity

A number of authors have argued that home ownership confers identity and is a marker of social status. As David Morgan in his recent book *Family Connections* puts it

> The idea of property points both to a location in physical and social space and to an individual or family life project which is increasingly bound up with individual identity . . . To have a 'good' address and to be a home-owner is to make certain kinds of status claims, which reflect on one's own sense of personal worth or achievement and, often, upon the identities of those with whom one is associated. (1996: 180)

If entering owner occupation confers such status it is perhaps not surprising that we have found that not being able to keep up with the requirements of owner occupation is linked to poor mental health. Qualitative research in this area has found that this may take the form of reduced levels of self esteem and social status. For example Ford (1994: 27) quotes respondents in her study who had experienced mortgage possession as saying:

> We lost respect, it was the best in the road . . . somewhere to show people. They couldn't believe I'd achieved so much.

and

> Pride, this has hurt my pride.

and again

> There [home that had been possessed], I wasn't embarrassed for the children when they brought their friends home.

A number of studies have therefore shown that the 'home' and, in particular the ownership of one's own home, may be bound up with notions of self and identity. Thus, owing money on a house that one has bought may well have different meanings from owing money on a home which is actually owned by someone else. To be an owner occupier has connotations of being an adult who is a responsible citizen able to fulfil obligations and someone who has property rights. Saunders (1990) takes this argument further when he argues that home ownership is something to which people universally aspire, he suggests that people have an innate desire to own their own homes. Drawing on R.D. Laing's notion of 'ontological security' developed by Giddens (1984) he maintains that within an increasingly turbulent and uncertain world a home of one's own serves to reinforce one's basic self identity. He suggests therefore that in a world characterised by change and instability home ownership provides a major source of

> ontological security, for a home of one's own offers both a physical (hence a spatially rooted) and permanent (hence temporally rooted) location in the world. (Saunders 1990: 293)

Essentially he refers to emotional security which, in turn, is contingent upon one's biographical continuity and freedom from real and perceived external threats. These factors are necessary for the formation of a stable sense of self and identity. Thus, he argues that home ownership facilitates a greater sense of ontological security:

> the privately owned home seems to represent a secure anchor point where the nerves can be rested and the senses allowed to relax [. . .]. When ordinary people own their own homes, they seem more confident and self reliant. (Saunders 1990: 311)

Whilst Saunders is possibly correct to argue that home ownership is for many people bound up with their social status and identity he is, as we have seen, wrong to presume that this is an invariably positive experience, and he is definitely wrong to suggest that home ownership guarantees emotional security.

Surveys of public opinion carried out in the 1980s and early 1990s would certainly confirm the widespread political claim that home ownership is 'what most people want' (Doling and Ford 1996). Home ownership has been perceived by the public, and promoted by successive governments as a means of gaining control over one's life and one's future. However, more recent research indicates that people's attitudes towards owner occupation might be changing (Memery *et al.* 1995, Doling and Ford 1996). Whilst the discourse of home ownership during the 1980s was littered with terms such as 'trading up', 'equity gain', and 'gentrification', the discourse of the 1990s has been dominated by terms such as 'negative equity', 'arrears', 'repossessions' and 'debt overhang' (Forrest and Murie 1994). As Forrest and Murie point out: 'There are households which are becoming impoverished rather than enriched by their experience of the tenure' (1994: 55). This may also impact upon gender inequalities. As households begin to experience difficulties with paying the mortgage it has been found that it is women who extend their responsibilities and take on financial responsibilities for debt management in the household (Ford 1988, 1991). This has also been found to be the case with other aspects of debt or where households experience significant reductions of income (Bradshaw and Holmes 1989, Pahl 1989, Parker 1992).

Individualisation and insecurity

As we indicated above, recent housing policies are premised on the idea that individuals should take responsibility for their own shelter. This ideology of individual responsibility is a feature which now underpins other welfare policies such as health, education, employment and social security. Over recent decades the balance has tipped in favour of individual responsibilities rather than social rights. Housing policies, or more especially the consequences of these policies, must be understood within the context of these broader policy trends. They have contributed towards the formation of what Wilkinson (1996) has called a 'cash and keys society':

> Increasingly we live in what might be called a 'cash and keys' society. Whenever we leave the confines of our own homes we face the world with the two perfect symbols of the nature of social relations on the street. Cash equips us to take part in transactions mediated by the market, while keys protect our private gains from each other's envy and greed . . . Although we are all wholly dependent on one another for our livelihoods, this interdependence is turned from being a social process into a process by which we fend for ourselves in an attempt to wrest a living from an asocial environment. Instead of being people with whom we have bonds and share common interests, others become rivals, competitors for jobs, for houses, for space, seats on the bus, parking places . . . We feel hurt, angry, belittled, annoyed and sometimes superior as the processes of social distinction and social exclusion thread their way between us. (1996: 226)

Contemporary sociologists have also theorised about such processes of what they call *individualisation*. Giddens (1992), Rose (1993) and Beck and Beck-Gersheim (1996) have argued that individualisation is one of the most profound features of late modernism. As the latter authors note:

one of the decisive features of individualization processes . . . is that they not only permit, but demand an active contribution by individuals . . . If they are not to fail individuals must be able to plan for the long term and adapt to change; they must organise and improvise, set goals, recognise obstacles, accept defeats and attempt new starts. They need initiative, tenacity, flexibility . . . (Beck and Beck-Gersheim 1996: 27)

Individuals are encouraged to be enterprising, to take advice so that they may calculate and negotiate their own risks, be they related to health or finance (Nettleton 1997). As in all spheres of welfare we see here examples of what O'Malley (1992) calls 'the privatisation of risk'. Within this context, when things start to go wrong individuals and/or individual households will invariably feel socially isolated. The social and welfare mechanisms to which they might hitherto have turned are being diminished. Today losing a job may mean losing a home if mortgage payments cannot be met. When possessions occur there are now fewer alternatives; for example, social housing has been diminished, it is restricted to those in 'priority need', and is increasingly of a poor quality (Burrows *et al.* 1997). Responsibility for basic welfare provision – both housing and health – is being placed in the hands of individual households and this means when there is any disruption to people's everyday lives, such as the reduction of income, or additional caring responsibilities, then people's circumstances are particularly precarious. For some, the experience of buying one's own home has contributed to, and compounded their circumstances, and as we have seen, the psycho-social consequences of it may be profound.

Conclusion

Mortgage indebtedness is socially patterned, with those groups who are already socio-economically disadvantaged being at most risk of problematic home ownership. Furthermore, our data suggest that the onset of mortgage indebtedness appears to be associated with higher scores on the GHQ12 – a tool designed to measure mental health status. The experience for men is also associated with increased rates of consultation with GPs. This chapter has been limited to the impact of mortgage debt and has not examined the possible health effects of those who actually have their homes possessed. It is likely that losing a home in this way will also have profound consequences for health and wellbeing of the members of the households involved (Nettleton 1998). Indeed, one of the aims of the research presented in this paper is to demonstrate that within contemporary Britain any analysis of current health and social inequalities must have an appreciation of the changing nature of housing policy and the increasingly diversified nature of owner occupation.

Furthermore, the rise in the numbers of people with mortgage arrears, and the number of people who have their homes possessed, will have an impact on all home owners and not just on those who are in debt. Indeed research into people's reactions to the changes in the housing market during the 1990s has found that people do not wholeheartedly adhere to the idea that there is nothing as secure as bricks and mortar (Memery *et al.* 1995). Inequality, poverty and insecurity make for what Wilkinson (1996) has called a 'cash and keys society' which is likely to impact upon all members of society and not just those who are not directly and materially affected by poverty. Anyone who has had experience of buying their own home during the last decade may well feel that this view reflects their experience. It is possible therefore that the rise in arrears is likely to generate a wider sense of unease amongst home owners, especially at a time of substantial economic and employment restructuring which are already invoking widespread feelings of insecurity.

Acknowledgements

Thanks are due to the anonymous referees and the editors of this volume for their advice and support.

Notes

1 The data used in this chapter were made available through the Data Archive at the University of Essex. The data were originally collected by the ESRC Research Centre on Micro-Social Change at the University of Essex. Neither the original collectors of the data nor the Archive bear any responsibility for the analyses or interpretations presented here. For further details of the BHPS see Buck *et al.* (1994).

2 'Council housing' refers to social housing, which is owned by a Local Authority and rented to tenants.

3 We must be cautious here. Statistics on mortgage possessions, like any others, are a product of social processes. The decline in the number of mortgage possessions in the 1990s may be due to a combination of factors, which include matters such as the changing attitudes of lenders to those in difficulty, and a change in the attitudes of judges in county courts who preside over possession hearings (for a fuller discussion see Ford 1997).

4 The authors are currently working on a Joseph Rowntree Foundation funded study of the social consequences of mortgage possession for families with children.

References

Arber, S. (1991) Class, paid employment and family roles: making sense of structural disadvantage, gender and health status, *Social Science and Medicine*, 32, 4, 425–36.

Bartley, M. (1994) Unemployment and ill health: understanding the relationship, *Journal of Epidemiology and Community Health*, 48, 4, 333–7.

Beck, U. and Beck-Gersheim, G. (1996) Individualization and precarious freedoms. In Heelas, P., Lash, S. and Morris, P. (eds) *Detraditionalization*. London: Blackwell.

Best, R. (1995) The housing dimension. In Benzeval, M., Judge, K. and Whitehead, M. (eds) *Tackling Inequalities in Health*. London: King's Fund.

Bradshaw, J. and Holmes, H. (1989) *Living on the Edge*. London: CPAG.

Buck, N., Gershuny, J., Rose, D. and Scott, A. (1994) *Changing Households*. University of Essex: ESRC Research Centre on Micro-Social Change.

Burrows, R. (1999) Residential mobility and residualisation in social housing in England, *Journal of Social Policy*, forthcoming.

Burrows, R. (1998) Mortgage indebtedness in England: an 'epidemiology', *Housing Studies*, 13, 1, 5–22.

Burrows, R. and Ford, J. (1997) Who needs a safety net? The social distribution of mortgage arrears in England, *Housing Finance*, 34, 17–24.

Burrows, R., Pleace, N. and Quilgars, D. (eds) (1997) *Homelessness and Social Policy*. London: Routledge.

Bury, M. (1982) Chronic illness as a biographical disruption, *Sociology of Health and Illness*, 4, 2, 167–82.

Davis, R. and Dhooge, Y. (1992) *Living with Mortgage Arrears*. London: HMSO.

Doling, J., Ford, J. and Stafford B. (eds) (1988) *The Property Owing Democracy*. Aldershot: Avebury.

Doling, J. and Ford, J. (1996) The new home ownership, *Environment and Planning*, 28, 157–72.

Ferrie, J., Shipley, M.J., Marmot, M., Stansfield, S. and Davey Smith, G. (1995) Health effects of anticipation of job change and non-employment: longitudinal data from the Whitehall II study, *British Medical Journal*, 311, 1264–9.

Ford, J. (1988) *The Indebted Society*. London: Routledge.

Ford, J. (1993) Mortgage possession, *Housing Studies*, 8, 4.

Ford, J. (1994) *Problematic Home Ownership*. Loughborough University/Joseph Rowntree Foundation.

Ford, J. (1997) Mortgage arrears, mortgage possessions and homelessness. In Burrows, R., Pleace, N. and Quilgars, D. (eds) *Homelessness and Social Policy*. London: Routledge.

Ford, J., Kempson, E. and Wilson, M. (1995) *Mortgage Arrears and Possessions; Perspectives from Borrowers, Lenders and the Courts*. London: HMSO.

Ford, J. and Kempson, E. (1997) *Bridging the Gap? Private Insurance for Mortgagors*. York: York Centre for Housing Policy.

Ford, J. and Wilcox, S. (1998) Can owner occupation take the strain? *Housing Studies*, forthcoming.

Forrest, R. and Murie, A. (1994) Home ownership in recession, *Housing Studies*, 9, 1, 55–74.

Giddens, A. (1984) *The Constitution of Society*. Cambridge: Polity Press.

Giddens, A. (1992) *Modernity and Self-Identity*. Cambridge: Polity Press.

Hopton, J. and Hunt, S. (1996) The health effects of improvements to housing: a longitudinal study, *Housing Studies*, 11, 2, 271–86.

Hogarth, T., Elias, P. and Ford, J. (1996) *Mortgages, Families and Jobs: an Exploration of the Growth in Home Ownership in the 1980s*. Warwick: Institute for Employment Research.

Hutton, W. (1995) *The State We're In*. London: Jonathan Cape.

Ineichen, B. (1993) *Homes and Health: how Housing and Health Interact*. London: E. and F.N. Spon.

Kempson, E. (1996) *Life on a Low Income*, York: Joseph Rowntree Foundation.

Memery, C., Munro, M., Madigan, R. and Gibb, K. (1995) Reacting to the housing market slump, University of Glasgow, *Economic Beliefs and Behaviour Programme*, Discussion Paper 10.

Morgan, D. (1996) *Family Connections*. Cambridge: Polity Press.

Nettleton, S. (1997) Governing the risky self: how to become healthy, wealthy and wise. In Petersen, A. and Bunton, R. (eds) *Foucault, Health and Medicine*. London: Routledge.

Nettleton, S. (1998) Losing homes through mortgage possesion: a 'new' public health issue, *Critical Public Health*, 8, 1, 47–58.

Nettleton, S. and Burrows, R. (1998) Individualization processes and social policy: insecurity, reflexivity and risk in the restructuring of contemporary British health and housing policies. In Carter, J. (ed) *Postmodernity and the Fragmentation of Welfare*. London: Routledge.

Oldman, C. and Kemp, P. (1996) *Income Support Mortgage Interest: An Assessment of Current Issues and Future Prospects*. London: Council of Mortgage Lenders.

O'Malley, (1992) Risk, power and crime prevention, *Economy and Society*, 21, 3, 252–75.

Pahl, J. (1989) *Money and Marriage*. Basingstoke: Macmillan.

Pahl, R. (1995) *After Success?* Cambridge: Polity Press.

Parker, G. (1992) Making ends meet: women, credit and debt. In Glendinning, C. and Miller, J. (eds) *Women and Poverty in Britain in the 1990s*. London: Harvester Wheatsheaf.

Rose, N. (1993) Government, authority and expertise in advanced liberalism, *Economy and Society*, 22, 3, 283–99.

Saunders, P. (1990) *A Nation of Home Owners*. London: Unwin Hyman.

Smith, S. (1989) *Housing and Health: a Review and Research Agenda*. Glasgow: ESRC Centre for Housing Research.

Smith, S. (1990) Health status and the housing system, *Social Science and Medicine*, 31, 7, 753–62.

Wilcox, S. (1996) *Housing Review 1996/97*. York: Joseph Rowntree Foundation.

Wilkinson, R. (1996) *Unhealthy Societies: the Afflications of Inequality*. London: Routledge.

Wilson, S.H. and Walker, G.M. (1993) Unemployment and health: a review, *Public Health*, 107, 153–62.

9. A lifecourse perspective on socio-economic inequalities in health: the influence of childhood socio-economic conditions and selection processes

H. Dike van de Mheen, Karien Stronks and Johann P. Mackenbach

Introduction

Socio-economic inequalities in health in adult life have been found in many European countries throughout a long period (Fox 1989, Illsley and Svensson 1990). Still largely unanswered is the question on the processes underlying the generation of these inequalities. The Black Report (Townsend and Davidson 1982) offers some explanations for these inequalities, of which the causal explanations via pathways of behavioural and materialist factors are suggested as the most likely. After more than a decade of research, however, the social processes underlying exposure to these risk factors and the mechanisms by which exposures lead to disease are still not properly understood (Davey Smith *et al.* 1994). As socio-economic health differences in adult life are probably partly explained by processes earlier in life, some authors have recently stressed the importance of studying health inequalities and their determinants over the lifecourse (Davey Smith *et al.* 1994, Vågerö and Illsley 1995).

In a life-time perspective, accumulation of adverse socio-economic circumstances and selection are important mechanisms, which successively may cause a downward spiral. Health problems in youth may be followed by a lower socio-economic position upon joining the labour force. A lower socio-economic status will lead to more health problems in adult life, which in turn may cause downward social mobility. Studying these mechanisms empirically seems worthwhile, but a further conceptualisation of the way in which these mechanisms might act over the lifecourse is required.

In this chapter a conceptual model is presented (Figure 1) which will be examined with empirical data.[1] Three processes will be emphasised. The numbers refer to the relations which will be dealt with in the chapter.

The first process concerns the contribution of *childhood socio-economic conditions* to socio-economic health inequalities in adult life. The central question is: are adult people in lower socio-economic groups less healthy

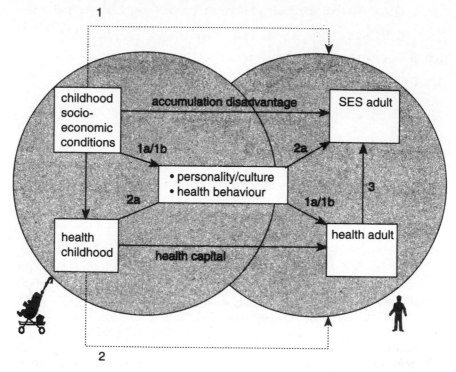

Figure 1: *Conceptual model*

1 contribution of childhood socio-economic conditions to socio-economic health inequalities in adult life
1a independent effect of childhood socio-economic conditions on adult health
1b independent effect of childhood socio-economic conditions on adult health through health behaviour and personality/cultural factors
2 contribution of childhood health to socio-economic health inequalities in adult life
2a contribution of childhood health to socio-economic health inequalities in adult life through selection on health in childhood
3 selection on health in adult life

than people in higher socio-economic groups because they have grown up in relatively poor socio-economic conditions? Important in this question is whether the effect of childhood conditions on adult health is produced independently of the socio-economic position in adulthood.

First, this might be a direct causal mechanism (Lundberg 1991a): childhood socio-economic circumstances may have a significant influence on childhood health, which in turn is related to adult health. As children from less privileged families are likely to become less privileged adults, and childhood illness is related to health status in adult life (Wadsworth 1986), this may partly explain socio-economic health inequalities in adult life.

In addition, adverse childhood conditions may influence chances of education, job opportunities and life chances in general, resulting in 'unhealthy life careers' (Lundberg 1993). The influence of childhood disadvantage on health can be described in terms of 'social programming': the effect of early social environment on adult health is mediated through social conditions during upbringing, educational achievement, entry into work and adult living conditions and lifestyle (Vågerö and Illsley 1995). Pathways in this 'social programming' may run through health-related behaviour and personality characteristics. Consequently, the subsequent question is: is it through intermediate factors such as behaviour and/or personality and cultural factors that the independent effect of childhood conditions is determined?

This leads to the question as to whether a process of accumulation exists. That is: the longer a person's exposure to poor circumstances, the greater the health risks? And also, is the adverse effect on adult health of a period of disadvantage both in childhood and adulthood stronger than just the sum of the separate effects of childhood and adult socio-economic conditions?

A second process concerns the contribution of *childhood health* to socio-economic health inequalities in adult life. Are people in lower socio-economic groups less healthy than people in higher socio-economic groups because they experienced more health problems in childhood? If so, as described above in the first process, this might be a causal mechanism: adverse childhood socio-economic circumstances may cause childhood health problems. In addition there may also be an effect of childhood health by means of health selection. Is it (also) through a selection process that the effect of childhood health on socio-economic health inequalities in adult life is produced? This selection process in childhood concerns so-called intergenerational social mobility; health problems in childhood may influence educational opportunities and consequently the occupational career and income level later in life.

The health capital accrued upon entering adulthood may also affect a person's socio-economic status throughout the rest of her/his life. So the third process in the model concerns *health selection* in adult life, the so-called intragenerational social mobility. The question is: are people in lower socio-economic groups less healthy than people in higher ones because they are more likely to experience downward mobility (with respect, for example, to occupation or income), or less likely to experience upward mobility, because of health problems which partly have their roots in childhood?

In this chapter the conceptual model described above will be examined empirically. Each of the processes identified will be discussed separately, using data from the Longitudinal Study of Socio-Economic Health Differences (LS-SEHD) in the Netherlands. In the LS-SEHD, data on childhood socio-economic conditions, childhood and adult health, adult socio-economic status, personality characteristics/cultural factors and adult health-related behaviour, are available to investigate the mechanisms whereby childhood socio-economic conditions and selection on health play a role in explaining socio-economic health inequalities in adult life.

Design of the study

The design and objective of the LS-SEHD are described in detail elsewhere (Mackenbach *et al.* 1994). The study is based on a cohort of 15–74-year-old, non-institutionalised Dutch nationals, living in the city of Eindhoven and surroundings (a region in the South East of the Netherlands). At the start of the survey a random sample of approximately 27,000 people was drawn from the population registers of the participating municipalities, stratified by age and postcode (45–74-year-old people and people from the highest and lowest socio-economic groups, as indicated by postcode, were overrepresented in order to enhance the statistical power of the study and the socio-economic contrast within the study population). People in this sample were sent a postal questionnaire in 1991. The response rate for the postal survey was 70.1 per cent, resulting in a study population of 18,973 respondents. Two subsamples were drawn to take part, if willing, in a subsequent oral interview. The first subsample was formed by a group randomly chosen (approximately 3,500 persons, again stratified by postcode) from the respondents to the postal survey. The response rate for this oral interview was 79.4 per cent (2,802 respondents). For the second subsample (also taken from the respondents on the postal survey), chronically ill people were overrepresented (approximately 4,000 persons). The response rate for this second group was 72.5 per cent (2,878 respondents). No significant differences in response rate for the postal survey or the first oral interview were found by sex, age, marital status, degree of urbanisation or socio-economic status (measured by postcode). For the second subsample, response was slightly lower among the younger people, unmarried persons and those living in the city. In 1995 a follow-up postal questionnaire was sent to the oral interviewees (response rate appr. 80 per cent).

We had to use different subsamples to answer the research questions as described in the introduction appropriately. More details can be found elsewhere (van de Mheen *et al.* 1997, 1998a, 1998b, 1998c). For example, the study population used in the analyses with respect to (socio-economic) childhood conditions was restricted to persons aged 25 and over, since the influence of childhood characteristics on behaviour and health, as well as on the socio-economic status finally attained, may not have worn off yet in younger persons. The study population used in the analysis on health selection was restricted to respondents aged 15–59. With a follow-up period of 4.5 years this population does not include respondents who reached the normal age of retirement (65 years).

Data

In the LS-SEHD several indicators of (self-reported) health, socio-economic status and intermediate factors were measured.

Socio-economic status was indicated by the highest level of education attained, the occupational level of the respondent and of the head of the household. Educational level was divided into seven categories (university, higher vocational, intermediate general, intermediate vocational, lower general, lower vocational and primary school). Students were classified by their current course. The occupational level was determined on the basis of the current occupation (or the most recent if not in paid employment) of the respondent and of the head of the household. Occupations were classified according to the Erikson, Goldthorpe and Portocarero (EGP)-scheme (1983, 1992) into seven[2] categories: higher grade professionals, lower grade professionals, routine non-manual, self-employed, high-skilled manual, low-skilled manual and unskilled manual).

Health problems were indicated by self-reported health and mortality. Self-reported health was measured by perceived general health, health complaints and by the presence of chronic diseases at the time of the survey. Perceived general health was measured by the question 'how would you rate your health in general'. A dichotomous variable was constructed ('very good, good' versus 'fair, sometimes good and sometimes bad, bad'). Health complaints were measured by a thirteen-item questionnaire, divided into two categories: 0–3 and 4 or more complaints. Chronic conditions were established according to a list of 23 chronic diseases. The answers were classified into two categories: none versus one or more chronic conditions. Mortality follow-up for the entire study population was completed by 15 July 1996.

Childhood socio-economic conditions were defined as socio-economic and material circumstances at the age of 12. Variables were the occupational level of the father (seven categories), the educational level of the mother (five categories) and the financial situation (no lack of money, sometimes lack of money, (very) often lack of money).

Personality characteristics were indicated by neuroticism and (external) locus of control, and *cultural factors* by 'orientation towards the future' and parochialism. We used validated questionnaires (Eysenck *et al.* 1985, Andriesen 1972, Ormel 1980, Tax 1982).

Health-related behavioural factors are smoking, alcohol consumption, leisure time physical exercise and Body Mass Index. Smokers were categorised into never smokers, earlier smokers and current smokers. Alcohol consumption was classified into abstainers, light, moderate and (very) excessive drinkers. Body Mass Index was categorised into under-weight (Quetelet-index < 20), normal (Quetelet-index between 20 and 27) and overweight (Quetelet-index > 27). Leisure time physical exercise was measured in four categories: no exercise, light, moderate and vigorous exercise.

Childhood health was assessed retrospectively by eliciting answers to the following question: 'Did you suffer from a severe disease or accident in childhood?' If the answer was 'yes', the subsequent questions were: 'Were you admitted to hospital for that disease(s) or accident(s)?' and 'What was your age at the time of hospital admission?' Only hospital admissions at the age of 25 or under were included, as later hospital admissions were not regarded as 'childhood' health.

The *demographic variables* age (5-year categories), sex, marital status, religious affiliation and degree of urbanisation were added as confounders, because these variables are probably related to both health and socio-economic status (in childhood and in adult life). One might assume that some of these factors are not just confounders, but also intermediary in the process between socio-economic status and health. Hence, adjusting for these demographic variables always means a conservative estimation of the relation.

Logistic regression was used to estimate the contribution of different variables to the explanation of socio-economic health differences in adult life.

Table 1 *Odds ratios[1] less-than-'good' perceived general health by current educational level, before and after adjusting for childhood living conditions, men and women, 25–74 years*

| | | less-than-'good' perceived general health | | |
| | | model A[2] | model B[2] | |
		OR [95% CI]	OR [95% CI]	Diff. with A (%)[3]
educational	1 (110)	1	1	
level[4] N	2 (278)	2.89 [1.31–6.37]	2.75 [1.24–6.08]	7.4
	3 (409)	3.52 [1.63–7.57]	3.26 [1.50–7.09]	10.3
	4 (715)	4.68 [2.20–9.95]	4.26 [1.97–9.20]	11.4
	5 (338)	8.44 [3.91–18.21]	7.41 [3.34–16.44]	13.8

[1] Odds ratios adjusted for age (5-years categories), sex, marital status, religious affiliation and degree of urbanization
[2] model A = educational level + confounders
model B = A + education mother + occupation father + financial situation
[3] (OR model A – OR model B)/(OR model A–1)
[4] 1 = university; 2 = higher vocational; 3 = intermediate vocational/intermediate general; 4 = lower vocational/lower general; 5 = primary school

Health differences between childhood socio-economic groups (indicated by father's occupational level) or adult socio-economic groups (indicated by respondent's educational or occupational level) are expressed in Odds Ratios (OR) with 95 per cent confidence intervals. The highest socio-economic level was used as a reference in all analyses. One or more explanatory factors were added to a model with childhood or adult socio-economic level and confounders only. The contribution of these explanatory factors was measured by the percentage reduction in the Odds Ratios of (childhood) socio-economic groups compared with the first model. The formula used is: (OR model A – OR model B)/(OR model A – 1).

In the analyses concerning the role of selection processes, the outcome variable was occupational mobility. Also by using logistic regression models we estimated the risk of occupational mobility for respondents who reported health problems at baseline. Respondents without health problems were used as reference category.

Overview of the results

The first step in testing our conceptual model empirically was to study the extent to which socio-economic health inequalities in adult life are explained by childhood socio-economic conditions (relation 1 in the model). In addition, we studied which childhood socio-economic conditions were the most important in this explanation (van de Mheen et al. 1997).

Table 1 shows the respondent's educational level and perceived general health. Findings on chronic conditions were highly similar (results not shown). It can be seen that approximately 10 per cent of the relation between adult socio-economic status and adult health may be attributed to childhood socio-economic conditions. An additional analysis (results not shown) indicated that the mother's education was the most important factor, followed by the father's occupation and the financial situation.

Unravelling the first process was further helped by looking at whether childhood socio-economic status had an independent effect (i.e. adjusted for adult socio-economic status) on adult health (relation 1a in the model) (van de Mheen et al. 1998a). In these analyses, we used perceived general health, health complaints and mortality as outcome variables. Results concerning perceived general health are presented in Figure 2, adjusted for confounders. For the other health outcomes results were comparable.

Childhood socio-economic status as indicated by the father's occupation had an independent effect on adult health, even after adjustment for the respondent's own occupation. Respondents with fathers in the lowest occupational class had a significantly higher risk of a less-than-good perceived general health, health complaints and mortality, although the latter was not statistically significantly different from unity. This means that the

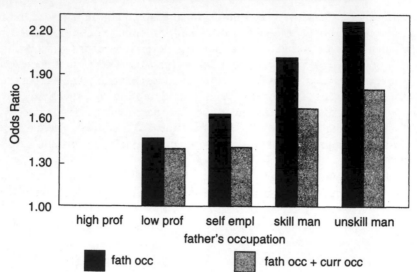

Figure 2: *Perceived health less-than-good by father's occupation*

risk of health problems was higher among respondents who had grown up in unfavourable socio-economic circumstances, irrespective of their current socio-economic status. People who had grown up in unfavourable circumstances, and who were still in unfavourable circumstances at adult age, ran the highest risk (results not shown). We found no interaction, however, between childhood and current socio-economic status: the influence of childhood circumstances was the same in all adult socio-economic groups.

In two subsequent analyses, we examined whether the influence of childhood socio-economic status on adult health (relation 1b in the model) operates through intermediate factors. We first concentrated on health behaviour: does childhood socio-economic status affect adult health through behavioural factors? (van de Mheen *et al.* 1998a). Results are presented in Table 2.

Again, the father's occupation was used as an indicator for childhood socio-economic status. The outcome variable in this table is perceived general health. Results for health complaints and mortality were comparable. It is evident that the relation between childhood socio-economic status and adult health decreased when behavioural factors were added to the model. After adjustment for behavioural factors, the effect of the father's occupational level was still statistically significant. This means that the effect of childhood socio-economic conditions on adult health is only partly determined by behavioural factors. Physical activity was the most important factor: an estimated 11.5 per cent of the increased risk of a less-than-good perceived general health for the lowest father's occupational group can be

Table 2 Odds ratios[1] less-than-'good' perceived general health by father's occupation, adjusted for current occupation and behavioural factors, men and women, 25–74 years

father's occupation	model A[2] OR [95% CI]	model A, adjusted for BMI OR [95% CI]	Diff. with A (%)[3]	model A, adjusted for alcohol consumption OR [85% CI]	Diff. with A (%)	model A, adjusted for physical activity OR [95% CI]	Diff. with A (%)
high prof	1	1		1		1	
low prof/ routine non-man	1.39 [1.13–1.68]	1.37 [1.12–1.66]	5.1	1.40 [1.14–1.69]	–	1.33 [1.09–1.61]	15.4
self-empl	1.40 [1.14–1.69]	1.41 [1.16–1.71]	–	1.38 [1.13–1.68]	5.0	1.29 [1.06–1.56]	27.5
skilled man	1.66 [1.38–1.97]	1.65 [1.38–1.97]	1.5	1.62 [1.33–1.97]	6.1	1.59 [1.30–1.93]	10.6
unskilled man	1.78 [1.45–2.15]	1.75 [1.43–2.11]	3.8	1.74 [1.43–2.11]	5.1	1.69 [1.38–2.-5]	11.5

[1] Odds ratios adjusted for age (5-yr categories), sex, marital status, religious affiliation and degree of urbanization
[2] model A = father's occupation adjusted for current occupation and confounders
[3] only reduction (red.) in Odds Ratio was calculated: (OR model A – OR model B)/(OR model A – 1)

attributed to this factor (Odds Ratio decreasing from 1.78 to 1.69). Smoking did not contribute to the relation between the father's occupation and health. The other behavioural factors (physical activity, alcohol consumption and BMI), taken together, explained a small part (approximately 10 per cent) of the differences in adult health between childhood socio-economic groups (results not shown).

Besides the role of health behaviour we studied the role of personality and culture. Does the influence of childhood socio-economic status on adult health operate through personality characteristics and cultural factors? The results are presented in Figures 3 and 4, adjusted for current occupational level and confounders.

All personality and cultural factors measured contributed to the higher risk of a less-than-good perceived general health among respondents whose fathers had a lower occupation level. For neuroticism and future orientation this is shown in Figures 3 and 4 as an example. For locus of control and parochialism, results were highly comparable. The reduction, except for parochialism, was statistically significant. When the four factors were put together in a model, the Odds Ratios of educational levels decreased by approximately 50 per cent (results not shown). The contribution of personality characteristics (neuroticism and locus of control) was more important than the contribution of cultural factors (parochialism and orientation towards the future). We found comparable results for health complaints (results not shown).

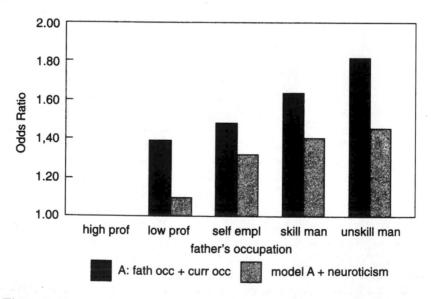

Figure 3: *Perceived health less-than-good contribution neuroticism*

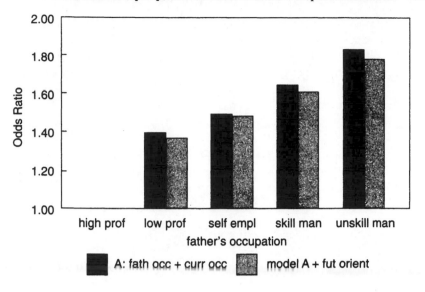

Figure 4: *Perceived health less-than-good contribution future orientation*

The second process in our conceptual model is the role of childhood health in explaining socio-economic health inequalities in adult life (van de Mheen *et al.* 1997) (relation 2 in the model). In this analysis, adulthood was defined as the period between 25 and 34 years. Older age groups were not analysed because of considerable recall bias (van de Mheen *et al.* 1998a). Therefore, the question mentioned above could only be answered with respect to early adult health. The results are presented in Figure 5 for severe disease in childhood, adjusted for confounders. Results for hospital admission showed the same picture.

The figures show that educational differences in perceived general health decrease if adjustment is made for childhood health. Childhood health accounted for approximately five to 10 per cent of the increased risk of having a less-than-good perceived general health. The analyses were repeated for occupational level: the results were highly comparable with those obtained from analyses for educational level (results not shown). Results with respect to chronic conditions were similar (results not shown).

In studying the role of health selection in childhood (intergenerational social mobility) (relation 2a in the model), we adjusted for the occupation of the father as an indicator of childhood socio-economic status. As stated above, a reduction in Odds Ratio of approximately five to 10 per cent was found when the association between educational level and less-than-good perceived general health was corrected for childhood illness. After adjustment for the father's occupation, we found similar reduction percentages in Odds Ratio when childhood illness was added to the model (results not

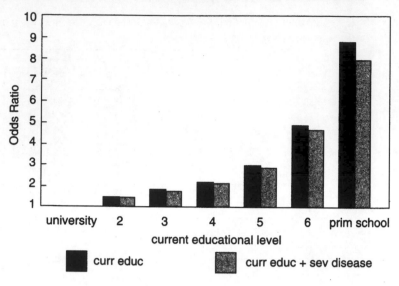

Figure 5: *Perceived health less-than-good contribution severe disease child-hood*

shown). Thus, the contribution of health in childhood cannot be accounted for by the occupation of the father. This means that selection on health in childhood would seem to account mainly for the extent to which childhood health determines socio-economic health differences in early adult life. We tested this by estimating the relation between health in childhood and educational level, adjusted for occupation of the father. Adjusting for the father's occupation did not change the relation significantly, which confirmed our hypothesis. We conclude therefore that it seems possible that the role of direct intergenerational selection is small but relevant, at least in early adult life.

The third process in our conceptual model was the role of the selection mechanism at adult age (intragenerational mobility, relation 3 in the model). To what extent are health problems in adulthood related to downward or upward social mobility? We used prospective data from the LS-SEHD from 1991 to 1995 to answer this question. We studied the influence of health in 1991 on change in occupational status in 1995. Analyses were performed separately for upward and downward mobility. The occupational mobility was determined among persons who had been in paid employment in both 1991 and 1995. During this period, 72 persons moved downward and 114 upward.

Table 3 shows the Odds Ratios for upward and downward mobility, related to three health indicators: perceived general health, chronic conditions and health complaints. It shows that health in 1991 was, during a

Table 3 *Odds ratios[1] occupational mobility 1991–1995 by health in 1991, paid job in 1991–1995, men and women, 15–59 years*

		decrease[2] OR [95% CI]	increase[2] OR [95% CI]	stable[2] OR [95% CI]
perceived general health[3]	less than good	1.06 [.56–1.99]	1.07 [.63–1.82]	0.92 [.59–1.42]
chronic condition[3]	> = 1	1.21 [.73–2.00]	1.29 [.84–1.96]	0.76 [.54–1.07]
health complaints[3]	> 4	1.04 [.59–1.82]	0.83 [.51–1.36]	1.09 [.73–1.62]

[1] Odds ratios adjusted for age (5-years cat.), sex, marital status, religious affiliation and degree of urbanization
[2] decrease resp. increase compared with stable plus increase resp. decrease, stable compared with increase plus decrease
[3] ref. cat = perceived general health (very) good, chronic condition 0, health complaints < = 3

follow-up time of 4.5 years, not related to occupational mobility. Neither decrease nor increase in occupational level was related to any of the health indicators.

Conclusions and discussion

In this chapter we have examined a conceptual model concerning the role of childhood socio-economic conditions and selection processes related to socio-economic health inequalities in adult life. We studied three processes: the influence of childhood socio-economic conditions, the influence of childhood health and the influence of intragenerational selection on adult health.

In this review of empirical results we used data from the Longitudinal Study of Socio-Economic Health Differences (LS-SEHD). In the analyses we had to use different subsamples, because some outcome measures or explanatory factors were not available for the total study population. This resulted in different numbers and, consequently, categorisation of variables which sometimes differed from the earlier results. It is not our purpose here to go into detail about methodological issues concerning data, data collection and methods of analyses. These subjects are discussed elsewhere (Mackenbach *et al.* 1994, van de Mheen *et al.* 1997, 1998a, 1998b, 1998c, Stronks 1997). However, we do raise briefly some general points about the nature of the data. First, non-response might bias the results. We observed only small differences in demographic variables between respondents and non-respondents on the postal survey and oral interviews. An additional survey among non-respondents showed that they did not differ from respondents regarding health and socio-economic variables. Overall, we expect that the respondents of both postal and oral interviews closely resemble the original sample. Response to the follow-up survey in 1995 was slightly lower in lower educational groups. We think, however, that this probably does not influence our results unduly.

Second, bias may have been introduced by the retrospective character of questions on childhood conditions and childhood health. We have concluded that the influence of childhood illness on socio-economic health inequalities in adult life could only be estimated as valid in the youngest age-group; when one is restricted, as we were, by a retrospective design, the report of this factor may be sensitive to memory failures in older age-groups. As our results in the youngest age-group seem to be in accordance with other studies (Power and Peckham 1990, Power *et al.* 1990, Starfield *et al.* 1984, Wadsworth 1986) a serious under- (or over-) estimation in this age group is not likely to have occurred. Systematic recall bias between socio-economic groups concerning father's occupation will less often occur, because it is less sensitive to memory failure. If it occurs, it may be more likely to underestimate the correlation between socio-economic status in adult life and childhood environment than to overestimate this correlation (Lundberg 1991b).

Third, the choice for self-reported health as indicator for adult health status may cause bias. It is recognised that self-reported health is a useful measure of health status because it is associated with morbidity (Power *et al.* 1991) and predicts mortality (Kaplan and Camacho 1983, Wannamethee and Shaper 1991). We tried to tackle the problem of self-reported health by using various health indicators, from the more subjective to the more objective. In addition, we used mortality data. Results were comparable for all health indicators and mortality. Summarising, we do not expect this bias to be considerable.

Childhood socio-economic conditions

We found that the relation between adult socio-economic status and adult health is influenced by childhood socio-economic conditions. This corresponds to relation 1 in the model. In our analysis almost 10 per cent of the relation could be explained. Others have found similar results (Power 1991, Lundberg 1991b). In this chapter, we have especially considered the influence of childhood socio-economic conditions on socio-economic health inequalities in adult life.

First of all, social disadvantage may exist throughout the course of life. Several authors have shown that both childhood and adult socio-economic status have an effect on adult health and mortality (Lundberg 1991a, 1991b,

1993, Vågerö and Leon 1994, Rahkonen *et al.* 1997). An accumulation of disadvantages may increase the effect of childhood socio-economic circumstances. This means that the adverse effect on adult health of a period of disadvantage might be stronger than just the sum of the separate effects of childhood and adult socio-economic conditions. Davey Smith *et al.* (1997) showed that the risk of mortality was higher in those who had experienced cumulative socio-economic disadvantages. They showed a graded association between cumulative social class and mortality: respondents who reported manual social class for three stages at the lifecourse (occupation of father, first job and occupation at the time of screening) had the highest death rates. Our results showed that social disadvantage indeed exists over the lifecourse: people who grew up in unfavourable circumstances, and who are still in unfavourable circumstances at adult age, run the highest risk. One might assume that the cumulative effect is not only additive, but also multiplicative. This means that the adverse health effect of living at social disadvantage during more periods over the lifecourse is stronger than just the sum of the separate effects of these periods. However, we did not find evidence for such a multiplicative effect, since we found no interaction between childhood and adult socio-economic status. This means that the influence of childhood circumstances is the same in all adult socio-economic groups and vice versa.

We found an independent effect of childhood socio-economic conditions on adult health (*i.e.* irrespective of adult socio-economic status). Vågerö and Illsley (1995) describe this influence of childhood disadvantage on health in terms of 'social programming': the effect of early social environment on adult health is mediated through social conditions during upbringing, educational achievement, entry into work and adult living conditions and lifestyle. One of the pathways in this 'social programming' may run through health-related behaviour. Since some of the backgrounds of health-related behaviour go back to childhood and early adulthood (Taylor 1991), this seems very likely. Results from the literature about this pathway are ambiguous. Blane *et al.* (1996) found no significant relation between childhood socio-economic status and behavioural factors. Lynch *et al.* (1997) found no differences between poor and rich parents with respect to smoking and alcohol consumption. Less physical activity, however, and less healthy diet, were more common among respondents with parents from lower socio-economic groups. Our results are partly in agreement with these studies. We found more unhealthy behaviour among respondents from lower childhood socio-economic groups, independent of their current socio-economic status, but the associations were not strong. Physical activity was the most important. The relation between childhood socio-economic circumstances and physical activity might also, however, partly reflect health selection: childhood socio-economic circumstances are related to health, and health problems (in childhood and adulthood) may lead to less physical activity. It is not to be expected that childhood health selection will explain the whole phenomenon, but it cannot be excluded. We need to explore the causal direction in more detail to understand the underlying mechanisms.

Our results show that the independent effect of childhood circumstances on adult health operates partly through unhealthy behaviour (approximately 10 per cent). This element, if rather small, cannot be ignored.

Vågerö and Illsley (1995) describe not only the interconnection between health development and social achievement by a process of 'social programming', but also the idea of common underlying causes. Their definition of 'co-evolution of health and social achievement' encompasses these two processes. The process of common underlying causes is called the process of indirect selection: not health problems in themselves, but common determinants may influence both social mobility and later health (Blane et al. 1993). Such characteristics have to be known or plausibly hypothesised determinants of social mobility and later health. Several characteristics have been suggested, such as behavioural factors, material deprivation during childhood and personality and cultural factors (Blane et al. 1993, Davey Smith et al. 1994, Sweeting and West 1995, Ranchor 1994). West (1991) suggests that the much greater effect on socio-economic inequalities in health is likely to result from indirect processes rather than from direct health selection: health and health potential will be distributed over classes by other associated factors which also influence social mobility.

What little literature there is on the relation of childhood socio-economic status and personality characteristics does not give a clear insight into the matter. Personality characteristics such as a sense of hopelessness or hostility were related to childhood socio-economic status; depression and a sense of coherence showed a non-significant trend (Lynch et al. 1997). Lundberg (1997) showed that a sense of coherence did not mediate effects of childhood factors on adult health.

Our results indicate that this pathway may be rather important: childhood circumstances proved to have an independent effect on both personality characteristics and cultural factors. This means that children growing up in socio-economically deprived groups face a higher risk of developing a neurotic personality and an external locus of control. These children are in adulthood also more orientated to the local culture than other children and less to a wider future. These factors were also associated with later health. From our analysis, it can be concluded that part of the independent effect of childhood socio-economic status on health leads to personality characteristics and cultural factors.

In the process of indirect selection, personality characteristics, and also behavioural and material factors, may act as common backgrounds, influencing not only adult health, but also social mobility. We shall explore the latter in further analyses.

In our analysis of personality and cultural factors, we adjusted for current social class. However, from a selection perspective, it seems that specific personality traits may affect educational and occupational achievement. Controlling for current social class would then imply overadjustment. However, the possibility that adult socio-economic conditions affect adult personality should not be excluded. It has been hypothesised that environmental conditions and experiences in adulthood may induce personality change and development (Funder et al. 1993, Heatherton and Weinberger 1994, Krahe 1992). Given this conceptual dilemma, we decided to adjust for current social class and present possibly conservative estimations.

Neuroticism appears to explain much of the relationship between childhood social conditions and self-reported adult health. It may be that self-reported health is systematically overreported by people with high neuroticism scores. The contribution of personality characteristics to the relation between childhood socio-economic status and subjective health might be overestimated if neuroticism would also affect the report of childhood socio-economic conditions. This is, however, not to be expected, since the report of father's occupation, for example, is not likely to be very sensitive for 'complaining'. On the contrary, one might argue that neuroticism is indeed formed by adverse childhood circumstances. In that case, neuroticism causally precedes adult health. Then, the contribution is not overestimated because it is part of the causal chain we are interested in.

Other explanations, according to Barker and colleagues, implies that the independent effect of childhood socio-economic conditions on adult health may point to biological determinants of health that operate in the early years. This perspective emphasises the early living conditions, which are not influenced by later socio-economic circumstances (Barker et al. 1989a, 1989b, Forsdahl 1977, 1978, Kuh and Wadsworth 1993). Because we did not measure early biological risk factors in our study, this mechanism could not be explored empirically. However, the hypothesis of 'biological programming' means that poverty affects later health via maternal constitution and health (through fetal in utero) and infant environment. Critics of this pathway argue that Barker et al.'s hypothesis refers to absolute poverty, relative poverty would hardly operate through this mechanism (Vågerö and Illsley 1995).

One might assume that the influence of personality characteristics and cultural factors on health act through health-related behaviour. However, as the association between childhood socio-economic circumstances and adult health was explained for approximately 10 per cent by behaviour, and for approximately 50 per cent by personality and cultural factors, it means that personality and cultural factors (also) have an independent influence on health, and not necessarily through unhealthy behaviour. Other mechanisms, e.g. through psycho-social stress-related factors, such as coping styles or social support, might be more plausible here. These possible explanations would have to be explored in further research.

Childhood health

The second process in our conceptual model is the explanation of socio-economic inequalities in adult life by childhood health. This corresponds to relation 2 in the model. In earlier results from the LS-SEHD it was shown that the risk of early adult health problems was approximately twice as high among people who reported health problems in childhood (van de Mheen *et al.* 1998a). In addition the risk of childhood health problems was higher in the less educated groups. In this review we have shown that childhood health plays a role in the explanation of socio-economic health differences in early adult life, although the contribution appeared to be rather small. Childhood health explains approximately five to 10 per cent of the increased risk of having a less-than-good perceived general health.

The process by which childhood health plays a role in the relation between adult socio-economic status and adult health is further explored in this paper from the perspective of health selection. Health problems in childhood can influence the socio-economic status in (early) adult life. In our analysis health selection in childhood seems to be more important than (biological or social) causation, at least in early adult life. The literature suggests a minor role of direct health selection in childhood, although evidence about the importance of intergenerational social mobility related to health in childhood is ambiguous. For example, Wadsworth (1986), in a prospective longitudinal design, reported a direct effect of health status on intergenerational mobility. Lundberg (1988, 1991a) found no evidence, however, that severe childhood illness increases the risk of downward intergenerational mobility. Power *et al.* (1986, 1996) argue that health-related intergenerational social mobility does exist, but does not have a major effect in the explanation of socio-economic inequalities in early adult life. We looked at the possible effect of health in childhood on educational achievement. Our results indicated that the role of direct selection with respect to education is small but relevant. It is possible that this is not necessarily followed (in the short term) by a downward intergenerational occupational mobility. Wadsworth (1986) found an effect of childhood illness on educational achievement for both men and women, but a downward occupational mobility only for men. Our results indicate that the selection mechanism (with respect to intergenerational social mobility) cannot be ignored and should still be explored in further research.

Health selection

The third process is that of health selection operating in adult life (relation 3 in the model). Health problems may lead to downward social mobility, or very good health toward upward social mobility. The literature suggests that the relative importance of direct (physical) health selection is small (Fox *et al.* 1985, Power *et al.* 1996, Davey Smith *et al.* 1994, Blane *et al.*

1993, Lundberg 1991a). Health-related social mobility is, however, not frequently studied with empirical data. Our results on intragenerational health selection indicated no effect of health problems on downward social mobility. This is in agreement with results from two other studies (*a.o.* Power *et al.* 1996, Lundberg 1988, 1991a). Lundberg also concluded that intragenerational mobility was not influenced by health status. Power *et al.* found that social mobility was influenced by health status. However, health selection was not important in the explanation of adult health differences, due to the small numbers of people who are socially mobile because of poor health, compared to the total population.

One might argue that the period for health-selective social mobility in this study is too short, because health selection may operate slowly. However, Lundberg (1988) did not find any health-related social mobility over a period of 13 years. This supports the idea that health selection is not very important in mobility between occupational classes.

In the EGP-scheme, physically light occupations, like administrative work are classified higher than heavy manual work. It is suggested in the literature, however, that health-related social mobility will be in the direction of lower non-manual jobs (because they are both physically and mentally less demanding) (Lundberg 1988, Dahl 1993, Bartley and Owen 1996). This does not support the idea that unhealthy people move into lower, *i.e.* manual occupations. On the contrary, one has to be 'healthier' to remain employed in manual occupations. We dealt with this problem by considering a change from EGP-class three a and b (lower non-manual) to seven (higher manual) not as downward social mobility. In addition, we studied the nature of the occupations, to which the mobility occurred. Taking into account the health status in 1991, the risk of downward mobility was higher for unhealthy people in the manual classes. In the non-manual classes there was no difference between people with and without health problems in 1991. The numbers were very small, so results have to be interpreted with caution (results not shown).

The contribution of health-related social mobility to the explanation of socio-economic health inequalities may be much more complicated than is usually suggested. Two questions are frequently mixed up. First, we have to examine if there is any health-related social mobility at all. The subsequent question concerns the net effect of health-related social mobility on the size of socio-economic health inequalities. It is normally assumed that social inequalities would widen as a consequence of health-related social mobility. This would narrow if downward mobile persons were less healthy than the class they leave but healthier than the class they join (and upwardly mobile persons would be healthier than the ones they leave but less healthy than the ones they join). We found no effect of health on occupational mobility at all. In a subsequent analysis, however, we found that ill-health influences the risk of mobility out of and into the labour force significantly (results not shown).

Furthermore, the health of people who both left the labour force and entered the labour force, was worse than in working people, but better than among those who stayed economically inactive (results not shown). This indicates that a lifecourse perspective is needed further to explore the mechanisms by which health selection affects the size of social inequalities in health.

In the theory of accumulation of disadvantage over the lifecourse, the mechanisms of social causation and health selection may act in succession in a downward spiral. Health problems in youth may be followed by a lower socio-economic position upon access to the labour force. A lower socio-economic status (or, for example, unemployment) will lead to more health problems in adult life. Supposing that these adult health problems might in turn cause downward social mobility, this downward spiral may lead to a cumulation of both socio-economic and health disadvantages, affecting each other. Our results indicate that the occurrence of a downward spiral is likely to be more significant during the period of childhood and youth than during adult life. In further exploring our conceptual model other aspects have to be taken into account, such as the mechanism of indirect selection and the process of health-related access to and/or exit from the labour force.

Acknowledgements

The LS-SEHD is financially supported by the Ministry of Public Health, Welfare and Sports and the Prevention Fund. It forms part of the GLOBE-study ('Gezondheid en Levensomstandigheden Bevolking Eindhoven en omstreken'). The GLOBE-study is being conducted by the Department of Public Health of the Erasmus University Rotterdam, in collaboration with the Public Health Services of the city of Eindhoven and the region of South-East Brabant.

The authors wish to thank Michael Provoost and Xandra Savelkouls for carefully constructing the data-base and collecting follow-up data.

Notes

1   This model is a specification of an extensive theoretical framework (Stronks *et al.* 1993), covering also other causal explanations of socio-economic health differences in adult life, such as through material and structural factors, adult behaviour and psycho-social stressors. In the conceptual model presented here, which emphasizes the influence of childhood conditions and selection processes, for ease of reference other causal factors have been left out. This does not deny the importance of these factors.

2   The Erikson and Goldthorpe scheme of 1992 contains 8 categories: category 3 (routine non-manual) was divided into skilled non-manual and semi-unskilled non-manual. The 1992 classification was used in the analysis with respect to health selection.

3 The percentage reduction in Odds Ratios is used as measurement for the explanation of health inequalities between socio-economic groups by a particular risk factor. This method is used by others, *e.g.* Power *et al.* (1991). It can be interpreted as the reduction in the Odds Ratio for an adverse health outcome among lower socio-economic groups when the prevalences of the risk factor would be the same in all socio-economic groups.

References

Andriessen, J.H.T.H. (1972) Interne of externe beheersing, *Nederlands Tijdschrift voor de Psychologie*, 27, 173–97 (in Dutch).

Barker, D.J.P., Osmond, C., Golding, J., Kuh, D. and Wadsworth M.E.J. (1989a) Growth in utero, blood pressure in childhood and adult life, and mortality from cardiovascular disease, *British Medical Journal*, 298, 564–7.

Barker, D.J.P., Osmond, C., Winter, P.D. and Margetts, B. (1989b) Weight in infancy and death from ischaemic heart disease, *Lancet*, 577–80.

Bartley, M. and Owen, C. (1996) Relation between socio-economic status, employment, and health during economic change 1979–93, *British Medical Journal*, 313, 445–9.

Blane, D., Davey Smith, G. and Bartley, M. (1993) Social selection: what does it contribute to social class differences in health? *Sociology of Health and Illness*, 15, 1–15.

Blane, D., Hart, C.L., Davey Smith, G., Gillis, C.R., Hole, D.J. and Hawthorne, V.M. (1996) Association of cardiovascular disease risk factors with socioeconomic position during childhood and during adulthood, *British Medical Journal*, 313, 1434–8.

Dahl, E. (1993) High mortality in lower salaried Norwegian men: the healthy worker effect, *Journal of Epidemiology and Community Health*, 47, 192–4.

Davey Smith, G., Blane, D. and Bartley, M. (1994) Explanations for socioeconomic differentials in mortality, *European Journal of Public Health*, 4, 132–44.

Davey Smith, G., Hart, C., Blane, D., Gillis, C. and Hawthorne, V. (1997) Lifetime socioeconomic position and mortality: prospective observational study, *British Medical Journal*, 314, 547–52.

Erikson, R., Goldthorpe, J.H. and Portocarero, L. (1983) Intergenerational class mobility and the convergence thesis: England, France and Sweden, *British Journal of Sociology*, 34, 313–42.

Erikson, R. and Goldthorpe, J.H. (1992) *The Constant Flux. A Study of Class Mobility in Industrial Societies.* Oxford: Clarendon Press.

Eysenck, S.B., Eysenck, H.L. and Barret, P. (1985) A revised version of the psychotism scale. *Pers Indiv Diff*, 6, 21–9.

Forsdahl, A. (1977) Are poor living conditions in childhood and adolescence an important risk factor for arteriosclerotic heart disease? *British Journal of Preventive Medicine*, 31, 91–5.

Forsdahl, A. (1978) Living conditions in childhood and subsequent development of risk factors for arteriosclerotic heart disease, *Journal of Epidemiology and Community Health*, 32, 34–7.

Fox, A.J., Goldblatt, P.O. and Jones, D.R. (1985) Social class mortality differentials: artefact, selection or life circumstances? *Journal of Epidemiology and Community Health*, 39, 1–8.

Fox, J. (ed) (1989) *Health Inequalities in European Countries*. Aldershot: Gower Publishing Company Limited.

Funder, D.C., Parke, R.D., Tomlinson-Keasey, C. and Widaman, K. (1993) *Studying Lives through Time. Personality and Development*. London: American Psychological Association.

Heatherton, T.F. and Weinberger, J.L. (1994) *Can Personality Change?* London: American Psychological Association.

Illsley, R. and Svensson, P.G. (eds) (1990) Health inequities in Europe, *Social Science and Medicine*, 31, 223–420.

Kaplan, G.A. and Camacho, T. (1983) Perceived health and mortality: a nine-year follow-up of the human population laboratory cohort, *American Journal of Epidemiology*, 117, 292–304.

Krahe, B. (1992) *Personality and Social Psychology. Towards a Synthesis*. London: Sage Publications Ltd.

Kuh, D.J.L. and Wadsworth, M.E.J. (1993) Physical health at 36 years in a British national birth cohort, *Social Science and Medicine*, 37, 905–16.

Lundberg, O. (1988) *Class Position and Health: Social Causation or Selection?* Stockholm: University of Stockholm.

Lundberg, O. (1991a) Childhood living conditions, health status, and social mobility: a contribution to the health selection debate, *European Sociology Review*, 7, 149–62.

Lundberg, O. (1991b) Causal explanations for class inequality in health – an empirical analysis, *Social Science and Medicine*, 32, 385–93.

Lundberg, O. (1993) The impact of childhood living conditions on illness and mortality in adulthood, *Social Science and Medicine*, 36, 1047–52.

Lundberg, O. (1997) Childhood conditions, sense of coherence, social class and adult ill health: exploring their theoretical and empirical relations, *Social Science and Medicine*, 44, 821–31.

Lynch, J.W., Kaplan, G.A. and Salonen, J.T. (1997) Why do poor people behave poorly? Variation in adult health behaviours and psychosocial characteristics by stages of the socioeconomic lifecourse, *Social Science and Medicine*, 44, 809–19.

Mackenbach, J.P., Mheen, H. van de and Stronks, K. (1994) A prospective cohort study investigating the explanation of socio-economic inequalities in health in the Netherlands, *Social Science and Medicine*, 38, 299–308.

Mheen, H. van de, Stronks, K., Bos, J. van den and Mackenbach, J.P. (1997) The contribution of childhood environment to the explanation of socio-economic inequalities in health in adult life: a retrospective study, *Social Science and Medicine*, 44, 13–24.

Mheen, H. van de, Stronks, K., Looman, C.W.N. and Mackenbach, J.P. (1998a) Does childhood socio-economic status influence adult health through behavioural factors? *International Journal of Epidemiology*, 27, 431–7.

Mheen, H. van de, Stronks, K., Looman, C.W.N. and Mackenbach, J.P. (1998b) The role of childhood health in the explanation of socio-economic inequalities in early adult life, *Journal of Epidemiology and Community Health*, 52, 15–19.

Mheen, H. van de, Stronks, K., Looman, C.W.N. and Mackenbach, J.P. (1998c)

Recall bias in self-reported childhood health: differences by age and educational level, *Sociology of Health and Illness*, 20, 2, 241–54.

Ormel, J. (1980) Moeite met leven of een moeilijk leven. Groningen: Rijksuniversiteit Groningen [dissertation] (in Dutch).

Power, C., Fogelman, K. and Fox, A.J. (1986) Health and social mobility during the early years of life, *Quarterly Journal of Social Affairs*, 2, 397–413.

Power, C. (1991) Social and economic background and class inequalities in health among young adults, *Social Science and Medicine*, 32, 411–17.

Power, C., Matthews, S. and Manor, O. (1996) Inequalities in self rated health in the 1958 birth cohort: lifetime social circumstances or social mobility? *British Medical Journal*, 313, 449–53.

Power, C. and Peckham, C. (1990) Childhood morbidity and adulthood ill health, *Journal of Epidemiology and Community Health*, 44, 69–74.

Power, C., Manor, O., Fox, A.J. and Fogelman, K. (1990) Health in childhood and social inequalities in health in young adults, *Journal of the Royal Statistic Society*, 153, 17–28.

Power, C., Manor, O. and Fox, J. (1991) *Health and Class: the Early Years.* London: Chapman and Hall.

Rahkonen, O., Lahelma, E. and Huuka, M. (1997) Past or present? Childhood living conditions and current socioeconomic status as determinants of adult health, *Social Science and Medicine*, 44, 327–36.

Ranchor, A.V. (1994) Social class, psychosocial factors and disease: from description towards explanation. Groningen: Rijksuniversiteit Groningen [dissertation].

Starfield, B., Katz, H., Gabriel, A., Livingston, G., Benson, P., Hankin, J., Horn, S. and Steinwachs, D. (1984) Morbidity in childhood – a longitudinal view, *New England Journal of Medicine*, 310, 824–9.

Stronks, K. (1997) Socio-economic inequalities in health: individual choice or social circumstances? Rotterdam: Erasmus Universiteit Rotterdam [dissertation].

Stronks, K., Mheen, H. van de and Mackenbach, J.P. (1993) Achtergronden van sociaal-economische gezondheidsverschillen. Een overzicht van de literatuur en een onderzoeksmodel, *Tijdschrift Sociale Gezondheidszorg* 71, 2–10 (in Dutch).

Sweeting, H. and West, P. (1995) Family life and health in adolescence: a role for culture in the health inequalities debate? *Social Science and Medicine*, 40, 163–75.

Tax, L.C.M.M. (1982) *Waarden, Mentaliteit en Beroep: een Onderzoek ten Behoeve van een Sociaal-Culturele Interpretatie van Sociaal-Ekonomisch Milieu.* Lisse: Swets and Zeitlinger BV (in Dutch).

Taylor, S.E. (1991) *Health Psychology.* New York: McGraw-Hill Inc.

Townsend, P. and Davidson, N. (1982) *Inequalities in Health: the Black Report.* Harmondsworth: Penguin Books.

Vågerö, D. and Leon, D. (1994) Effect of social class in childhood and adulthood on adult mortality [letter], *Lancet*, 343, 1224–5.

Vågerö, D. and Illsley, R. (1995) Explaining health inequalities: beyond Black and Barker, *European Sociology Review*, 11, 1–23.

Wadsworth, M.E.J. (1986) Serious illness in childhood and its association with later-life achievement. In Wilkinson, R.G. (ed) *Class and Health: Research and Longitudinal Data.* London: Tavistock.

Wannamethee, G. and Shaper, A.G. (1991) Self-assessment of health status and mortality in middle age British men, *International Journal of Epidemiology*, 20, 239–45.

West, P. (1991) Rethinking the health selection explanation for health inequalities, *Social Science and Medicine*, 32, 383–84.

Notes on Contributors

Dr Jon Bernardes is Principal Lecturer in Sociology at the University of Wolverhampton, author of Family Studies: An Introduction (Routledge, 1997), he teaches across family and marriage. Jon has a wide range of research interests around family life and more recently prostate ill-health (he suffers from Chronic Prostatitis).

Nicola Brimblecombe has a background in social policy. Previously a Researcher in Education, she is currently a Research Associate at the University of Bristol, researching geographical inequalities in health, part of the ESRC Health Variations Programme. Her research interests include health inequalities, housing and health, and sexual health.

Roger Burrows is Assistant Director of the Centre for Housing Policy at the University of York. His most recent book is the co-edited Homelessness and Social Policy (Routledge, 1997). He is currently working on 3 ESRC funded projects on: the sociological analysis of computer mediated social support, the housing circumstances of young people; and lay perceptions of equity in relation to health and health care.

Elaine Cameron is Senior Lecturer in Sociology at the University of Wolverhampton, her teaching includes sociology of health and older age. Elaine has a wide range of research interests and activities, especially in older age and health.

Dr Sarah Curtis is Reader in the Department of Geography, Queen Mary and Westfield College, University of London. Her research interests include national and international geographies of health and health care focusing on health inequalities, equity and access to health services. This has involved research in Britain, France and Russia. At a more local level her research interests focus on community and locality planning, the determination of need for services and the evaluation of appropriate and acceptable health care.

Danny Dorling is a Lecturer in Human Geography in the School of Geographical Sciences, Bristol University. Following several years spent in full time research as a Joseph Rowntree Foundation Fellow and subsequently British Academy Fellow at Newcastle University. His research interests include mapping and the visualisation of spatial social structure, the economic and political geographies of Britain and medical geography.

Jon Ivar Elstad is a sociologist currently employed as Research Director at NOVA – Norwegian Social Research, Oslo. His research interests include social inequalities in health, health services, medical sociology, social stratification and class theory.

Anthony Gatrell is Professor of the Geography of Health at Lancaster University and also Director of the Institute for Health Research. His research interests are in geographical epidemiology and health inequalities.

Dr Ian Rees Jones is Lecturer in the Department of Geography, Queen Mary and Westfield College, University of London. His research interests focus on inequalities in health and the use of health care services at a variety of spatial levels. His research also addresses urban environments and health, including housing, homelessness, social exclusion and their relation to public health policies. At a local scale his research addresses needs assessment, community development and the evaluation of services appropriate to local populations. He is currently working on a sociology of rationing and rationality in health care.

Ichiro Kawachi is an Associate professor in the Department of Health and Social Behavior at the Harvard School of Public Health. His research interests are focused on social determinants of health, specifically, the relationship of income inequality and social capital to health.

Bruce P. Kennedy is the Deputy Director of the Division of Public Health Practice at the Harvard School of Public Health where he teaches courses on adolescent health and the social determinants of health. Dr. Kennedy's current research focuses on developing models of the social determinants of health such as income inequality and social capital. He is the recipient of a Robert Wood Johnson Investigator Award in Health Policy Research for his work.

Johan Mackenbach is professor in Public Health at the Erasmus University Rotterdam. His research interests include medical and social determinants of public health, especially socio-economic health inequalities, medical demography and health care as determinant of public health. He is coordinator of the Dutch National Program Committee of socio-economic inequalities in health.

James Nazroo is senior lecturer in sociology in the Department of Epidemiology and Public Health at University College London. His research activities have focussed on the relationship between ethnicity, class and both physical and mental health, gender differences in mental illness, gender differences in career progression, and marital power and violence.

Dr Sarah Nettleton is a Senior Lecturer in the Department of Social Policy and Social Work at the University of York. Her most recent book is the co-edited The Body in Everyday Life (Routledge, 1998). Her current research interests include the health and social consequences of mortgage possession for families and children (funded by the Joseph Rowntree Foundation) and the sociological analysis of computer mediated social support (funded by the ESRC).

Jennie Popay is Professor of Sociology and Community Health at the University of Salford and Director of the Public Health Research and Resource Centre. She is also an Associate Director of Research and Development at the National Primary Care Research and Development Centre. She has published widely in the fields of health and social policy. Her particular research interests include, gender and social class, inequalities in health, and the sociology of knowledge, with particular reference to the relationship between lay and professional knowledge in the sphere of public health. Recent publications include the edited collections 'Dilemmas in Health Care' (with Basiro Davey, Open University Press, 1993), 'Researching the People's Health' (with Gareth Williams, Routledge, 1994) and 'Men, Gender Divisions and Welfare' (with Jeff Hearn and Jeanette Edwards, Routledge, 1998).

Mary Shaw has a PhD in Sociology from the University of Queensland and is currently a researcher on the ESRC Health Variations Programme at the University of Bristol. Her research interests include the sociology of food, spatial and social inequalities in health, and housing, homelessness and health.

Karien Stronks is lecturer in Public Health at the University of Amsterdam and registered as epidemiologist. Her research interest include socio-economic and ethnic inequalities in health.

Carol Thomas is a Lecturer in the Department of Applied Social Science at Lancaster University. Her research interests are in disability, health inequalities, the experience of illness, and women's health.

H. Dike van de Mheen is lecturer in public health at the Erasmus University Rotterdam and registered as epidemiologist. Her research interest include socio-economic inequalities in health and the lifecourse. In addition she works as policy advisor at the Municipal Health Service of the city of Rotterdam.

Richard Wilkinson is professorial research fellow at the University of Sussex and visiting professor at University College London where he is also Associate Director of the International Centre for Health and Society. He has worked for many years on the social and economic determinants of health inequalities and has focused particularly on the relation between the extent of income inequality and population health.

Gareth Williams is Professor of Sociology and Deputy Director of the Public Health Research and Resource Centre at the University of Salford. He has published extensively in sociological and health journals, and is co-author of Understanding Rheumatoid Arthritis (Routledge) and Markets and Networks (Open UP) and co-editor of Challenging Medicine and Researching the People's Health (both Routledge). He is currently one of the principal investigators on a study funded by the ESRC under its Health Variations Programme.

Index

Printed in Great Britain
by Amazon.co.uk, Ltd.,
Marston Gate.